C0-CCO-150

THE SPRING THUNDER AND AFTER

A SURVEY OF THE MAOIST AND ULTRA-LEFTIST MOVEMENTS IN INDIA

1962-1975

THE SPRING THUNDER AND AFTER

A SURVEY OF THE MAOIST AND ULTRA-LEFTIST MOVEMENTS IN INDIA : 1962-75

ASISH KUMAR ROY M.A., PH.D.

SOUTH ASIA BOOKS
Box 502
Columbia, Mo. 65201, U.S.A.

First Published: December 1975

ISBN: 0-88386-536-X

Printed in India by M. K. Mukerjee at Temple Press, 2, Nayaratna Lane, Calcutta-700 004 and published by T. K. Mukherjee for and on behalf of South Asia Books, Columbia, Mo. 65201, U.S.A.

TO LITTLE PAPPA

AND HIS

MAMANI

INTRODUCTION

The Institutionalisation of political extremism and violence in Bengal synchronised with the first partition of the province in 1905. West Bengal also witnessed a short spell of political violence during 1948-1949 when the Communist Party of India embarked on a "Left adventurist programme under the leadership of B. T. Ranadive. But the phonemenon of *ultra-leftism* which had been growing in the politics of West Bengal since the early 1960's and found its acutest manifestation in 1967 in a peasant uprising at Naxalbari, earned for the State a mark of distinction, because with the Naxalbari uprising the split in the Indian Communist movement took a final and defined shape. This is so because the Naxalbari peasant uprising signalled the recrudescence of Maoism in India, thereby providing the mission extreme of the left political spectrum, and with the formation of the Communist Party of India (Marxist-Leninist), the only Maoist party in India, the process became complete.

The scope of the present study includes the two older Communist parties—exclusive attention has been paid to the study of the origin and growth of the phenomenon of *ultra-leftism* in West Bengal. This is largely because of the fact that although the CPI (M-L) and other Maoist factions declared on many occasions that their movements had spread to as many as ten Indian States, their activities were primarily confined to West Bengal and later extended into some parts of Andhra Pradesh and Bihar. An attempt has also been made to analyse how the gradualist and constitutional approach of the CPI faced challenge from the Maoist groups in West Bengal and later in Andhra Pradesh. And as a result of this, politics took a definitely violent turn especially in West Bengal. Violence, this time, put on an ideological garb, furnished by the Maoist strategy of armed agrarian revolution.

There are several shades in the whole spectrum of *ultra-leftist* politics in West Bengal, and in the absence of any term that describes them accurately, the *ultra-leftists* came to be known as "Naxalites" after the 1967 peasant uprising in Naxalbari in West Bengal.

The terms *ultra-leftism*, 'Maoism' and 'Naxalism' have

therefore, been used as more or less synonymous and interchangeable. But the term *ultra-leftism* has earned preference for itself in this work for two main reasons. In the first place, it indicates the complex and pre-Naxalite origin of left extremism in West Bengal, and generally in India, within the broad frame-work of the Indian Communist movement. Secondly, it highlights the plural and spectroscopic character of contemporary left extremism in West Bengal as well as in India.

Although there is a wealth of literature on the Indian Communist movement in general, writings on the recent Maoist and the *ultra-leftist* movements in India, especially in West Bengal, are rather few and unsatisfactory. Mohan Ram's *Communism in India—Split Within A Split*[1] and *Maoism in India*[2] are fairly exhaustive analysis of the origin and development of Maoism in India in general. It may, however, be pointed out that Mr Ram's studies have not gone deep into the phenomenon in so far as West Bengal is concerned. Further, Mohan Ram's works seem to be somewhat superficial, because they have simply analysed the ideological bases of Naxalism without any reference to its social roots.

Another book of particular importance is *Radical Politics in West Bengal*[3] *by* Dr Marcus F. Franda. This book provides an exhaustive account of the Communist movement in West Bengal and is "an attempt to understand the various forces impinging on the Communist movement in Bengal by focusing both on the factors and on the setting, on the Communists as political calculators and on the environment (regional, national and international) in which they have their origins."[4] While Dr Franda has commendably analysed the social roots of Bengali Communism and left extremism, he has confined his study of the Maoist and other *ultra-leftist* groups in the West Bengal Communist movement to only one chapter (Chapter: VI). Similar is the case with Dr Bhabani Sen Gupta who has made a very sketchy reference to the Naxalbari Peasant Uprising and the CPI (M-L) movement in his book *Communism in Indian Politics*.[5]

1. Vikas Publications, New Delhi, 1969.
2. Vikas Publications, New Delhi, 1971.
3. Cambridge, Massachusetts, and London, England, 1971.
4. *Ibid.*, p. 5.
5. Columbia University Press, Columbia, 1972.

There are still a few books like *Naxalite Politics in India* by J. C. Johari. *The Naxalite Movement*[7] by Sankar Ghosh and also *The Naxalite Movement*[8] by Biplab Das Gupta. While the first two are more or less running commentaries on the Naxalite activities in India, the third book constitutes a "subjective" assessment of the Naxalite movement, 'subjective" because the author claims to have been associated with the Communist movement in India for twenty years.

It is the contention of the present author that while all such studies have significantly contributed to an understanding of the origin and development of Maoism in India, they have not traced the social roots of the Naxalbari peasant uprising and the subsequent Maoist and *ultra-leftist* movements in West Bengal; and this is what the present author seeks to investigate, for the first time, it is believed, in this work. He attempts to trace the origin, both ideological and social, of the Maoist movement in West Bengal, leading to the formation of the CPI (M-L); and to analyse the organisational structure, mode of operation, personnel, and programme of the new party, as well as how it has acted upon, and in turn has been acted upon by its environment.

Thus understood, the present work is a study in both macrocommunism and microcommunism. It is partly a study of macrocommunism because the author has tried to place India in the international communist strategy, especially in the Maoist strategy, and to trace the evolution of the Chinese line for India, leading to the call for a Maoist revolution in the mid-1967, as part of the general srategy of people's war for the Third World. But it is mainly a case study in microcommunism, as it seems to analyse the various forces involved in the Maoist movement in West Bengal, where the movement had originated.

The author does not pretend to have written a comprehensive history of the Communist movement in West Bengal. His modest aim has been only to bring into bold relief the so-called Maoist movement in West Bengal as well as in the adjoining states during the period between 1962 and 1975. In particular, the work represents an attempt to answer the following queries:

6. Research, ICPS, New Delhi, 1972.
7. Firma K. L. Mukhopadhyaya, Calcutta, 1974.
8. Allied Publishers, New Delhi, 1974.

1. What was the ideological basis of the so-called Maoist movement or the Naxalite movement ?
2. To what extent was this movement a Chinese-inspired phenomenon ? In other words, what are the Chinese ideological-diplomatic needs that prompted the CPC to project a Maoist revolutionary line towards India and why was West Bengal chosen as the testing ground for that purpose ?
3. Did the Naxalbari Peasant Uprising and the subsequent CPI (M-L) movement have any social roots ?
4. How did the Maoists organise themselves and what were their operational techniques ?
5. What did the "Maoists" try to accomplish and to what extent did they succeed in achieving their objective ?
6. Does *ultra-leftism* represent merely a passing phase in the contemporary political processes of India or is it likely to be a recurrent phenomenon ?

The work is divided into eight chapters. Chapter I briefly analyses the first Maoist revolt of the Telengana peasants in Andhra Pradesh in the late 1940's, and then deals with the history of the resurrection of Maoism in the Indian Communist movement, especially in West Bengal, in the context of the Sino-Soviet ideological rift and with special reference to the Chinese diplomatic needs. Chapter II analyses the social roots and the history of the Naxalbari peasant uprising. Chapter III studies the circumstances under which the Chinese Communist Party precipitated the split in the Communist Party of India (Marxist) in 1968-1969. Chapters IV, V, VI and VII analyse the formation, organisational structure, mode of operation and disintegration of the Communist Party of India (Marxist-Leninist). Chapter VIII sums up the findings of the entire study and attempts to arrive at certain conclusions regarding the prospects of the Naxalite movement. The book contains appendices which include the General Programme and Constitution of the CPI (M-L), and a biographical dictionary on the leaders connected with the Naxalbari Peasant Uprising and the CPI (M-L) movement.

A brief explanation of the methodology adopted is in place. For a better understanding of the whole political phenomenon in West Bengal the author has taken an historical-analytical approach to interpret the political dynamics of the State in terms of key analytic concepts of political sociology like "social mobilisation", "political development", "modernisation" etc. Through this approach an attempt has been made to link the Maoist and *ultra-leftist* movements in the State with the social structure, tradition, ideological setting, culture and environment within which they have operated. In this respect field work and empirical observations have been of great use. And for a closer look at the movements, the author has gone deep into the textual materials and inner-party documents of the CPI (M-L) and other Maoist groups.

The author owes a debt of gratitude to Dr Jayantanuja Bandyopadhyaya, Professor, Department of International Relations, Jadavpur University, Calcutta, and to Dr G. P. Bhattacharjee of the same department, whose suggestions and criticisms have been of immense value to him while planning the book. Thanks are due to Hiralal, Jiban and Amal, all assistants in the Department of International Relations, Jadavpur University for their most cordial cooperation.

I acknowledge my profound gratitude to my wife, Shrimati Geeta Roy, Lecturer, Department of History, Victoria Institution, Calcutta, without whose insistence and valuable assistance the work could have never taken shape at all.

Finally, I am grateful to Professor A. N. Bose, Vice-Chancellor, Jadavpur University for extending me financial assistance towards the project.

proach to interpret the political dynamics of the State in terms of key analytic concepts of political sociology like "social mobilisation", "political development", "modernisation" etc. Through this approach an attempt has been made to link the Maoist and ultra-leftist movements in the State with the social structure, tradition, ideological setting, culture and environment with which they have operated. In this respect field work and personal observations have been of great use. And for a closer look at the movements the author has gone through the original materials and unpublished documents of the CPI (M-L) and other Naxalite groups.

The author owes a [illegible] Department of [illegible] University of Calcutta [illegible] Dr. [illegible] Bhattacharya [illegible]

[illegible]

Finally [illegible]

CONTENTS

ABBREVIATIONS

AICCR	..	All-India Co-ordination Committee of Revolutions
AICCCR	..	All-India Co-ordination Committee of Communist Revolutionaries
APCCR	..	Andhra Pradesh Co-ordination Committee of Communist Revolutionaries.
BPSF	..	Bengal Provincial Students' Federation
CC	..	Central Committee
CPGB	..	Communist Party of Great Britain
CPC	..	Communist Party of China
CPI	..	Communist Party of India
CPI(M)	..	Communist Party of India (Marxist)
CPI(M-L)	..	Communist Party of India (Marxist-Leninist)
CPSU	..	Communist Party of the Soviet Union
CSP	..	Congress Socialist Party
CUSF	..	Calcutta University Students' Federation
GPCR	..	Great Proletarian Cultural Revolution
EPCP(M-L)	..	East Pakistan Communist Party (Marxist-Leninist)
LPPD	..	For Lasting Peace For People's Democracy
MCC	..	Maoist Communist Centre
NCNA	..	New China News Agency
PB	..	Polit Bureau
PCSC	..	Presidency College Students' Consolidation
PHQ	..	Party Headquarters
POC	..	Provincial Organization Committee
PCZ	..	Code initials of an underground organization of the Left Communists in West Bengal in 1963-1964
PPH	..	People's Publishing House
PSCC	..	Progressive Students' Coordination Committee

PULF	..	People's United Leftist Front
RSP	..	Revolutionary Socialist Party
SSP	..	Samyukt Socialist Party
SUCI	..	Socialist Unity Centre of India
UF	..	United Front
ULF	..	United Leftist Front
WPP	..	Workers' and Peasants' Party

CHAPTER I

MAOISM IN INDIA : IRRUPTION-RETREAT-RESURRECTION

EARLY MAOIST TREND IN INDIA AND ITS RETREAT : 1948-50

THE FIRST irruption of a Maoist movement in India, it would be seen in the following pages, came as a sharp reaction to the abortive bid of B. T. Ranadive, the then General Secretary of the Communist Party of India, to translate the Zhdanovist strategy of urban insurrection into a massive revolutionary upsurge in India. For a fair understanding of the activities of the pioneer Maoists in India it is necessary to analyse briefly the interaction of forces —national and international—which contributed towards the growth of a viable, though transitory, Maoist movement in India at a time when the tactics and strategy of revolution adopted by Mao Tse-tung himself in his own country had been at a strictly experimental stage and was as such yet to be formalised into what came to be known as "Sinified Marxism" at a later date.

It may be recalled that till the late 50's since independence the history of the Indian Communist movement is a complicated story of the CPI's difficult trek through a zig-zag course from Calcutta to Amritsar[1]. Another interesting feature of this decade is that during a period of five years between the end of World War II in 1945 and the take-over of the CPI central leadership by the Andhra Communists, the party had undertaken its major experiments on the tactics and strategy of the Indian revolution. And this is abundantly clear from the three striking shifts in the

1. During the period under review the general line of the CPI evolved from the strategy of armed uprising initiated at its Second Party Congress held in Calcutta in 1948 to a policy of peaceful transition to Socialism, adopted at the Fifth Congress held at Amritsar in 1958. For an outstanding analysis of the Indian Communist movement during this period, see Overstreet, G. D. and Windmiller, M., *Communism in India*, Berkeley, University of California Press, 1959.

general policy line of the CPI—first, constitutional Communism under the leadership of General Secretary P. C. Joshi until 1948; second, a strategy of Zhdanovist left-adventurism inaugurated at the Party's Second Congress in Calcutta in 1948 and followed by B. T. Ranadive who had then succeeded P.C. Joshi; and finally, the adoption of the Maoist strategy of peasant revolution under the leadership of C. Rajeswar Rao, who had replaced Ranadive after the latter's failure to bring about "a revolution in six months." Thus it should be clearly understood that in the post-independence days when the CPI leadership was on the lookout for a definite programme of a socialist revolution in India, the Maoist ideology came to be accepted by a section of the Indian Communists during a short interlude of 1949-1950, even before it was recognised as a valid revolutionary strategy.

During the years from 1945 until the party's Second Congress held in Calcutta in February 1948 the CPI under the guidance of P. C. Joshi attempted to gain respectability by burying the anti-national disrepute it had incurred during World War II while opposing Gandhiji's "Quit India Movement" and helping the British Government's war efforts. He sought to build an image for the CPI as a national and constitutional force and as a democratic party functioning through parliamentary and peaceful means.[2]

Although to many Indian Communist leaders the country appeared on the brink of a major revolutionary upheaval, Joshi estimated that it would be unrealistic to expect the CPI to establish its control over this revolutionary ferment which had been sweeping many parts of the country,[3] harness it into a full-fledged revolutionary war against the new Congress Government. And the immediate reflection of this view could be found in the attitude taken by the Communist leadership towards the Congress

2. For this change of policy of the CPI, see Joshi, *Congress and Communists,* People's Publishing House, Bombay, 1944.

3. The ferment manifested itself in a mutiny in the Royal Indian Navy in February 1946, the revolutionary tendencies among the Indian personnel of the Royal Air Force, demonstrations against the court-martialing of the I.N.A. officers, a series of strikes by workers, the Tebhaga Movement of the Bengal peasants, the peasant unrest in Malabar and in a pitched guerrilla war fought by the peasants of Telengana and other places against the Nizam of Hyderabad.

Government as the successor of the British Government, following the announcement of the Mountbatten Award by the British Prime Minister Clement Attlee in the House of Commons on June 3, 1947, which set the deadline of formal British pull-out from the sub-continent on August 15, 1947.

Though the Award was initially characterised as "a diabolical plan" to balkanise India and a "manoeuvre" to perpetuate imperialist influence over the sub-continent, the CPI Central Committee recognised in its resolution adopted on June 29, 1947 that the Award did represent certain "important concessions" and "new opportunities for national advance". In the same breath it recognised the fact that since the "extreme right wing of the Congress leadership" over which British imperialism had great influence and control, did no longer represent or dominate the Congress as a whole, the Indian National Congress was "the main national democratic organisation" in the country. In other words, the resolution suggested that the Congress under Jawaharlal Nehru's leadership was a rather progressive force. Therefore, the resolution pledged the Party's fullest cooperation to the Congress Government "in the proud task of building the Indian Republic on democratic foundations, thus paving the way to Indian unity."[4] Such cooperation, it observed, should be carried through "a broadest joint front" of all "progressive forces—the CPI, the left elements in the Congress and the League." The resolution thus prescribed a united front from above with the Nehru Government.

The "Intertwined Revolution" that Failed

Although the CPI official line of cooperation with the Congress government continued to prevail, the leftist elements in the party began to voice sharp criticism against Joshi and to press for a radical change in the party line. The central question was whether Joshi's policy of "right opportunist" support to the Congress government would not emasculate the CPI and reduce it into a "harmless appendix" of the Congress, and whether the CPI should not promote and then channel the already existing revolutionary ferments into a fullscale revolutionary war against

4. Central Committee of the CPI "Statement of Policy", *People's Age,* June 29, 1947, pp. 6-7, quoted in Overstreet, G. D., and Windmiller, M., *op. cit.,* p. 260.

the government. The reference was obviously to the violent peasant struggle that had been raging since 1946 in Telengana in the eastern half of the princely state of Hyderabad under the Nizam.

The attack on Joshi's line was spearheaded by B. T. Ranadive, leader of the left radicals within the CPI. The ideological-tactical foundation of Ranadive's political thesis was provided by the theoretical and practical experience which the Yugoslav Communist leaders had accumulated through their struggle for state power in the course of World War II.[5] The essence of these ideas formulated by Tito and Kardelj came to be officially known as the "Theory of Intertwined Revolution". The theory held that it was possible to combine a national democratic revolution and a socialist revolution into one revolutionary process, which would eliminate the otherwise sustained period of time separating these two revolutions and drive the Communist Party straight to power. Thus the establishment of a People's Democracy would be made possible through this short-cut of "intertwined" revolutionary strategy.[6]

In his final assault on Joshi's policy of constitutional com-

5. The extent to which Ranadive was influenced by the writings of the Yugoslav Communist leaders may be clearly understood from his own admissions in his "Self-critical Report" presented before the Central Committee of the CPI in May 1950, when he was removed from the post of General Secretary of the party. He declared:

It is difficult to write an adequate criticism of one's own mistakes when one has piled up a record of mistakes and crimes in a short period (1948-1950)....In the past also I had been guilty of worst kind of left-sectarian error—left-sectarianism was natural to me. For this and other important extracts from the "Self-critical Report" dated May 20, 1950 and the report of self-critical speeches made by B. T. Ranadive on May 28, 29 & 31, 1950, see Chaudhuri, Partha, "I Will Unmask Myself—Ranadive", *Liberation,* February 1968, pp. 83-89.

6. For details of the ideological-tactical line of the Yugoslav Communists, see "Character of the New Democratic State in Yugoslavia", *Communist* (the Yugoslav Communist Party organ), January, 1947, reproduced in *Communist* (the CPI English organ), Vol. I, No. 3, September 1947; Tito, *On the People's Front in Yugoslavia,* an address to the Second Congress of the People's Front of Yugoslavia held on September 27, 1947, People's Publishing House, Bombay, 1948; Kardelj, *Problems of International Development · A Marxist Analysis,* People's Publishing House, Bombay, 1947.

munism, Ranadive's hands were further strengthened by the decisions taken at the Conference of the Nine Communist and Workers' Parties, held in Poland in September 1947 to establish the Communist Information Bureau of the Cominform. At that Conference the Soviet delegate, A. A. Zhdanov set the world upon a radical course by working out the strategy against imperialism in the epoch of the general crisis of the colonial system amidst a weakening of the imperialist system as a whole following its failure to crush the national liberation movements in the colonies. In the new international situation he held, "the chief danger to the working class . . . lies in underrating its own strength and overestimating the strength of the enemy." The Communist parties, therefore, must lead national resistance to "the plans of imperialist expansion and aggression along every line."[7]

The victory of Ranadive was clearly reflected in the decisions of the Second Congress of the CPI, held in Calcutta from February 28 to March 6, 1948. The Congress replaced Joshi by Ranadive as the General Secretary of the Party and approved a programme of revolutionary war on the Yugoslav pattern presented by Ranadive himself.

The hard core of *Political Thesis* adopted at the Second Congress was that a "revolutionary upsurge" was in motion in India and that the final phase of the revolution, the phase of armed struggles had arrived. This "people's democratic revolution", it held, involved the intertwined revolutionary process of "the completion of the tasks of democratic revolution and the simultaneous building up of socialism". The socialist revolution would be generated by promoting the class struggle, waged by the industrial proletariat in many cities, into a general strike; this would then merge with the armed struggle of the peasantry, spreading out from Telengana to other rural areas of India. The armed struggle would be the chief form of the operations to achieve a people's democratic state.[8]

In the months following the Calcutta Congress which had given a clear mandate for revolution, the CPI under the radical

7. Zhdanov, A. A., *The International Situation,* Moscow, Foreign Languages Publishing House, 1947, pp. 46-47.

8. *Political Thesis,* adopted at the Second Congress of the CPI, held in Calcutta, February 28 March 6, 1948.

Ranadive leadership went into an all-out adventurist spree. But in no time the whole movement received a big jolt as it proved wellnigh impossible to touch off the initial stage of the socialist revolution, i.e. a general strike in the cities which would spill over to the rural areas, would merge with the peasant revolution and set the whole country ablaze. This failure of the party greatly isolated it from the masses. As a result, the party switched to terrorism and subversion in many parts of the country[9].

The Government of India immediately responded to the large-scale violence with a heavy crackdown on the CPI. Although the Central Government did not declare the party illegal on a national scale, following the Centre's directive many provincial governments took stern measures against the local Communists and banned the state party organisations of the CPI. On March 26, 1948 under the Public Safety Act the West Bengal Government banned the state unit of the CPI. In the following week the party units were declared illegal in Mysore, Indore, Bhopal and Chandernagore. With scores of important Communist leaders rounded up and others taking shelter in the underground cells in the face of intense police repression, the party apparatus throughout the country had gone almost out of commission.

It should be noted that Ranadive had committed a tactical blunder by placing at the heart of his strategy a total reliance upon the revolutionary potential of the urban proletariat, and relegating the raging peasant struggle in Telengana and other parts of Andhra Pradesh to a secondary position.

The Maoist Challenge

The failure of urban proletariat to bring about an "intertwined" socialist revolution "within six months" through a series of lightning strikes, on the one hand, and the successful operation[10] of the Telengana peasant revolt under the leadership of

9. For a detailed account of the insurrectionary activities of the CPI during 1948 and 1949, see Government of India (Ministry of Home Affairs), *Communist Violence in India,* New Delhi, Government of India Press, 1949.

10. The extent of the success of the Communist-led peasant gurrillas in Telengana was borne out by the fact that by July 1948 they brought under their control as many as 2,500 villages, with "Communes"

the Andhra Communists since 1946, on the other, totally discredited the Ranadive leadership. An instant challenge came from the Andhra Communists, led by Rajeswar Rao, who condemned the basic strategy underlying Ranadive's policy as "utterly left opportunist." Rao contended that the Ranadive faction had imagined that its left-opportunist strategy of the People's Democratic revolution in India, of its class alliance and tactics, which it had borrowed from the Titoist literature, "was the last word in the application of Marxist-Leninist theory to the problems of the new stage of the colonial movement."

On the other hand, Rao insisted that the future revolutionary struggle in India must be based upon a self-supporting agrarian revolutionary base from where the industrial proletariat could be revolutionised. The Andhra Communists argued that the only way to the victory of Communism in India was the outright application of the strategy of agrarian revolutionary war, which had been innovated by Mao Tse-tung and successfully carried out in China.

The new tactical line of India's revolution set forth by the Andhra Provincial Committee of the CPI was contained in a document entitled, the "Andhra Letter", submitted to the Central Executive Committee of the party in June 1948. This document laid down in absolutely unambiguous terms a revolutionary strategy based on Mao Tse-tung's New Democracy in order to translate the Second Congress programme of the CPI into action.[11]

functioning in most of them. See J. M., "The People Fight Back", *World News and Views"*, Vol. XXIX, No. 35, August 27, 1949, pp. 416-417.

11. Later, commenting on the contributions of the Andhra Provincial Committee of the CPI, the Editorial Board of *Communist* wrote:

The Comrades from Andhra had submitted a document to the Editorial Board soon after the Second Congress (in June 1948) in which they very correctly proposed that the concrete formulations of the strategy and tactics, to be pursued by the Party in its struggle to realise the programme and objectives set forth by the Second Congress, should be made on the basis of the ideas developed by Comrades Mao Tse-tung in his classical work, the New Democracy.... See Statement of the Editorial Board of *Communist* on "Anti-Leninist Criticism of Comrade Mao Tse-tung," in *Communist,* Vol. III, (July-August 1950), pp. 7-8, quoted in Fic, Victor M., *Peaceful Transition to Communism in India,* Nachiketa Publications, Bombay, 1969, p. 22.

Applying the Chinese experience as the guide to the Indian situation and drawing parallels between the class compositions of the Chinese and the Indian societies, the Andhra thesis identified feudalism and imperialism as the main enemies of the Indian people and the stage of revolution as the "new democratic" stage as distinct from that of a proletarian revolution.

Summing up, the Andhra Communists argued:

Our revolution in many respects differs from the classical Russian Revolution; and it is to a great extent similar to that of the Chinese Revolution. The perspective is not that of general strikes and general rising leading to the liberation of the rural sides; but dogged resistance and prolonged civil war in the form of an agrarian revolution culminating in the capture of political power by the democratic front.[12]

It is revealing that even before the formal victory of the Maoist revolution in mainland China itself, the Andhra Communists led by Rajeswar Rao were second to none in visualising the prospects and relevance of a revolutionary strategy exclusively based on the Chinese experience. In fact, after the triumph of the Chinese Communist Party in October 1949, there had been a complete polarisation of Marxism-Leninism (which is intrinsically a European current of thought) between the Europocentric and Asiocentric forms. The victory of the Chinese revolution exercised a decisive influence on the national liberation struggles in South and South-East Asia in that it presented a definite model of Communist revolution by de-Europeanising Marxism.[13]

In fact, the shift in the centre of gravity of revolutionary activities from the European to the Afro-Asian scene was accelerated by the victory of the Maoist revolutionary strategy in China

12. "Struggle for People's Democracy and Socialism—Some Questions of Strategy and Tactics," *Communist,* Vol. II, No. 4, (June-July, 1949), p. 83, quoted in Overstreet and Windmiller, op. cit., p. 287.

13. It was not long after the victory of the Chinese Revolution that the Cominform placed the Communist parties of South and South-East Asia under the strategic direction of the Chinese Communist Party. This vital shift in the operational control of the Asian Communist parties took place during Mao Tse-tung's six week state visit to Moscow from December 1949 to January 1950, when the Moscow-Peking Axis was formed. See Boorman, H. L. *et al, Moscow-Peking Axis: Strength and Strains,* Council on Foreign Relations, Harper Brothers, New York, 1957.

in 1949. And the Chinese themselves were not unconscious of this breakthrough in the World Communist movement. Even as far back as 1945 the Chinese Communists started claiming rather boastfully that the adaptation of Marxism to the peculiar conditions prevailing in China as one of the "greatest" theoretical exploits in the history of international Communist movement. Speaking at the Seventh Congress of the Chinese Communist Party in May 1945 Liu Shao-ch'i proclaimed that Mao-Tse-tung's "Thought", which was the "highest example" of "Sinified Marxism," was particularly well-adapted to the needs of all the people of the East. He further held:

The general Programme of the Party Constitution stipulates that the Thought of Mao Tse-tung shall guide all the work of our Party. The Constitution itself provides that it is the duty of every Party member to endeavour to understand the fundamentals of Marxism-Leninism and the Thought of Mao Tse-tung. This is a most important historical characteristic of our amendment of the Constitution at this time .... The Thought of Mao Tse-tung is a further development of Marxism in the national-democratic revolution in the colonial, semi-colonial and semi-feudal countries of the present epoch. It is an admirable model of the nationalisation of Marxism (Ma-ko-szu-chu-i ti min-tsu-hua) ... It is Chinese, at the same time it is thoroughly Marxist .... What Comrade Mao Tse-tung had done as a disciple of Marx, Engels, Lenin and Stalin is precisely to unite Marxist theory with the practice of the Chinese revolution, thus giving rise to Chinese Communism —the Thought of Mao Tse-tung. And Mao Tse-tung's Thought, too has guided and is guiding the Chinese people to achieve complete emancipation; it will, moreover, make great and useful contributions to the course of the emancipation of the peoples of all countries, and of the peoples of the East in particular. The Thought of Mao Tse-tung, from his world view to his style of work, is sinified Marxism (Chung-kuo-hua ti Ma-K'o-szu-chu-i) in the process of development and perfection ... These theories and policies are thoroughly Marxist, and at the same time thoroughly Chinese. They are the highest expression of the wisdom of the Chinese nations, and its highest theoretical achievement.[14]

14. Liu Shao-ch'i, *Kuan-yu hsiu-kai tang-chang ti pao-kao*, Wuhu, Hsihua Shutien, n.d. (1945?). For this English translation of the Chinese text, see Helene Carrérè d'Encausse and Stuart R. Schram,

At a meeting of the World Federation of Trade Unions held in Peking in November 1949, shortly after the establishment of the Chinese People's Republic Liu Shao-ch'i declared most emphatically in his opening speech that the Chinese way was applicable throughout Asia. He proclaimed :

"The way taken by the Chinese people in defeating imperialism and its lackeys and in founding the People's Republic of China is the way that should be taken by the peoples of many colonial and semi-colonial countries (in Asia and Australasia) in their fight for national independence and people's democracy. This way, which led the Chinese people to victory, is summarised in the following formula:

1. The working class must unite with all other classes, political parties and groups, organizations and individuals, who are willing to oppose the oppression of imperialism and its running dogs, form a broad nation-wide united front and wage a resolute fight against imperialism and its running dogs.

2. This nation-wide united front must be led by and built round the working class which opposes imperialism most resolutely, most courageously and most unselfishly, and its Party, the Communist Party, with the latter as its centre. It must be not led by the wavering and compromising national burgeoisie or petty bourgeoisie and their parties.

3. In order to enable the working class and its Party, the Communist Party, to become the centre for uniting all the forces throughout the country against imperialism, and to lead competently the national united front to victory, it is necessary to build up through long struggles a Communist Party, which is armed with the theory of Marxism-Leninism, understands strategy and tactics, practises self-criticism and strict discipline and is closely linked with the masses.

4. It is necessary to set up wherever and whenever possible a national liberation army which is led by the Communist Party and is powerful and skilful in fighting the enemies, as well as

Marxism and Asia, London, Allen Lane, The Penguin Press, 1969, pp. 259-261. For some recent studies on the Maoist revolution in China, see Mark Selden, *The Yenan Way in Revolutionary China,* Cambridge, Mass., Harvard University Press, 1971 and Richard H. Solomon, *Mao's Revolution and the Chinese Political Culture,* Berkeley, University of California Press, 1971.

the bases on which it relies for its activities, and to coordinate the mass struggles in the enemy-controlled areas with the armed struggles. Armed struggle is the main form of struggle for national liberation in many colonies and semi-colonies.

This is the basic way followed and practised in China by the Chinese people in winning their victory. This way is the way of Mao Tse-tung. It may also be the basic way by which the peoples of other colonial and semi-colonial countries where similar conditions prevail achieve emancipation. . . ."[15]

It seems quite obvious that the Andhra Communists had been profoundly influenced by Liu's proclamation at the Seventh Congress of the CPC, which marked a decisive stage in the development of the Neo cult in China and other parts of Asia. The Andhra leaders suggested a four-class strategy of revolution by uniting the entire peasantry under the working class leadership for sustained "guerrilla warfare." Viewing Imperialism and Feudalism as its main class enemies, the strategy would include a section of the bourgeoisie in the united front because only the big bourgeoisie and the big landlords had turned out to be reactionary. Thus understood, the Andhra leadership was advocating a two-stage revolution by including the middle bourgeoisie along with the poor peasantry for armed struggle.

In fact this was the first occasion in the international Communist movement when outside China Mao Tse-tung's thought was upheld publicly by the Andhra Communists as an integral part of Marxism-Leninism. Paying their tribute to Mao Tse-tung, they observed that "Mao, the leader of the historic Chinese liberation struggle, from his unique and rich experience and study, has formulated a theory of new democracy. This is a new form of revolutionary struggle to advance towards socialism in colonies and semi-colonies." With this formal declaration of their attachment to Maoism the Andhra Communists simply replaced Ranadive's allegiance to the Soviet tactical line with equal allegiance to the Chinese general line.

Initially, the Political Thesis of the Andhra Communists had a severe setback in the face of the bitter counter-offensive by Ranadive on the Andhra leadership and his anti-Maoist polemics

15. For this English translation of Liu Shao-ch'is speech, see *Ibid.*, pp. 271-72.

through a bunch of four articles. In the first three articles[16] which appeared in the CPI's English organ, *Communist,* there was no direct reference to the Andhra Thesis, Maoism or the Chinese experience, but they contained veiled attacks on all the three.

The fourth and the final document[17] constituted a total rejection of the Andhra Thesis and a bitter attack on Mao Tse-tung. Assailing the Andhra strategy of combining four agrarian revolution in India as "reformism in its most naked and gross form" and a "shame-faced theory" of class capitulationism, Ranadive claimed that the experience of the Soviet revolution provided the model for India's People's Democratic revolution. He argued that because of certain specific conditions obtaining in India, the Chinese pattern of revolutionary war was totally inapplicable and that a People's Democracy could be established in India only through the strategy of an "intertwined" revolutionary process, combining the national democratic revolution with the socialist revolution.

Denouncing Maoism, Ranadive held :

It must be admitted that some of Mao's formulations are such that no Communist Party can accept them; they are in contradiction to the world understanding of the communist parties.

He even characterised these formulations as "reactionary", "counter-revolutionary" and "horrifying."

Finally, in support of his argument that the entire experience of the Russian Revolution was fully valid for India, Ranadive wrote :

Firstly, we must state emphatically that the Communist Party of India has accepted Marx, Engels, Lenin and Stalin as the authoritative sources of Marxism. It has not discovered new sources of Marxism beyond these. Nor for the matter of

16. (a) "On People's Democracy," *Communist,* II, January 1949, pp. 1-12. (b) "On the Agrarian Question in India", *Communist,* Vol. II, January 1949, pp. 13-53; and (c) "Struggle Against Revisionism Today, in the Light of Lenin's Teachings," *Communist,* Vol. II, February 1949, pp. 53-66. For detailed analyses of these articles, see Overstreet, Gene. D., and Windmiller, M., op. cit., pp. 288-290.

17. "Struggle for People's Democracy—Some Questions on Strategy and Tactics," *Communist,* Vol. II. June-July 1949, pp. 21-89.

that is there any Communist Party which declares adherence to the so-called theory of New Democracy alleged to be propounded by Mao and declared it to be a new addition to Marxism. Singularly enough, there was no reference to this new addition to Marxism in the Conference of Nine Parties in Europe (Cominform) .... It is impermissible for Communists to talk lightly about new discoveries, enrichment, because such claims have proved too often to be a thin cloak for revisionism (Tito, Browder).[18]

Though Ranadive held on to power and went on defending his policies tenaciously throughout 1949, events both at home and abroad started crowding so thick and fast between July 1949 and January 1950 that at one stage the Maoist model of revolution seemed to have gained virtual legitimisation through international Communist sanction. In 1950 the Cominform which had been exercising guidance over the CPI since its formation in September 1947, came out with its approval of the Chinese revolutionary strategy as the model for the colonial and dependent countries.[19] To this smart shift in Moscow's revolutionary strategy vis-a-vis the colonial and newly independent countries may be adduced two important reasons. First, it may be pointed out that in the years immediately after World War II the policy formulations of the CPSU were characterised by an almost total priority to the foreign policy, which to a great extent deformed the Leninist theory of revolution in the East. This priority to foreign policy objectives did not, of course, rule out vigorous efforts to extend Soviet influence. On the contrary, revolutions improvised in the haversacks of the Red Army during the first post-war years, led to the establishment of direct Soviet hegemony over the whole of Eastern Europe. But the Colonies and the newly independent nations of Asia and Africa were quite another question. Because they were beyond the reach of direct military intervention by the Soviet Union.

18. *Ibid.*, pp. 77-78.

19. In an article entitled, "Mighty Advance of the National Liberation Movement in the Colonial and Dependent Countries", published in the January 27, 1950, issue of the Cominform organ, *For A Lasting Peace, For A People's Democracy*, it was declared that the CPI must draw heavily on "the experience of the national liberation movements in China and other countries."

Even more significant, perhaps, was the fact that Stalin, who had already burnt his fingers once in China in 1927, was not particularly serious of engineering revolutionary movements in these countries, whose inhabitants appeared to him quite strange and unpredictable. Moreover his primary concern was the prevailing cold war tensions between the United States and his country and he, therefore, judged all other matters in terms of their immediate repercussions on this central question. In Asia, the policy advocated by Moscow beginning in 1947 was a policy of armed insurrection by the workers and peasants directed not only against the colonial powers but also against the local bourgeoisie. Such a line, by which the Communist parties and other left militant groups cut themselves adrift from the struggles of the Asian peoples could only lead to failure. On the other hand, the vigour with which the newly formed national governments in Asia repressed the Communists was greatly increased by the fact that these groups, blindly applying Zhdanov's thesis to the effect that real independence was impossible under bourgeois leadership, bitterly opposed the new governments. The universal hostility of the socialist camp towards such governments drove them, quite regardless of their own wishes, more and more towards the capitalist camp, thus reinforcing the latter.

It thus had the great advantage for Stalin of allowing him to be revolutionary and intransigent in words, without running any great risks of fostering a situation in Asia that might disturb his own tranquility.[20]

This primary foreign policy objective along with the failure of sundry Communist insurrectionary activities in different parts of Asia, it may be suggested, might have mollified the revolutionary zeal of Stalin who, somewhat prudently and somewhat constrained by the *force majeure,* passed the buck of guiding revolutionary struggles in the colonial and the semi-colonial countries to the Chinese Communist Party, which had by this time, led a successful revolution in China itself.

Another plausible explanation of this sharp orientation of the Soviet strategy vis-a-vis the revolutionary struggles in Asia

20. Carrérè d'Encausse H, and Schram, Stuart, R., *op. cit.,* p. 64.

was Stalin's anxiety to maintain the national and territorial integrity of his own motherland. Shortly after World War II the Soviet ruling elite was faced with a very delicate situation in the peripheral republics and that was the growing nationalist aspirations—a sentiment which had been carefully developed and systematically exploited by resistance to the Nazi invaders. In fact, the national aspirations of the non-Russian peoples of the USSR which had never been totally hammered out by the Bolshevik revolution, had been one of the persistent problems facing the Soviet leadership especially during the period from the end of the Second World War in 1945 to Stalin's death in 1953. In this situation it would have been a costly adventure for Stalin adopt a policy based on the encouragement of national liberation movements in Asia (particularly in the Islamic countries) without further aggravating the problem of national frustration of the minorities in the Soviet Union, who were in large part Muslims, keenly watching the developments in the neighbouring countries.

Thus understood, it was becoming too obvious that the circumstances required a quick shift in the Soviet revolutionary strategy for Asia and, for that matter, both the international situation and the domestic milieu seemed to have prompted the Kremlin to concede to the Chinese the main role in the Asian drama in the early fifties. To this one must not forget to add the fact of the growing Chinese pretensions on the question of the specificity of Chinese experience over the Soviet vis-a-vis the Asian situation. It should, however, be pointed out that the Soviet leaders were never inclined to hand over to the Chinese, of their own free will, the responsibility of guiding revolutions in Asia and never accepted with pleasure Peking's pretensions of having found an original way for the revolution in non-European countries. Nor at the same time was Moscow prepared to precipitate an immediate schism in the international Communist movement over this issue which, however, subsequently matured into a formidable question in the Sino-Soviet ideological rift.

Although the Chinese were gradually stepping into the shoes of the Soviet leaders insofar as revolutionary movements in Asia were concerned, what had, however, already strengthened the hands of the Andhra Communists under the leadership of

Rajeswara Rao in their ideological assault upon Ranadive was the voice of the Chinese leader Liu Shao-Ch'i from China.[21]

Thus with the prescription for a Maoist line from Liu Shao-ch'i and finally with the green signal from the Cominform in early 1950,[22] the outster of Ranadive from the post of General Secretary of the CPI became only a matter of time, although in a last desperate bid to save himself from this inevitable fate he came out to admit disarmingly his faith in Maoism. He declared:

The path taken by the Chinese people . . . in the path that should be taken by the people of many colonial and dependent countries in their struggle for national liberation and People's Democracy . . . . For the Indian liberation struggle, headed by the working class and the Communist Party, the lessons of the Chinese revolution, the reaching of its great leader Comrade Mao Tse-tung, will be an unfailing guide.[23]

At a meeting of the CPI Central Committee in May 1950—the first in two years—the Andhra leaders staged a "palace revolution" in the party. The old Committee removed Ranadive and elected C. Rajeswara Rao the new General Secretary. In the new Politbureau of nine members four were taken from the Andhra Secretariat. The public announcement of the shake-up in the CPI Central Committee came only on 23 July 1950 in the shape of a Central Committee statement published in the Soviet Papers

21. It has already been mentioned that in the opening session of the Trade Union Conference of the Asian and Australasian countries held in November 1949 in Peking Liu declared that the road of Mao Tse-tung "is the path that should be taken by the peoples of the various colonial and semi-colonial countries in their fight for national independence and People's Democracy". See "Speech by Liu Shao-ch'i at the Conference of Trade Unions of Asia and Oceania", *op. cit.*, in fact, when Liu declared in November 1949 that the Chinese way should be followed by the peoples of many colonial countries, he was acting in tacit agreement with Moscow, which shortly came to accept officially a variant of the Chinese tactical line. *op. cit.*, p. 96.

22. During this time another interesting development in the international Communist movement also played into the hands of the Andhra Communists. As a result of the growing rift between Stalin and Tito Yugoslav theory was declared as "revisionism of worst character." The Communist parties all over the world received a warning to be on guard which had fallen under the spell of the "revisionist" theories of the Yugoslavs.

23. *Crossroads,* Vol. 1, No. 31, April 7, 1950.

Pravda and *Izvestia* in July 1950. The statement declared the CPI's adherence to the Maoist strategy of revolution. It said :

> The new policy will be based on the national liberation movement in China. The course China is taking and which the countries of Southeast Asia are following is the only correct course before our people.[24]

Again, the newly constituted Editorial Board of *Communist*, official organ of the CPI which had sent greetings to the CPC on the occasion of the latter's 29th anniversary declared that "the Communist Parties in the colonial world are looking upon the Communist Party of China as their model." At the same time the Editorial Board publicly apologised to Mao Tse-tung for Ranadive's invectives against him.[25]

Retreat of Maoism in India

The victory of the Maoist line of peasant partisan warfare as the valid strategy of Indian revolution for which the Andhra Communists had so ardently fought, was to be rather ephemeral. In the face of severe mopping up operations of the Indian army the base areas of the peasants guerrilla warfare in and around Telengana were virtually liquidated. Thus agrarian revolution proved no more successful than urban insurrection. And when criticism started mounting fast against the Rao leadership in the party circles[26], the Telengana movement was finally shelved in pursuance of Moscow's directive, first indirectly through the Communist Party of Great Britain and later directly in consultation with an Indian Communist delegation visiting Moscow.

It may be pointed out that the success of the national liberation struggles was virtually dependent upon the active guidance and material support of the Moscow-Peking Axis. But as a result of the involvement of Moscow and Peking in the Korean

24. See Overstreet and Windmiller, *op. cit.*, pp. 298-299.

25. Statement of the Editorial Board of *Communist*, *op. cit.*, pp. 1-26.

26. The main fire of the criticism was directed against Rajeswara Rao by P. C. Joshi, who had been removed from the post of the General Secretary in the Second Congress of the CPI held in 1948 for his alleged "class collaborationist" policy. See P. C. Joshi, *For A Mass Party: Problems of the Mass Movement*, Allahabad, N. C. Jain, 1950, pp. 71-73.

war, the revolutionary movements in India, Burma, Malaya, Indo-China and Indonesia suffered severe setbacks, because the diversion into the Korean theatre of those material resources and other assistance which had been kept ready for the support of the national liberation struggles in South and South-East Asia, deprived these Communist parties of the much-needed help. Thus the preoccupation of Moscow in the Korean war brought about a major shift in the policy of the Soviet leadership. The new policy called upon the Asian Communist parties to support the ruling bourgeoisie, which had started taking an anti-American and anti-Western stand in foreign policy.

In view of this background of the Soviet diplomatic needs, it may be pointed out that what had compelled the Kremlin to intervene in the affairs of the CPI was not so much the anxiety to set the faltering party right on its track, but to placate the Nehru government in an already changed cold war situation. When Nehru's foreign policy of non-alignment showed signs of independence of the Anglo-American bloc, Moscow thought it expedient to suspend the three-year-old cold war against his government and to neutralise his future moves before his non-alignment switched into any alliance with the "Capitalist" bloc. Thus understood, the new diplomatic requirements of Moscow demanded an immediate moratorium on class struggle in India.

This time, however, the directive from Moscow came not through the usual channel of the *IPPD* editorial, but through a letter of the Political Committee of the Communist Party of Great Britain to the CPI towards the end of 1950. The latter urged the CPI to give up the policy of armed struggle and instead, to concentrate on exploiting all chances of renewed legal activity in view of the forthcoming general elections to be held in early 1952. As the first step towards this change of policy line, the letter called for a total purging of the "Trotskyite-Titoite Cancer" and recommended a party conference for the selection of new leaders.[27]

Then in early 1951, a top-level CPI delegation consisting of S. A. Dange, A. K. Ghosh, C. Rajeswara Rao and M. Basavpunniah visited Moscow and returned with a new Draft Pro-

27. *"PHQ Unit Covering Note to the Letter of the Political Committee of the CPGB to the CPI,"* December 6, 1950, pp. 6. For a convenient summary of this document see, Overstreet and Windmiller, *op. cit.*, pp. 303-304.

gramme of the Party along with a highly secret document entitled the "Tactical Line", both drawn in consultation with the Soviet leaders. The Draft Programme which formalised Moscow's stand on the strategy and tactics of the Indian revolution was to cast aside both the lines of urban insurrection and of peasant partisan warfare. A four-class alliance[28] and a two-stage revolution was to be the strategy but armed revolution was not to be part of the immediate programme.

The Draft Programme was formally adopted at the Third Congress of the party held at Madurai from December 27, 1953 to January 3, 1954. The Congress gave the green signal to the shift in the direction of lawful activities[29] including the use of legislatures and other political institutions for securing partial demands as well as for strengthening the influence of the CPI. The shift had already taken place on the eve of the first general elections held in 1952, and it had helped the party to win legitimacy for itself in the Indian political process.

It should be noted that although armed peasant struggle as a tactic had been officially abandoned by the end of 1950, the flames of the peasant partisan warfare were still flickering in parts of Telengana. The finale of the Andhra leadership's hegemony over the party, however, came with the resignation of Rajeswara Rao in May 1951, when a new leadership headed by Ajoy Ghosh as General Secretary was elected. In October 1951, A.K. Gopalan, on behalf of the Central Committee and the Andhra Committee, announced the withdrawal of the struggle.[30]

Thus from all indications it became clear that since 1950 the CPI, following Moscow's directives was steadily moving away from the strategy of armed struggle and gradually staging a come-

28. The Programme declared: Our party calls upon the toiling millions, the working class, the peasantry, the toiling intelligentsia, the middle classes as well as the national bourgeoisie interested in the freedom of the country and the development of a prosperous life . . . to unite into a single democratic front in order to attain complete independence of the country, the emancipation of the peasants from the oppression of the feudals . . . See *Programme of the Communist Party of India,* Bombay, People's Publishing House, 1951, pp. 23-24.

29. This shift, however, had to be made possible in the teeth of great opposition within the party. See *Indian Communist Party Documents, op. cit.,* p. 75.

30. "CPI Advises Stoppage of Partisan Action in Telengana," *Crossroads,* October 26, 1951.

back in favour of constitutional communism. And it should be noted that although the 20th Congress of the CPSU in a way formalised the CPI's shift to peaceful parliamentarism, a great stir was created when the CPI came out victorious in the 1957 general election in Kerala and proceeded to form a government in that State—the first occasion in the history of World Communist movement that a communist party had achieved even this limited degree of power through a parliamentary election. Kerala came to be regarded as the first apparent confirmation of the 20th Congress thesis on the peaceful transition to power. And with this the CPI quickly moved from the April 1956 line of the Fourth Party Congress of Palghat, where the party had somewhat tentatively acknowledged the practicability of transition to socialism through parliamentary path, to the April 1958 line of the Fifth *Extra-ordinary* Party Congress held at Amritsar, which declared its new-found faith in peaceful change. The central paragraph of the Preamble to the constitution of the CPI, adopted at the Amritsar Congress read :

> The Communist Party of India strives to achieve full Democracy and Socialism by peaceful means. It considers that by developing a powerful mass movement, by winning a majority in Parliament and backing it with mass actions, the working class and its allies can overcome the resistance of the forces of reaction and ensure that Parliament becomes an instrument of People's will for effecting fundamental changes in the economic, social and state structures.[31]

PRELUDE TO NAXALBARI : MAOISM RESURRECTED, 1957-1966

Although Telengana failed to be the Yenan of India in the early 50's, interest in Maoism was never lost to the Indian Communists. In fact, serious homework in the Maoist strategy and tactics of armed agrarian revolution became a regular habit with a section of the Communists in India, especially in West Bengal, during the next decade. And it was in West Bengal that Maoism was resurrected by a group of young Maoist enthusiasts with the launching of the Naxalbari peasant uprising in Darjeeling district in the spring of 1967. But before this vigorous reassertion of

31. *Constitution of the Communist Party of India,* adopted at the Extra-ordinary Party Congress, Amritsar, April 1958, Communist Party of India, New Delhi, May 1958, p. 2.

the Maoist tactical line as a model for Indian revolution, certain concrete indications were there that some extremist factions in the undivided CPI had been persistently fighting within the party circles for the adoption of Maoism as the valid strategy of a people's democratic revolution in India.

The Dual Environment

It should be noted that for a period of six years from the Fifth Party Congress at Amritsar in 1958 to the final split in 1964 the CPI was locked in an excruciating interlude, which helped Maoism to consolidate itself within the Indian Communist movement, because it was at this stage that the Sino-Soviet ideological dispute broke out in the open and the Sino-Indian border dispute which was building up into an armed confrontation, also got linked up with the ideological rift. During this interlude, again, the CPI became gravely affected by the divergent Soviet and Chinese assessments of the Indian bourgeoisie and the potential of the Indian revolution. The sharp deterioration in Sino-Indian relations was accompanied by the Soviet soft-pedalling of the Nehru government and even implied diplomatic support to India against China, first over the question of the Khampa uprisings in Tibet leading to the flight of the Dalai Lama to India in April 1959, and then, during the India-China border controversy culminating in a full-scale war in late 1962. It is interesting to note that the Soviet attitude towards the Sino-Indian border dispute definitely irked the Chinese and as such acted as one of the main sources of strains on the Sino-Soviet relations as it was admitted by the Chinese at a later date:

> One of the main differences of principle between the Soviet leaders and ourselves turns on the Sino-Indian boundary question.[32]

It was against the background of the increasingly divergent Soviet and Chinese policies that the rightist and the leftist factions of the CPI began to identify themselves publicly either with Moscow or Peking. Thus understood, the interjection of the

32. "Truth About How the Leaders of the CPSU Have Allied Themselves with India Against China," *People's Daily*, November 2, 1963, quoted in Mohan Ram, *Indian Communism: Split Within a Split,* Vikas Publications, New Delhi, 1969, p. 79.

ideological debate of the two Communist giants into the already complex situation in the CPI let loose the disruptive forces within the party.

Apart from the mounting India-China border crisis since 1959 what had simultaneously precipitated the surfacing of the vital differences within the CPI, thereby strengthening the pro-China lobby in the party, was the fall of the first communist regime in Kerala. The Indian Government's dismissal of the Communist government in Kerala came in July 1959, almost synchronising with the Sino-Indian controversy caused by Communist China's armed suppression of the Khampa uprising in April and the opening of the border tensions in August when Nehru revealed the Chinese occupation of 15,000 square miles of Indian territory in Ladakh and the NEFA.

The most important consequence of the toppling of the communist regime in Kerala was the augmentation of the influence of the pro-China left elements in the CPI, who contended that the Amritsar thesis of peaceful transition to power through parliamentary path was totally belied. Following this, intra-party tensions in the CPI continued to mount with the further deterioration of the India-China relations over the boundary questions.[33]

It may be pointed out that in West Bengal a sudden spurt of speculations on the Maoist tactics and strategy of revolution among the Left Communists could be detected in late 1960 and the instigation came from none other than Harekrishna Konar, leader of the Left radicals in West Bengal. In September 1960, he along with K. Damodaran of Kerala, led an Indian Communist delegation to Hanoi to attend the Congress of the North Vietnamese Lao Dong Party. From Hanoi Konar slipped into Peking on an invitation from the Chinese leaders even though he had been expressly instructed by the CPI Central Committee not to accept any invitation from the CPC to visit Peking.[34] On his return to India Konar started disseminating the Chinese views

33. For a fairly exhaustive account of the India-China border dispute and the conflicts within the CPI, see Harry Gelman, "The Communist Party of India; Sino-Soviet Battleground" in A. Doak Barnett (ed.) *Communist strategies in Asia,* Praeger, New York, 1963.

34. When Konar was censured by the Central Secretariat and asked to explain why disciplinary action should not be taken against him, the West Bengal State unit rallied behind line, arguing that censure of Konar

with regard to both the India-China border dispute and the Sino-Soviet ideological conflict among the party members in West Bengal. Konar was reported to have told the Calcutta District Committee of the party that while the Indian Communists knew only the Soviet point of view, he could place the Chinese position before them, which he deemed his duty even if that amounted to "a technical breach of party discipline." He presented to the Committee a list of Chinese grievances against Moscow dating back to the CPSU's Twentieth Congress and reiterated the Chinese contention that Khrushchev's peaceful-coexistence line was "sowing illusions" about imperialism.[35] Konar also strongly argued for the adoption of the Maoist strategy of armed agrarian revolution in India. This left a profound influence on the party members, a large section of whom became seriously interested in Maoism.

Soon after Konar's visits to Hanoi and Peking a five-men CPI delegate led by Secretary Ajoy Ghosh left for Moscow to attend the conference of 81 Communist Parties. While at the Soviet capital, the delegation was received by Mikhail Suslov, who criticised the CPI for its anti-Chinese policy and urged the party to follow the Moscow conference declaration in its relations with the CPC. The outcome of the talks represented a clear victory for the pro-Chinese wing of the Indian party. When the CPI National Council met again in January 1961, the pro-Chinese elements demanded the repudiation of the Council's Meerut resolution, citing Suslov's advice in support of their stand. Ghosh, however, mustered enough right-wing support to block the demand. Enraged at this, Promode Das Gupta, Secretary of the West Bengal State unit, circulated a document entitled "Revisionist Trend in the CPI", which attacked the policy of the Ghosh leadership as a "surrender" to the bourgeoisie and imperialism and demanded that the CPI "follow the lead" of the Chinese Communist Party.[36]

amounted to censure of the entire unit of the party. See *Indian Affairs Records,* No. 10, p. 229.

35. *Link* (New Delhi Weekly), October 15, 1960.

36. *Ibid.,* February 5, 1961. It may be recalled that the CPI National Council which had met at Meerut in Uttar Pradesh in November 1959 unequivocally endorsed the Indian Government's claim to the McMahon Line as the rightful border between India and China and rejected the

Thus, from the foregoing analysis a particular trend could be discerned clearly in the Communist movement in West Bengal, viz., a pro-Chinese faction had got itself deeply entrenched in the party organisation by the end of 1960. But this phenomenon should not necessarily lead one to conclude that this faction was formally committed to the Maoist ideology of peasant revolution. An observer, who has depicted the situation quite aptly and accurately, writes:

> After Konar's visit to North Vietnam and China in 1960, the regular party organisation in West Bengal was labelled by almost everyone, both within the party and outside, as the most vociferous pro-Chinese element within the party, a label, that was both accurate and misleading. The leadership of the regular party organisation in West Bengal did support the Chinese position in the ideological debate at the party center, but it would be difficult to attribute this support solely to the ideological convictions of the state's left faction. . . . This is not to argue that there were no genuine pro-Chinese elements within the regular party organisation in the years before the split, but as later events were to point out in a very dramatic way, the leadership of the regular party organization was much more motivated by pragmatic considerations than it was by the wish to adopt a consistently pro-Chinese ideological stance. When in 1967 the leadership of the state party was faced with a choice between support of pro-Chinese elements in the state party and support of the electoral wing, it chose to support the latter, thereby alienating the CCP.[37]

Thus, reconstructing the events at this late date, one is inclined to believe that though the leadership of the regular party organisation in West Bengal had pretensions regarding the acceptance of Maoism, this should, however, be construed more as a "manoeuvre" to intensify their splitting activities in the CPI, thereby breaking the monopoly of power enjoyed by the rightists in the party than to seriously go in for a pure Maoist tactical line. On the other hand, the genuine Maoist elements in the party were largely drawn from the middle-order leadership in

Chinese claims in the NEFA area. See *New Age* (Weekly), 22 November, 1959.

37. Marcus Franda, *op. cit.*, p. 95.

the district committees in the West Bengal state unit. This leadership had been relentlessly propagating the Maoist strategy of agrarian revolution in India since the early 60's, particularly after the Chinese invasion of India in late 1962.

The massive armed confrontation between India and China in the North-East Frontier Agency and Ladakh sectors of India on October 20, 1962, precipitated a fresh crisis in the CPI and led to a decisive show-down between the dominant right-wing forces and the so-called pro-Chinese faction. S. A. Dange, now occupying the newly-created post of Chairman in the party, and other right-wing CPI leaders promptly reacted with public demonstrations of the Chinese action. However, it took the party full eleven days to adopt a resolution on the situation. On November 1 the CPI National Council finally passed a resolution which branded China as an aggressor, repudiated the Chinese claims to Indian territory, endorsed the Indian government's decision to buy arms abroad and gave full support to the government's conditions for entering into negotiations with China on the border issue.[38] The resolution was vehemently opposed by the leaders of the left group and when it was forced through, three leading left-faction spokesmen on the Central Secretariat, Jyoti Basu, P. Sundarayya and Harikishen Singh Surjeet resigned. The division of the party into the right and left factions thus became clear.

In the next few months the split between the two groups in the CPI became more pronounced. It was accelerated by the efforts of the rightists to establish their control over state committees dominated by the leftists by taking advantage of the latter's inability to function owing to arrests and detentions. This happened particularly in West Bengal, Punjab and Andhra, the three states where the leftists were very strong. There was also a struggle for control over party journals and for the possession of office premises. This led to the organisation of parallel party centres, for example, the Provincial Organising Committee (POC) set up by the central leadership of the party and the underground P.C.Z. set up by the left faction in West Bengal.[39]

38. *Indian Express* (New Delhi), November 2, 1962.

39. For further details, see Marcus Franda, *op. cit.*, pp. 98-102.

Maoism Consolidates Itself : The West Bengal Scene

While the senior Communist leaders of both factions in West Bengal busied themselves throughout 1963 in preparation for the impending split, inner-party documents upholding Maoist thought started appearing in Calcutta, Burdwan, Darjeeling and other districts of West Bengal where the pro-Chinese Communists had their strongholds. The authors of these documents always used pen names for fear of disciplinary action by the party.

The first ever inner-party ideological document to appear in West Bengal during this period was one drawn up under the pen name of "Prithviraj",[40] dated December 20, 1962.

The document contained a tactical line the main object of which was to create a strong pro-Chinese base in India by fomenting unrest among the peasants and workers. Reiterating the Chinese views on the India-China border dispute it held that the Nehru government was a reactionary government, and had surrendered to the US imperialists, and further, that it was India, and not China, which was unwilling for a settlement of the border dispute. Analysing the situation within the CPI the document contended:

"A sense of dissatisfaction is prevailing among the left-minded members and they want a concrete line of action. The party is facing a grave crisis as Dange has completely surrendered to militant nationalism and joined bourgeois chauvinism by extending full support to each and every step taken by the Government of India."

The circular analysed in the light of the pro-Chinese group's thinking on the economic situation of the country; how far it was controlled by private capital—both Indian and foreign and how the Anglo-American bloc had been trying to make India a strong base against socialist China. "Prithviraj" declared:

"In the conflict between India and China, on one side, there are the monopolists who in collaboration with the Imperialists want to exploit the people and check the spread of Communism,

40. Another document entitled *"Chanakya's Document"* (*Chanakyer Dalil*) also appeared about this time. The authenticity of these two documents was admitted at a later date by the Home Ministry, Government of India. See *Hindusthan Standard* (Calcutta), January 3, 1965.

and on the other side, there is the Communist regime in China which wants to crush the Imperialist design in Asia and preserve its independence, democracy and socialism. The politics of the working class is for peace, and that is why China has resorted to undeclared ceasefire and is showing its willingness to settle the matter round the table. But it is monopolists and war-mongers who want to keep up a war tempo and do not want to sit for a settlement."

In the context of the prevailing political situation, "Prithviraj" urged the Communists to shake off all doubts and stand against the policy of long-term war with China. "The main political aim," he declared, "would be to capture political power by putting an end to the dictatorship of Big Bourgeoisie and big landlords . . . ., and in this it is not the unity of the CPI and the Congress, but the unity of the working class and the peasants that should be the main prop of the struggle."

Another inner-party document written in Bengali, "Bartaman Paristhiti O Communist Partyr Karmaniti" (The Present Situation and the Communist Party's Policy), was surreptitiously circulated by the pro-Chinese elements in the CPI in the middle of 1963. The booklet outlines a detailed action programme for the party along the lines advocated by the CPC. It may be pointed out that this document for the first time expressed the growing dis-illusionment of a section of West Bengal Communists towards the CPI's strategy of peaceful transition to socialism through parliamentary means. The document contended:

"Parliamentary politics and electioneering organisations have reduced the party into an organisation of middle-class people and provided scope for opportunists, eager for seats in the Vidhan Sabha, Lok Sabha etc. to join the party . . . . The old leadership stands in the way of the party's progress. A new force must take over the leadership in a new historical background . . . . To give up parliamentary politics we shall have to oppose and change the current that has been set in motion inside the party . . . . We shall have to lay stress mainly on mass movements by mobilising the workers and peasants.[41]

It may be pointed out that though this was not the general

41. For further details, see A. K. Roy, "Ideological Bases of the CPI(ML)", *Journal of Constitutional and Parliamentary Studies*, October-December 1971, pp. 465-66.

line of thinking of the "32" who now constitute the central leadership of the CPI (M), a large section of the rank and file members in the undivided CPI, specially the party's Andhra Pradesh and West Bengal State Units wholeheartedly subscribed to that view. In fact, while in the days following the India-China border war of 1962, the West Bengal State Unit of the CPI presented a squalid scene of unprecedented factionalism between the Bhowani Sen—Somnath Lahiri faction, on the one hand, and the Promode Das Gupta-Jyoti Basu-Harekrishna Konar faction, on the other, it was the second grade leaders of the party in West Bengal who were carrying on a struggle on the ideological front against the "revisionist" leadership of the party. And this was admitted by none other than Promode Das Gupta, the unquestioned leader of the left faction in West Bengal before 1964 and now, Secretary of the West Bengal State unit of the Communist Party of India (Marxist).

In his article entitled "An Aspect of Left Opportunism in West Bengal" in the 1967 Annual Number (published during the Pujas) of the *Desh Hitaishi,* organ of the CPI (M) West Bengal State Unit, Das Gupta traced the growth of extremism within the Communist movement in West Bengal in early 60's. He said that the extremist trend first emerged in 1963 when the left faction leaders of the CPI in West Bengal had been in jail. Till May that year there was not much difference of opinion among the left Communists in jail. But afterwards vital differences cropped up over the Colombo Proposal on the India-China border war, the Nuclear Test-Ban Treaty, and a circular issued by the PCZ, the underground centre of the left Communists in West Bengal. The differences became so acute that the jail committee of the left Communists had to be dissolved. Both in jail and outside two separate groups started working. One came to be known as the "Jyoti Group" and the other, as the "Promode Group".

The majority of the left Communists in the "Promode Group" were of the view that without making any compromise with the "Centrist" Jyoti group in the political field they should work in unision with the followers of Jyoti Basu[42] on the orga-

42. It may be remembered that though Basu had joined the Left Communists in West Bengal before the split, he all along maintained his

nisational level to fight the Right Communists. Others in the Promode group held that the sooner Basu and his group joined the "Revisionist" group led by Bhowani Sen and Somnath Lahiri the better. This sub-group which was more powerful and vociferous in its pro-Chinese stand was led by Charu Mazumdar, Sushiltal Ray Chowdhury, Saroj Datta, Kanu Sanyal and Sourin Bose, who identified themselves as the Maoist leaders in the CPI (M) in 1967, and engineered the Naxalbari peasant uprising in Darjeeling district of West Bengal in the spring of 1967.[43]

Thus it is rather striking to note that following the India-China border war of 1962 the ideological debate among the Communist leaders in West Bengal had been caught up in the contest for factional advantages within the party, a very small but powerful group was steadily consolidating its position in the districts to prepare for the final assault on the ideological front of the Indian Communist movement. It was in the midst of those two trends that the formal split took place in the CPI in 1964. The immediate issue, it may be remembered, was not an ideological one, but a letter that the party Chairman Dange had reportedly written to the British authorities prior to independence offering to work for the government in exchange for his release from prison. The National Council of the party which had met in April 1964, refused to consider this allegation. Thereupon 32 left-wing and centrist members walked out, and issued an appeal to party members to repudiate Dange and "his group" and their "reformist political line". On April 15, the National Council expelled from party membership all the signatories of this appeal. This marked the final split in the party. On July 7 the leftist leaders met at Tenali in Andhra Pradesh, and formed the second CPI.[44]

centrist position until the split was complete at Tenali in the Summer of 1964.

43. Promode Das Gupta, "An Aspect of Left Opportunism in West Bengal," *Desh Hitaishi,* Annual Number, October 21, 1967. All the copies of this number were withdrawn by the party. The reason was that the party thought it undesirable to make any official admission of the existence of two opposing groups among the Communists who now form the CPI (M) organisation in West Bengal. For biographical details of the important Maoist leaders, see Appendix III.

44. For details of the series of events that led to the split in 1964,

Battle for Programmes

The militant section of the Indian Communists which had broken off from the CPI in 1964, reorganised itself under the banner of the CPI (M) with the simmering enthusiasm of building a "truly" revolutionary party based on Marxism-Leninism and the thought of Mao Tse-tung. The largest defection of these 'ultra-left' elements took place in the West Bengal unit, where more than 70% of the 17,600 members of the pre-split CPI identified themselves with the new party.[45] But these militants recorded their initial frustration at the Seventh Congress (the foundation Congress) of the breakaway Communists held in Calcutta from October 31 to November 7, 1964. In the Programme that was adopted at the Congress it was declared, "the Communist Party of India strives to achieve the establishment of people's democracy and socialist transformation through *peaceful means*, by developing a powerful mass revolutionary movement by combining parliamentary and extra-parliamentary forms a struggle, the working class and its allies will try their utmost to overcome the resistance of the forces of reaction and to bring about these transformations through peaceful means."[46]

The advocacy of the "peaceful means" came as a rude shock to the extremists in the new party, who were expecting their leaders to launch a serious revolutionary movement on the Marxist-Leninist and Maoist lines.[47] Another factor which

see Mohan Ram, *Indian Communism: Split Within A Split,* New Delhi, Vikas Publications, 1969, Chapter V.

45. It was estimated that at the end of 1963 in West Bengal a sharp decline took place in the CPI membership from 21,000 to 17,600 and after the split only 7,460 members out of 17,600 remained loyal to the CPI in West Bengal, while a few hundred did not renew their party cards. See *Amrita Bazar Patrika* (Calcutta), December 30, 1964.

46. *Programme of the Communist Party of India,* adopted at the Seventh Congress, Calcutta, 1964, pp. 53-54, emphasis added.

47. The disenchantment of these revolutionaries came all of a sudden because in order to catch the imagination of this section by assuring them of the party's revolutionary potential, a huge portrait of Mao Tse-tung had been displayed in the conference hall at Tenali. But only within five months their leaders descended over Calcutta as "apostles" of peaceful transition. For example, M. Basavpunniah, a member of the then newly constituted 9-man Politbureau came out disarmingly to set at rest all doubts regarding his party's real character and form. He declared

deepened the frustration of the extremists was the party's "utter reformist" character, laid bare in the 97th paragraph of the Programme which deals with the anti-feudal role of the People's Democratic Revolution in India. It declares that "the anti-feudal and anti-imperialist People's Democratic Revolution will have to take upon itself, first and foremost, the task of carrying out radical agrarian reforms in the interests of the peasantry, so as to sweep away the remnants of feudal and semi-feudal fetters on our productive forces of agriculture as well as industry".[48]

What these "radical agrarian reforms" could at their best mean in the estimate at the Indian Communists had been summarised by E.M.S. Namboodripad on the eve of the Second General Elections in 1957. While suggesting that the installation of a Communist Government in Kerala would be followed by legislative measures providing for prevention of evictions, rent reduction, fixation of ceilings, distribution of surplus and waste lands etc., he admitted in the same breath that these measures were so modest in their character that they would not go beyond what had been agreed to in the Land Reform Panel of the Planning Commission.[49] With this "bourgeois reformist" character of the CPI (M) leaders already in view, the extremists came out sharply against the party Programme.[50]

It was not, however, only at the Seventh Congress of the party, but on more than one occasions many of its leading members came out openly in support of "peaceful transition to socialism" and parliamentary democracy. Even in their occasional exchanges with the Government of India, they had been found very much anxious to prove how slender was their difference—ideological and tactical, with the "revisionist" CPI. For instance, immediately after the all-India swoop by the police on

that "the talk of an armed struggle—a scandal about us—is infantile nonsense; the CPI's new programme does not envisage such struggle in future." *Statesman* (Calcutta), November 9, 1964.

48. *Programme of the Communist Party of India, op. cit.*, p. 46.

49. For details, see Namboodiripad, E. M. S., *Agrarian Reforms—A Study of the Congress and Communist Approaches,* People's Publishing House, Bombay, 1956.

50. For a summary of the attitudes of the dissidents in the CPI (M) towards the party Programme, see Manab Mitra, "The Revolutionary Path Is The Only Path," *Liberation* (English organ of the CPI (ML), May 1968, pp. 65-85.

the entire leadership of the new Communist Party in the last week of December 1964, Shri G. L. Nanda, the then Union Home Minister, made a serious charge in an AIR broadcast to the nation that the left Communist Party had been preparing for "armed revolution" and guerrilla warfare "to synchronise with a fresh Chinese attack, destroying the democratic government of India through a kind of pincer movement. which was hoped for but could not materialise in 1962". Later on, in a statement in Parliament he charged the Left Communists with supporting China over Tibet and the India-China border dispute, disloyalty to the country during the Chinese invasion, dissemination of pro-Chinese and anti-national documents, splitting the CPI at Peking's call and preparation for subversion and violence.[51]

While refuting the charges of the Home Minister as "baseless" and "highly concocted", P. Sundarayya, now General Secretary of the Communist Party of India (Marxist), contended that programmatically his party hardly had any differences with the CPI. He wrote :

"It will be interesting . . . to note that the relevant passages regarding the possibilities for, and the limitations of, the peaceful path are almost similar in our Programme and the Programme of the revisionists. This is the most telling refutation of the canard by the Congress rulers . . . that our Party stands for the insurrectionary methods while the revisionists are the champions of the peaceful parliamentary path".[52]

Countering Nanda's charge of "subversive activities" he further wrote somewhat self-apologetically :

"When I met Nanda in the first week of December (1964), ... I told him : Do not believe your police reports. Use your political judgement. We are not thinking of any armed struggle of any type . . . . We are a legal party and function openly .... Let me once again categorically deny the slander that we are preparing to go underground for making preparations for a Telen-

51. For the full text of the 45 page statement of the Home Minister, see Government of India, Ministry of Home Affairs, *Anti-National Activities of Pro-Peking Communists and Their Preparations for Subversion and Violence*, New Delhi, 1965.

52. "Sundarayya Answers Nanda", *People's Democracy*, September 12 & 19, 1965.

gana-type armed struggle . . . . if we had any thought of going underground, I would not have gone to Nanda.[53]

Again, while rejecting the allegations of Nanda sometime later, another CPI (M) stalwart, M. Basavapunniah, was arguing much in the same vein. Agreeing with the right communists that "there has been a new orientation in the world Communist movement in favour of peaceful transition," he wrote :

"Unlike the earlier rare and exceptional possibilities of the peaceful transition of socialist revolution, new additional possibilities of it in some countries have been visualised under the new world conditions that are obtaining today .... it is expected that all this would greatly restrain the ruling classes from resorting to the adventures of violence, and in some countries at least certain possibilities have arisen for such a peaceful path to be explored and utilised by the Communists of those countries. It is exactly on the basis of this new assessment that we have introduced this new concept of peaceful transition to socialism in our party programme. The formulation of this concept as well as the general warning against the danger of violence, usually unleashed by the ruling classes, is exactly similar to the one put forth in the Programme of the Dangeites".[54]

It should be remembered that even before the foundation of Congress of the new party in Calcutta, the state conference of the West Bengal unit had already left sufficient indications that the China-wing had developed as a well-organised third force in the Indian Communist movement. The necessary spade-

53. *Ibid.,* September 19, 1965.

Immediately after the Home Minister's statement in Parliament, Jyoti Basu and P. Sundarayya met President Radhakrishnan and the Home Minister and openly challenged the validity of the statement. Basu stated publicly on a number of occasions that he would resign from the party if the Home Minister could provide convincing evidence that the Left Communists were engaged in subversive activities. In June 1969, after the CPI(M) came to power in West Bengal, Nanda admitted that his decision to arrest the Left Communists in 1964-1965 had been made on the basis of "faulty intelligence." See, *Hindusthan Standard* (Calcutta), June 18, 1969.

54. M. Basavapunniah, "Reply to Nanda", *People's Democracy,* January 30, 1966. For a detailed analysis of the two Programme approaches, see Analyst, "Battle of Programmes", *Mainstream,* (New Delhi Weekly), July 18, 1964, and E. M. S. Namboodiripad, *The Programme Explained,* Communist Party of India (Marxist), Calcutta, 1966.

work for this breakthrough had been done in the district-level conferences and group meetings throughout the state. After Tenali this extremist wing was careful enough not to display any portrait of Mao Tse-tung or to raise any Maoist slogans when the district conferences were held in preparation for the Foundation Congress of the Left Communists. The only exceptions were the Darjeeling and Murshidabad District Committees where portraits of Mao Tse-tung and quotations from his writings adorned the Conference halls.[55] This, at any rate, showed the slow process of organising the third force in the West Bengal Communist movement. This Maoist group became very active at the state conference of the party, where they clamoured for a programme of armed struggle led by workers and peasants alone. The extremist wing insistently demanded the deletion of a significant phrase in the draft programme, viz., "peaceful transition to socialism." In fact, the blue print of a Chinese style revolution was drawn up by Sushital Ray Chowdhury in the "Alternative Draft Programme" to the Conference.[56] Ray Chowdhury later played a key role in organising the Indian Maoist under the banner of the CPI (M-L) 1969.

Miscalculated Ostrichism

It has already been pointed out that since the Tenali Convention of July 1964 when the draft Programme of the Left Communist Party had been broadly endorsed, the Party's official stand on most of the ideological issues regarding the world communist movement stood in suspense. At the Seventh Party Congress in Calcutta in 1964 a party discussion on the ideological issues was promised. But the Central Committee which later met at Tenali in June 1966 to review the developments since the founding of the Party, did not initiate the long-awaited

55. For this report, see *Hindusthan Standard,* (Calcutta), October 31, 1964.

56. In this battle for programme, Ray Chowdhury was joined by Parimal Das Gupta, Saroj Datta, Suniti Ghosh, Asit Sen and others, all of whom were later expelled by the West Bengal State Committee of the CPI (M) in 1967. For further information on the activities of the extremists in the CPI (M), see *On Left Deviation,* Calcutta, Communist Party of India (Marxist), 1967, pp. 1-25.

ideological debate. It, however, noted that during the eighteen months since the party Congress "divergent views have been expressed by some fraternal Communist Parties of various countries on the Indian situation." But the whole issue was put into cold storage by the Central Committee which observed that what had been said in the party's programme proved correct and sound and the party should be guided by the Programme. All views divergent or deviating from it should be rejected. The State Committees were directed to "publish the authoritative pronouncements of fraternal parties", but in so doing "it should be made clear that our party is not committed to any one of them. Care should also be taken to avoid as much as possible the publication of such material as undermines faith in the socialist system".[57]

This calculated ambivalence of the CPI (M) central leadership towards ideological issues injected a deep sense of frustration in the minds of the extremist elements in the party. Because ever since their secession from the CPI in 1964 the CPI (M) leaders had never taken interest either at the Tenali Convention of July 1964 or at the Foundation Congress (the Seventh Congress), held in Calcutta in November, to clearly define their party's ideological position. On the other hand, the Right Communists had got their position legitimised by firmly committing themselves to the Soviet ideological position. And this was never better clarified than in S. A. Dange's article, "Neither Revisionism nor Dogmatism Is our Guide," by which he countered the Chinese attack on himself and his party in an editorial in the *People's Daily*, March 9, 1963, entitled, "A Mirror For Revisionist" in the dual context of the struggle against modern "revisionism" and the Sino-Soviet ideological rift. Dange retorted:

"It is well known that all world parties in their Party Constitutions abide by Marxism-Leninism. But the Chinese Party found it necessary to add something else to it, basing themselves on their own experience and the needs of their revolution. In the constitution of their Party adopted at the Seventh National Party

57. *Resolution of the Central Committee of the Communist Party of India,* Calcutta, 1966, pp. 26-27. It is interesting to note that even in 1966 the Left Communist Party was still calling itself the "Communist Party of India."

Congress in June 1945, Article 2, under the head "Duties of a Party Member," lays down the following:

(a) to endeavour to raise the level of his consciousness and to understand the fundamentals of Marxism-Leninism and the Thought of Mao Tse-tung."

It may be pointed out that the "Thought" is with a capital T and hence is something very concrete.

"So the Chinese Party has, in addition to the fundamentals of Marxism-Leninism, also the 'Thought' of a great national leader of theirs, Comrade Mao Tse-tung. What other parties enjoy such good fortune? We certainly are nowhere within the neighbourhood of such a personality or its cult and 'Thought'... Why should we be asked to follow Chinese lessons of 'thirty years before' which have no validity for us? And if we do not do so, why, please why interfere in our work and force on us the 'Thought' of Mao Tse-tung to the exclusion of our own, which however poor it may be, is our own understanding of our situation and Marxism-Leninism?"[58]

All such ideological issues, however, were left open to various interpretations in the CPI (M), because the new-born party then comprised both moderate and extremist elements who had vital differences regarding the issues in the international communist movement. The CPI (M) leaders— the "32"[59] who had broken off from the CPI in 1964, sought to shelve any such confrontation between the two groups on the ideological front, because it was then apprehended that if the ideological issues had been taken up either at Tenali or at the Calcutta Congress, the

58. For full text of Dange's article see *The Great Debate, Selected Writings on Problems of Marxism-Leninism Today*, New Delhi, People's Publishing House, 1963.

59. P. Sundarayya, M. Basavapunniah, E. M. S. Namboodiripad, A. K. Gopalan, M. Hanumanthia Rao, T. Nagi Reddy, C. H. Kararan, E. K. Nayanar, V. S. Achutanandan, E. K. Imbich Bava, Promode Das Gupta, Muzaffar Ahmad, Jyoti Basu, Abdul Halim, Harekrishna Konar, Saroj Mukherjee, P. Ramamurthi, M. R. Venkataraman, M. Sankaraiah, K. Ramani, H. S. Surjeet, J. S. Lyallpuri, D. S. Tapalia, Dr Bhag Singh, Sheo Kumar Mishra, L. N. Upadhyaya, Mohan Punamiya, R. P. Saraf, D. Venkatateswaran Rao, N. Prasada Rao, G. Papanayya and A. V. Kunhambu.

party would have foundered then and there and a fresh spectrum of Communist factions would have mushroomed.[60]

It is rather striking to note that the Indian Communist movement has been led exclusively by the same leadership for the last four decades. The intellectuals in the CPI were largely recruited in Indian and European colleges and universities, while the organisational leaders were drawn from among the "terrorist" prisoners in the jails. When the CPI held its first Congress in 1943, more than two-thirds of the delegates (92 out of 139) listed themselves as landlords, traders and members of the intelligentsia, and at least 70% of the delegates were less than 35 years of age.[61]

Subsequently, during the post-independence days the same leadership managed to retain their grip on the mainstream of the Indian Communist movement by excluding the younger generation from almost all the prominent party positions. There has been little or no infusion of new blood into the party leadership. The extent to which the older, pre-independence leadership now dominates the Central Executive Committees of both the CPI and CPI (M) is illustrated by the average age of the members of the CPI Central Secretariat which in February 1968 was just over 60. Similarly, the average age of the CPI(M) Politbureau in January 1969 was just under 60. In order to keep their power-political positions intact, these leaders have always tried to ward off any ideological challenge to their political wisdom.

It may be pointed out that the most self-deceiving decision taken at the Tenali Convention of 1964 was the one excluding any discussion on the ideological questions from the agenda of the proposed foundation Congress at Calcutta. This was surely a concession to the moderates like E. M. S. Namboodiripad and Jyoti Basu who had all along been pleading that the party should not take sides in the Sino-Soviet ideological dispute until

60. For this observation, see *New Age* (Weekly), July 11, 1965. In fact this prospect could only be arrested until 1967, when the inevitable came in an endless and bewildering train of splinterisation of the Indian Communist movement.

61. Figures for the First Party Congress delegates are taken from *People's War,* Vol. II, June 13, 1943, p. 1, and also *People's War,* Vol. II, August 1, 1943, p. 8.

it had sorted out its own ideological problems. Thus understood the decision at Tenali aimed at dissociating the new-born party in advance from either of the two extreme ideological positions and to leave the issue open for the future. The official report on the Convention observed:

> Our Party as an independent sovereign unit of the Communist movement shall arrive at its own independent decisions after a full democratic discussion in the entire party. No question of either pro-Peking or Pro-Moscow shall arise whatever our enemies shout to slander the cause of Communism. We should not resort to open criticism and attack either on C.P.S.U. or C.P.C. until our party concludes its inner-party discussions and arrives at its own conclusions.[62]

At the height of this strange ideological ostrichism practised by the CPI (M) leadership, E. M. S. Namboodiripad, while refuting a CPI charge that his party was following the Chinese line, declared that it was beyond controversy that his party had not taken up any position on the disputed questions in the international Communist movement. He further observed:

> My answer is that our party members and sympathisers knew very well that the party having taken no stand on these issues, whatever views are expressed by individual leaders and members of their party are their own.[63]

Later blasted by the Andhra Pradesh State unit's attack on the CPI (M) Central Committee's draft on ideological issues presented at the all-India plenum held at Burdwan in April 1968, the Central leadership of the party officially came out for the first time with a disarming confession that from 1964 to 1967 the party had been waging ideological crusade against revisionism without defining its own ideological position:

> One of the principal reasons (for the left-adventurist deviation in the party) is the undue though unavoidable delay caused in clinching the ideological questions that are under debate in the world Communist movement. Since our Tenali Convention of July 1964 when our Programme was broadly endorsed, for full three years up to August 1967,

62. Surjeet, H. K., *Tenali Convention of the CPI*, 1964 (Mimeographed).

63. For the text of this statement, see *People's Democracy*, August 29, 1965.

our C.C.'s official stand on these ideological questions, more or less, stood in suspense, with the result that in the name of fighting modern revisionism and defending Marxism-Leninism every syllable coming from the Chinese Communist press has come to be swallowed as an infallible piece of Marxism-Leninism, as used to be the case with most of us in regard to the C.P.S.U. for a long time in the past...... The non-committal stand of the Central Committee on the ideological issues in the international dispute, until they were discussed and decided by the party, was in reality utilised by this section of comrades, more and more, to commit themselves to each and every Chinese position, leaving no open mind whatsoever on any issue that was yet to be discussed and decided through organised inner-party discussions and debates. Positions were taken, convictions were formed and confirmed—and what remained was to carry on the inner-party struggle for the victory of these positions.[64]

This quotation proves beyond doubt that despite the deepening inner-party ideological crisis the CPI (M) Central Committee leadership never realised "the urgency or necessity of elaborating them and educating the entire party on them".[65]

As an inevitable result of this complacent ideological liberation of the CC leadership, groups sprouted like mushrooms in the party with commitment towards the Chinese position,—both tactical and ideological, and started waging inner-party struggle for the victory of their positions. This process was facilitated by the weak control of the party over its members at the initial stages.

One of such Maoist groups which had its origin in late 1964, came to be known as "Revolutionary Council," the leading figures[66] of which were Parimal Das Gupta, Kanai Chatterjee (known as Rahman in the party circle), Subhas Bose, Md. Latif, Azizul Haque, Saibal Datta, Sudhir Bhattacharya and others. This group carried on systematic attacks on the party Programme

64. *Why the Ultra-'Left' Deviation*? Document adopted by the CPI(M) Central Committee at its meeting held from October 5 to 9, 1968 in Calcutta, pp. 43-44.

65. *Ibid.*, p. 44.

66. See *On Left Deviation, op. cit.*, pp. 19-20.

and the leadership. In the middle of 1964 another institution was set up under the name "Marx-Engels Institute".[67] This Institute turned out to be the breeding ground of extremists, who were given thorough schooling in Marxism-Leninism and the thought of Mao Tse-tung. Sushital Ray Chowdhury was in charge of this Institute. Closely connected with this was another extremist organisation—the "Chinta" group,[68] mainly represented by Amulya Sen and Sudhir Bhattacharya. During the Calcutta Congress of the party in 1964 this group brought out a paper entitled "Chinta" (Thought) challenging the draft programme. Only six issues of this journal were brought out during 1964-65. Immediately after the general round up of the all-India leadership of the left communist party, sundry other splinter groups came to surface in West Bengal and became very active in bringing out numerous pamphlets, news sheets and leaflets attacking the "neo-revisionist" leadership of their party.

THE IMMEDIATE CHINESE INFLUENCES

A. *The Lin Piao Thesis, 1965*

Two events of great significance in international Communist movement gave a direct spurt to the rapid growth of thinking on the Maoist line in the CPI (M) organisation, particularly in West Bengal since 1965. First was the vigorous reassertion of the Maoist strategy of "people's war" by Lin Piao, a former CPC ideologue and Defence Minister, on September 2, 1965 in a lengthy thesis entitled "Long Live The Victory of The People's War", which upheld the Maoist model of revolution for the third World.[69] The second and the more sensational event was the Proletarian Cultural Revolution in China starting in August 1966.

It may be mentioned here that the CPC's reading in early 1967 of the "excellent" revolutionary situation in India, Burma and Indonesia[70] marked a rather significant break-through in the

67. *Ibid.*, p. 21.

68. *Ibid.*, p. 20.

69. Lin Piao, "Long Live the Victory of the People's War", *Peking Review*, September 3, 1965.

70. See "Great New Era of World Revolution", *Peking Review*, January 13, 1967, and "Imperialist Camp Enters Glooming New Year", *Ibid., January* 20, 1967.

Sino-Soviet ideological struggle. The series of developments in India, Burma and Indonesia[71] in the aggregate warranted, in the CPC's view, a new coordinated strategy to ensure the defeat of the "peaceful transition" line and to shift the struggle against the United States and the ideological crusade against the CPSU to the Third World. It is in this context that Lin Piao's article on the strategy of the people's war assumes much significance. In short, Lin's thesis highlights his global revolutionary strategy for the encirclement of the "cities of the world by the rural areas."

Starting with the main line of distinctions between the October Revolution and the Chinese Revolution, Lin Piao observed that the October Revolution began with armed uprisings in the cities and then spread to the country-side, while the Chinese Revolution was nationwide victory through the encirclement of the cities from the rural areas and the final capture of the cities. Commending Mao Tse-tung's theory of the people's war as the "common asset of the revolutionary people of the whole world", he declared that it had "characteristics of our epoch" and that it "has been proved by the long practice of the Chinese revolution to be in accord with the objective laws of such wars and to be invincible. It has not only been valid for China, it is a great contribution to the revolutionary struggle of the oppressed nations and peoples throughout the world."

Lin Piao further pointed out that Mao Tse-tung's theory of people's war solved not only the problems of people's war but also those of waging it. He wrote :

> It must be emphasised that Comrade Mao Tse-tung's theory of the establishment of rural revolutionary base areas and the encirclement of the cities from the country-side is of outstanding and universal practical significance for the present revolutionary struggles of the oppressed nations and peoples in Asia, Africa and Latin America against imperialism and its running dogs . . ..
>
> The basic political and economic conditions in many of these countries have many similarities to those that prevailed in China. As in China the peasants constitute the main

71. In India, in particular, the CPC ideologues saw a qualitative change in the revolutionary situation in the persistence of the CPI(M) in its equivocation on peaceful transition and the consequent Naxalbari peasant uprising engineered by the extremists in that party in the spring of 1967.

force of the national-democratic revolution against the imperialists and their running dogs. In committing aggression against these countries, the imperialists usually begin by seizing the big cities and the main lines of communication, but they are unable to bring the vast countryside completely under their control. The countryside, and the countryside alone, can provide the revolutionary basis from which the revolutionaries can go forward to final victory. Precisely for this reason, Comrade Mao Tse-tung's theory of establishing revolutionary base areas in the rural districts and encircling the cities from the countryside is attracting more and more attention among the people in these regions.[72]

Lin's strategy aimed at linking all the people's wars in the Third World into a global front against the United States, reinforcing each other and merging into a "torrential world-wide tide." His thesis concludes with a frontal attack on the Soviet "revisionist" ideological positions highlighting the general line of "Three Peacefuls"—peaceful coexistence, peaceful competition and peaceful transition. Peaceful transition to socialism through the parliamentary process, it may be pointed out, was Khrushchevian innovation at the 20th Congress of the Communist Party of Soviet Union held in February 1956, and finally refined in the Declaration of the Twelve Communist and Workers' Parties held in Moscow in November 1957. Khrushchev's concept of peaceful transition, repeated and endorsed by Anasthas Mikoyan and Mikhail Suslov, was, in fact, a corollary to his declaration that peaceful coexistence was the "general line of the Soviet policy."[73]

To the Chinese, the strategy of peaceful transition to socialism amounted to a "clear revision of the Marxist-Leninist teachings on the state and revolution and a clear negation of the universal significance of the road of the October Revolution." Precisely, the CPC's views on the question of peaceful transition were: It would be more flexible to refer to both peaceful and non-peaceful forms because that would leave the political initiative with the Communists but referring only to peaceful transi-

72. Lin Piao, "Long Live The Victory of The People's War", *Ibid.*

73. For details, see N. S. Khrushchev, *Report of the Central Committee of the Communist Party of Soviet Union to the XX Party Congress* February 14, 1956, Moscow, 1956, pp .42-46.

tion would tie their hands; it might be tactically advantageous to refer to peaceful transition but it would be inappropriate to over-emphasize its possibility; to the best of their knowledge there was still "not a country where this possibility is of any practical significance"; should such possibility arise the Communists could always take advantage of it; to obtain majority in parliament was not the same as smashing the old state machinery and establishing the new state machinery; peaceful transition to socialism should not be interpreted in such a way that it solely meant transition through parliamentary majority.[74]

As it emerges from the foregoing analysis, Lin Piao's article marked the culmination of the Chinese attack on Soviet "revisionism" and insofar as the Third World was concerned, the attack was to be carried out through an escalation of national liberation movement.

Lin Piao's thesis left a powerful impact on the growing Maoist movement in India, because it reaffirmed the faith of the Indian Maoists in the revolutionary strategy of Mao Tse-tung. And the article was immediately seized by them as the green signal for a people's war in India.

In fact, the publication of the Lin Piao thesis should be viewed as the beginning of the series of attempts made by the Chinese ideologues throughout 1966 and 1967 to project a Maoist revolutionary line to India where they saw an "excellent" revolutionary situation.

Towards the end of 1965 what acted as the major determinant of China's policy and strategy for the Indian sub-continent was the India-Pakistan armed conflict in September. The war quickly stirred up Peking to make a fresh strategical-ideological appraisal of the power-political situation in the sub-continent, especially from the perspective of China's own diplomatic and geo-political interests in the area and her assessment of the role played by India in an anti-China alliance system, supposedly sponsored by Moscow and Washington. Peking seemed to be witnessing "an eastward shift" of the American global strategy

74. See "Outline of Views on the Question of Peaceful Transition," in Editorial Departments of *People's Daily* and *Red Flag*. "The Origin and Development of Differences Between the Leadership of the CPSU and Ourselves : Comment on the Open Letter of the Central Committee, CPSU —1", *Peking Review*, September 13, 1963.

with active Soviet connivance, in which India was playing an increasingly important role.[75]

The Indo-Pakistani war prompted sharp Chinese attack on India, which tended to emphasize the convergence of the American and Soviet interests in India. Premier Chou En-lai condemned "India's aggression" "a threat to Asian peace" and saw "consent and support of the United States" and encouragements of the "modern revisionists" to the "military adventure".[76]

Later on, Peking came to "discover" finally Washington's link with the Indo-Soviet anti-Chinese alliance, following the talks in New Delhi on the occasion of Shastri's funeral, between Kosygin and Humphrey.

Thus by early 1966, Peking's strategic views on Asia had been clearly formulated:

"Asia, not Europe, is now the focal point for US Aggression ..... Confrontation with China, instead of the Soviet Union is the military strategy Washington now subscribes to....As part of this strategy, a US-dominated anti-China front is being patched up".[77]

In another article it was observed that "the policy of the new leaders of the CPSU is to unite with US imperialists and the reactionaries of various countries in forging a counter-revolutionary ring of encirclement against China."[78] India, in the Chi-

75. It appears that the theme of a US-Soviet-Indian alliance system against China began to be formulated by the Peking ideologues just after Premier Shastri's visit to Moscow in May 1965. In an article, entitled "What Shastri's Soviet Trip Reveals" in *Peking Review* on June 4, 1965, the *Observer* wrote that Shastri was toeing the "Nehru Line" such as the new Soviet leadership was following the old "Khrushchevian Line" in aligning itself with the Indian "reactionaries" against China. Shastri was further described as a "rare anti-China cavalier" and "Washington's pet". Again, in an article published in *Peking Review* on August 13, entitled "Non-Aligned India's Double Alignment" Shish Yen wrote that by receiving military aid from the Soviet Union, the Indian government hoped to conceal its alliance with Washington, claiming that between the two it is 'nonaligned' and 'neutral'. Military aids from the United States and the Soviet Union to India were of the "same nature" aimed against China and helping war preparation, which threatened India's neighbours and peace.

76. *Peking Review*, September 17, 1965.

77. "The Shift in US Global Strategy", *Peking Review*, February, 1966.

78. Commentator in *Hung Ch'i* (*Red Flag*), translated in *Peking Review*, February 18, 1966.

nese thinking, was the major base for a US-Soviet joint strategy for "encirclement and containment" of China. The fear of a so-called alliance between U.S.A., U.S.S.R. and India against China motivated China's Pakistan policy which was primarily designed to keep the subcontinent divided and weak and to keep Pakistan out of the so-called "anti-China" alliance. At the same time the Chinese leaders adopted a picture of extreme hostility towards India. Economic and political weakening of India by inciting discontent and movement against the Indian government became the sole objective of Peking's propaganda machinery in early 1966. The Chinese championed the "national self-determination struggles" in Kashmir, by the Nagas and Mizos in eastern India and also the independence and sovereignty of Sikkim and Bhutan.

On a fresh appraisal of the Indian domestic scene in the beginning of 1966 the Chinese ideologues found the Indian situation almost "ripe" for a revolutionary upsurge[79] and started prescribing the Maoist strategy and tactics for the oncoming Indian revolution. It was, however, only with the formal launching of the Great Proletarian Cultural Revolution in China in August 1966 that the CPC's projection of a clear ideological line became more pronounced.[80]

While analysing the Chinese motivation pattern behind the projection of the Maoist revolutionary strategy for the Third World as a whole, and India, in particular, an Indian writer has observed that "it is inconceivable that the projection of the Maoist line to Asian Communist movement was preceded in 1966-67 by careful objective assessment of actual social, economic and political situations obtaining in individual countries.

79. Two successive drought years and the resulting economic recession created political ferments in India in 1966. The Chinese media saw in all this "a sharpening of class contradictions." See "Indian People Rise up in Resistance," *Peking Review,* November 16, 1966, and "Student Movement in India." *Ibid.,* December 2, 1966.

80. Amidst the ravages of the Cultural Revolution the CPC commemorated the first anniversary of Lin Piao's thesis published in September 1965 with the declaration that "revolutionary military strategy of people's war, created by Mao Tse-tung, is the only correct and victorious strategy for the oppressed people to defeat all enemies." See Tung Ming, "The People's Revolutionary Strategy Will Surely Triumph Over U.S. Imperialism's Counter Revolutionary Strategy", *Peking Review,* September 9, 1966.

Revolutionary fervour apparently got the better of Marxist-Leninist homework. This seems to be borne out by the Chinese assessment of the Indian situation in 1966-67; evidently, the CCP saw a revolutionary political upheaval in India because it wished to see it."[81]

This, however, appears to be too oversimplified an assessment of the CPC's revolutionary strategy to promote Maoist parties in the Third World. It has already been elaborately pointed out that with the victory of the New Democratic revolution in China under the leadership of Mao Tse-tung in 1949, the CPC on its own took up the responsibility of guiding revolutionary movements in Asia, Africa and Latin America, and in the crucial 20th Congress of the CPSU it asserted its responsibility as a "right." Thenceforth the CPC sought to build an international Communist movement parallel to the one led by the CPSU. Since the Chinese claimed that the Maoist model of revolution was more relevant and suitable than the Soviet model for the Third World, sustained labour was put into developing, not quite subjectively, a revolutionary strategy for these countries. Thus understood, Lin Piao's "Long Live the Victory of the People's War" is not to be construed as a casual routine reassertion of the Maoist model of revolution, but as the net result of the foreign policy debate that had began early in 1965 in the Communist Party of China.[82] In fact, the Cultural Revolution simply brought about a brainwave which forced the CPC ideologues to take a rather optimistic note of the happenings in India, in which they quickly read an objective revolutionary situation. Now, of the reasons that can be adduced to the Chinese projection of a revolutionary line to India, in particular, in 1966-67, the more significant ones are first that the Chinese motivation for promoting revolutionary struggles was their rivalry with the Soviet Union and India was picked up as the testing ground because of their hostile relations with that country arising out of the border issues and because of India's position in the Sino-Soviet ideological rift. So the CPC calculated that by building a Maoist revolutionary movement in India first they could strike

81. Bhabani Sen Gupta, *Communism in Indian Politics,* Columbia University Press, New York and London, 1972, p. 388.

82. See Uri Ra'anan, "Peking's Foreign Policy Debate," *op. cit.*

at the Indian citadel of the CPSU's worldwide "revisionist" operations; and second, the immediate occasion for this testing operation was provided by the Great Proletarian Cultural Revolution in China in August 1966.

B. *The Great Proletarian Cultural Revolution, 1966*

The Cultural Revolution which was initiated with the rampage of the militant Red Guards, gave a good shake-up to the Communist Party of India (Marxist), which had been already deeply embroiled in a serious inner-party ideological crisis. The sharpening of the Mao-Liu feud[83] acted as a potent factor in forcing an informal schism in the CPI (M) leadership. It was reported that the party leaders were unofficially divided into two groups, viz., the "Peking Group" and the "Shanghai Group." The "Peking Group", led by B. T. Ranadive, Hare Krishna Konar and Promode Das Gupta, backed up by the Maoists in the party, moved ideologically much closer to the pro-Mao-group. Other prominent CPI (M) leaders like A. K. Gopalan, E. M. S. Namboodiripad and Jyoti Basu, on the other hand, belonged to the "Shanghai Group" which sympathised with Liu Shao Ch'i and his anti-Mao followers. The effect of this division in the party was very far-reaching as it further encouraged fissiparous tendencies which had already assumed disruptive proportions in the party. By exploiting this delicate situation the extremists in the CPI (M) came out openly in favour of Mao Tse-tung in order to challenge their "neo-revisionist" leadership. They contended that Mao Tse-tung had been fighting for inner-party ideological purity—a claim they had been voicing for quite a long time. They explained the growth of the Red Guards as

83. The Mao-Liu feud, itself a formidable issue in the Great Proletarian Cultural Revolution, was primarily attributed to Lin Shao Ch'i's deviation from Mao's ideological line on the very basic issue—whether the regime should rapidly implement its revolutionary programme or give priority to the consolidation of revolutionary gains. Mao has always been the promoter and initiator of new radical policies while Liu always tried to consolidate the gains and tended to move more slowly. For this and sundry other reasons Liu Shao Ch'i came to be ironically called "China's Khrushchev". For details, see S. H. Peter and J. M. Malconey, *Communist China. The Domestic Scene,* 1949-57, South Orange, New Jersey Seton Hall University Press, 1967.

a manifestation of the need to prevent China's younger generation from going the way of the Soviet "social imperialists.[84]

From the foregoing analysis it appears quite evident that Maoism returned to Indian politics after an interlude of two decades, first through the instrumentality of Lin Piao's thesis in 1965, which spells out the strategy of people's war on a global basis, and secondly, and perhaps more immediately, through the Proletarian Cultural Revolution which brought new relevance and dimension for Maoism before the Communist revolutionaries in India, especially in West Bengal. The recrudescence of Maoist thought set in motion a very fast proliferation of Maoist groups within the fold of the CPI (M). To these external factors responsible for the growth of Maoism in the Indian Communist movement one may further add the fact of domestic failure of the left Communist leadership to adopt extra-parliamentary methods in order to wreck the parliamentary system from outside. In fact, the CPI (M)'s choice of working within the parliamentary system could be seen to be partly dictated by the enormous punitive power at the disposal of the system, because working within the system with the objective of wrecking it may not bring the party to a direct confrontation with the armed forces of the State. Moreover, there is a tactical disadvantage for the party to launch largescale insurrectionary movement in India, because in a segmented society like India's the possibility of anarchy in one State spreading to other States is minimised considerably. The organisational growth of Communism in West Bengal since independence for example, has not been accompanied by a parallel growth even in the States adjoining West Bengal.

It is for this reason that CPI (M) leaders were not ready in the early 1960's to view the political situation in India as "an excellent revolutionary situation." It was precisely because of their conviction that India was not passing through a period ripe for a one-stage revolution, the CPI (M) leaders argued at a later date that "any further weakening or disorganising of the Party from a sectarian and left-opportunist deviation, we are of opinion, would only result in greater harm to the cause of the

84. For this interesting development in the CPI(M) in early 1967, see *Amrita Bazar Patrika* (Calcutta), February 15, 1967.

Indian revolution, and would come as a boon to the reactionary ruling classes".[85] This unwillingness of the CPI (M) leaders to go in for summary revolution in India was viewed by the Maoists within the party as a "neo-revisionist" trick of the leaders. And in their bid to throw an open ideological challenge to the leadership the Maoists were further reinforced first by the Lin Piao's thesis and then by the Cultural Revolution in China.

The penetration of Maoism into the CPI (M) rank and file membership could go much deeper because of the fact that most important members of the party's top leadership, especially M. Basavapunniah, P. Sundarayya, H. K. Konar and Promode Das Gupta not merely shut their eyes rather indulgently to these Maoists in the party but actually encouraged them by taking an anti-Soviet posture in the international Communist movement and an ultra-left stance within the party. They raised the slogan of a People's Democracy as the attainable goal without a transitional form of government in the intervening period. This attitude served two distinct purposes : first, it clearly demarcated the Marxist Party from the "revisionist" CPI after the formal split; and secondly, it projected the CPI (M) as the main challenge to the Congress system. Obviously, this was the only possible way for the new party to keep its following intact and insulated from the influence of the CPI. It also helped to augment the influence of the CPI (M) in the traditional Communist strongholds like Kerala, Andhra Pradesh and West Bengal.

85. *Ideological Debate Summed Up By Politbureau*, Calcutta, Communist Party of India (Marxist), 1968, p. 183.

CHAPTER II

NAXALBARI—I : THE HUNAN OF INDIA

WHILE THE inner-party ideological struggle in the CPI (M) was fast gaining momentum in and around Calcutta, the situation in the Darjeeling District Committee of the party had already assumed an all the more disquieting proportion. Before analysing the series of events leading to the peasant revolt in Darjeeling in the spring of 1967, it would be quite relevant to make a few observations on the socio-economic conditions of the three tracts of Naxalbari, Kharibari and Phansidewa where a group of extremists in the CPI (M) lit up the sparks of a Maoist revolution in India after an interlude of two decades.

PHYSICAL AND DEMOGRAPHIC FEATURES

Naxalbari[1] is a police station of 206.7 square kilometres in area under the Siliguri Sub-division of the Darjeeling District of West Bengal. It is situated in the slender 'neck' which is India's only vital land corridor that connects Bhutan, Sikkim and the country's north-east zone comprising Assam, Nagaland, Manipur, Tripura, the Mizo Hills, the Arunachal and the Meghalaya regions with the rest of the country. It has two international borders—in the west is Nepal at a distance of 4 miles, and in the east is the Democratic Republic of Bangla Desh[2] (formerly East Pakistan) at a distance of 15 miles. The People's Republic of China is also not very far off from this area on the northern side as China's Tibet is only 60 miles away. It

1. It should be noted that before February 1960 there was no existence of Naxalbari as a separate police station. It was by the Notification No. 416 Pl., dated the 3rd February 1960 that a new police station styled as Naxalbari Police Station was created with J.L. Nos. 55 to 85 & 97 of Kharibari Police Station and J.L. Nos. 17, 18, 64 to 72, 80 to 92 and 116 to 166 of Siliguri Police Station. See *The Census of India Report*, 1961, Vol. XIV, W. Bengal & Sikkim Part II-A, p. 75.

2. On one side, beyond Naxalbari, is the river Mechi, across which is Nepal. On the other, across the Mahananda from Phansidewa is Bangladesh.

is, however, the international border lying between the two Bengals that concerns us most in the present context because of the attitudes and interests of the Communists in India and elsewhere towards this part of the sub-continent.

After the partition of India in 1947 the convergence of the India-Pakistan borders at the eastern part of West Bengal made this State an area of special interest for the Communists on the either side of the international border. It may be pointed out that Bengal, being the strongest base of the Indian Communist movement in the pre-independence days, had always been in the calculation of the CPI leaders, and the Comintern as well, as the most advanced area which could lead the whole of India in the future revolutionary struggles. This strategy of the CPI was clearly reflected in its nationality policy adopted in the pre-partition days. The Muslim League's adoption of the Pakistan slogan apparently aroused great interest in the CPI. This was obviated by the party's stand on the Congress-League dispute over the fate of two important regions—Bengal and Punjab. Apparently, the C.P.I. line offered major concessions to the Muslim League and this was put forward by P. C. Joshi in 1944. In his thesis Joshi advocated not only two independent States of India and Pakistan but a third one—a "Sovereign and Independent State of Bengal".[3] Though a "Sovereign and Independent" Bengal did not come into existence in 1947, the CPI strategy of making Bengal the centre of the Indian Communist movement was not given up at that time. In fact, the CPI leadership took greater interests in building strong party organisations in the eastern wing of Bengal in the days following the partition, because they thought the peculiar geographical position of the new-born States of Pakistan and the fluid political situation in its both the wings, separated by 1000 miles of Indian territory, would give them greater scope and opportunity of building a revolutionary base in East Bengal. In that case, East Pakistan could be used both as a rear base and a sanctuary for spreading armed struggle in West Bengal first, and then, throughout the Indian sub-continent. Thus the geographic location of the two Bengals after 1947 suggested to the Communists on either side of the international

3. Joshi P. C., *They Must Meet Again,* Bombay, People's Publishing House, 1944, p. 44.

border the feasibility of guerilla warfare in this region. Moreover, the topographic condition of this area also strengthened their conviction as much of it consists of hilly terrain, covered with dense forests and criss-crossed by numerous fast-flowing streams. This probably accounts for the spate of the Communist insurrectionary activities that had swept many parts of the two Bengals during the late 40's and early 50's. That the Communists never give up the idea of a "Communist Bengal" became evident again in 1964 when it was reported that the "pro-Chinese" Communists in the CPI had planned to form a so-called People's Republic of Bengal covering West Bengal, the then East Pakistan, Assam and Nagaland (with headquarters at Calcutta) with the help of the People's Republic of China.[4]

Thus understood, the geographical position of Naxalbari and its adjoining areas has endowed it with a special strategic importance. Wiping out of this vital communication link by any military action or violent agitation in this area is likely to cost the whole country rather dearly. And the choice of this strategic area for the theatre of an armed peasant uprising engineered by the Maoists in the CPI (M) in early 1967 was thus highly significant. In the pages that follow what, therefore, the author seeks to emphasise is that the strategic position of Naxalbari coupled with the prevailing agrarian problems, which had been carefully and systematically capitalised by the Maoist ideologues in the CPI (M) in that area, helped the peasants to launch a violent agitation, largely modelled on the Hunan Peasant Uprising in China in the spring of 1927. It is the author's contention, in a word, that though there have been agrarian problems in other areas of West Bengal, no less acute than those of Naxalbari, the situation in Naxalbari was complicated by a host of socio-economic factors only peculiar to the area itself. To this must be added the strategic location of the tract, which made the situation all the more volatile for a violent uprising.

Apart from Naxalbari two other police stations of the Siliguri Sub-division, which shot into prominence in the spring of 1967 are Kharibari and Phansidewa.[5] These three police sta-

4. For full information, see *Hindusthan Standard* (Calcutta daily), May 3, 1964.

5. Siliguri, Naxalbari, Kharibari and Phansidewa—these four police stations constitute the Siliguri Sub-division of the Darjeeling District.

tions cover a total area of 256 square miles backward sub-montane terai. The whole area is very sparsely populated with a density of only 504 persons per square miles, much lower than the average density of 606 in the hill districts of the State. The total population as enumerated in the 1961 census is 126,725 of which Naxalbari accounts for 42,195, Kharibari 25,957 and Phansidewa 58,573.[6] The whole area is strewn with dense forests and rivulets. Communications, therefore, are difficult, especially during the rainy season which starts fairly early and persists till late October, with an average annual rainfall of about 127.5 inches, characteristic of the Duars region.

The major segments of the population of Naxalbari (57.7%), Phansidewa (64.5%) and Kharibari (72.2%) are composed of the scheduled castes and tribes; their total in Darjeeling district is 82,381 and 96,444 respectively. Among the scheduled castes and tribes in the three police stations the Rajbanshis (locally known as "Bahes") and the Adivasis are 50% and 25% respectively and the rest chiefly are the Nepalese. The Adivasis of the local origin like the Lepchas and the Bhutiyas mingle with the tribals like the Santhals, the Oraons and the Mundas, who hail from the Chotonagpur region of Bihar.

The backbone of the peasanty in this area is provided by the Rajbanshis, a scheduled caste. They speak a host of local dialects. The Lepchas and the Bhutiyas use a language of the Indo-Tibetan group. The Santhals, Oraons and Mundas mainly speak a broken Hindi. Many tribal groups have their own dialects also, including one which is rather close to Maithili and Bengali. They practise diverse religions. Some of the tribes are Christians, while there are a few Muslim families also in the Chaterhat area of Naxalbari. The Lepchas and Bhutiyas adhere to Lamaism of Tibetan origin. Table I[8] shows the break-up of the religious groups in the three police stations under study:

6. For a detailed analysis of the census figures of the three police stations concerned, see *The Census of India Report,* 1961, Vol. XVI part II-A, West Bengal and Sikkim, pp. 178-179.

7. For a detailed account of the scheduled castes and the scheduled tribes in these three police stations, see *Darjeeling District Census Handbook,* 1961, pp. 64-74.

8. *Ibid.,* p. 41.

TABLE I

Police Stations	Buddhist	Christian	Hindu	Muslim
Phansidewa	0.12	8.08	74.25	17.52
Kharibari	0.06	1.00	95.27	3.65
Naxalbari	1.14	4.68	91.31	2.87

Compared with West Bengal as a whole (32.90) and the district of Darjeeling (28.70), the percentage of literacy in the three police stations, according to the census data of 1961, is remarkably poor as shown in Table II.[9]

TABLE II

Police Stations	Percentage of Literacy
Phansidewa	16.55
Kharibari	19.57
Naxalbari	22.86

Land Problems :

In the three police stations there are as many as 44 tea estates employing about 25,000 workers. The brown podzolic soil that helps the growth of tea plantation here makes agricultural productivity very low. Water quickly drains away from the sandy and heavily leached gravelly soil, leaving the fields dry almost instantly.[10] There is no government scheme for the conservation of water for irrigation purposes. Fertiliser is almost unknown except in the tea gardens. The results in crops failure almost every year.

The land problem in the three tracts presents an even more complicated picture. First, the Terai region was never permanently settled with the zaminders under the British Raj. It was marked as "Non-Regulated Area," that is, regular tenancy laws of the British Indian Government were not enforced in the area.

9. *Census of India,* 1961: *West Bengal & Sikkim, Vol. XVI, Part I-A,* p. 116.

10. For an analysis of the physical background of the area, see *West Bengal*: *Land and People,* published by the City College Commerce Department, Calcutta, 1956, pp. 15-24.

Two different acts were in vogue: the Act of 1859 and the Act of 1879. According to these Acts the Bengal Government had leased out the land to its "subjects" for specific periods. These subjects were known as "Jotedars". There were 860 small and big jotedari in the region before the land Acquisition Act of 1954.[11]

The land tenure system in these areas has been even more irregular and a source of extra misery for the appallingly poor peasantry. Under the existing system in the Terai region, a jotedar employs "adhiars" (share-croppers) to cultivate his land on contractual basis every season. All the transactions are made orally and there are, therefore, no legal documents to establish any rights for the tillers. The jotedars have been legally free to exploit the peasants as they like. Naturally, bitter feuds accumulated for years and created acute tensions. The jotedars often started criminal cases against the "adhiars" and evicted them from their lands. A new situation arose after the Estate Acquisition Act and the Land Reform Act were passed in 1954 and 1955. As there were no land records, the jotedars took advantage of this and started a larger number of malafide transfers of holdings in excess of the ceiling. This was followed by large-scale evictions of the peasants and share-croppers, who did not get any protection from the law of the land or the administration.

Secondly, these three police stations of Naxalbari, Kharibari and Phansidewa are strewn with tea gardens. The owners of these tea gardens have retained under their possession vast stretches of land. Under the provision of the West Bengal Estate Acquisition Act of 1954, the tea planters were required to use their land for the purpose of tea plantation only. But now they have either kept a major portion of their land as fallows or are using it for producing jute and maize. This has created a standing problem for the poor landless peasants in the area where land is very much in short supply.

It may be pointed out that tea plantation was first systematically started in the Terai region in 1870, and as a result, the whole area underwent quick transformation within a decade. For

11. For further information see "The Naxalbari Story", *Link* (New Delhi, weekly), August 15, 1967, p. 84.

example, in the census report of 1871 the population breakups of Kharibari, Phansidewa and Siliguri police stations were 13,828, 12,668 and 21,489 respectively. Naxalbari, it has already been noted, was then under the administrative jurisdiction of the Siliguri police station. It was carved out of Siliguri and given the status of a separate police station only in 1960. According to the 1891 census report the total population of these three police stations was 72,997. Thus understood, during the two decades following 1871 these areas registered an overall increase of 25,000 people, whereas during the seventy years since 1891 the whole region had a population growth of about 55,000.[12] This steady increase in population is due, first, to the import of more plantation labour from outside the region, especially from Bihar; second, to the steady influx of refugees from what was formerly East Pakistan in the post-partition days, and third, to the inclusion of a section of population from Bihar as a result of the entry of some portion of Purnea district of Bihar[13] into West Bengal. This high rate of population growth put an extremely heavy pressure on the limited capacity of the total cultivable land in the Terai region.

According to the Siliguri sub-division land settlement records, the total amount of vested land of the area in 1967—just before the peasant struggle was launched—was a little above 19,089 acres, out of which only 10,875 acres were cultivable. Again, about 1,000 acres of cultivable land had already been handed over to the Defence Department for military purposes.[14] It could, therefore, be seen that only about 9,715 acres of arable land would be made available for distribution among the landless peasants—an amount too little to satisfy their land hunger.

Now, what made the situation as explosive in these three tracts of Naxalbari, Kharibari and Phansidewa in the spring of 1967 ? This might be explained in terms of the cob-webbed, dis-

12. For an account of the population growth in these areas during the period between 1901 and 1961, see *Darjeeling District Census Handbook*, 1961, p. 26.

13. An area of about 147.6 square kilometres of the Purnea District of Bihar was transferred to the Darjeeling District and included in the Phansidewa police station. See the *Census of India Report*, 1961 : West Bengal and Sikkim, Vol. VI, Part II-A, p. 120.

14. See *Jugantar* (a Bengali daily published from Calcutta), July 28, 1967.

cretely shadowed corner of India's socio-economic life—the world of the landless labourers and share-croppers. The mass of these people, looked down upon by most of the political parties and dismissed till recently as serfs beyond redemption from the influence of the landed gentry, remained at a distance from the main currents of political struggles.

In underdeveloped countries like India, the rural proletariat consisting of the landless peasants and share-croppers are the worst exploited. The industrial proletariat, particularly in the public sector today, suffer less as a result of the manipulative capacity of the trade unions to win some palliatives for them from the management or the state. Quite understandably the industrial workers are not so much concerned with the acquisition of political power as with gaining a fair share of economic wealth. On the other hand, a change in the lot of the agricultural workers is inextricably bound up with the basic question of changing the entire rural economic set-up.

As is now widely recognized, the land reforms of the 1950's and 1960's did not bring about any structural change in agrarian relations but merely abolished semi-feudal "intermediary" tennures. Again, while these laws regulated and protected tenancy rights of land-owning cultivators, they did almost nothing to protect the rights of share-croppers. On the contrary, they permitted owners to resume land from share-croppers in certain circumstances.[15]

It has been observed by Gunnar Myrdal that the Indian countryside "is like a complex molecule among whose ports extreme tensions have been built up" and that the tensions "may reorganize in a way that would explode the molecule".[16] It is from this perspective of the growing agrarian crisis in India that the Naxalbari peasant struggle has to be analyzed.

To understand the extent of operational possibilities of any underground movement in North Bengal it is necessary to get a clear picture of the sector-wise distribution of employed persons.

15. For different aspects of land reforms in India, see Daniel Thorner, *The Agrarian Prospect in India,* London, Oxford University Press, 1958: and Bhowani Sen, *Evolution of Agrarian Relations in India,* New Delhi, People's Publishing House, 1962.

16. Gunnar Myrdal, *Asian Drama,* New York, Tantheon, 1968, Vol. II, pp. 1063-64.

Insofar as the police stations of Naxalbari, Kharibari nad Phansidewa are concerned, there are three important sectors where the local tribal population is gainfully employed. First among these are the plantations (tea), where the lot of wage-earners is much better than that of the mass of the peasantry. Forest labourers constitute the second sector of employment. The major segment of the population is engaged in cultivation.

Table III[17] shows the relative importance of the three major sectors of employment in the different police stations of the area.

TABLE III

Incidence of major sectors of employment (% of total population)

Police Stations	Cultivators	Agricultural labour	Persons engaged in mining, forestry and Plantations
Naxalbari	37.5	4.6	40.0
Phansidewa	54.4	6.1	38.8
Kharibari	67.7	5.4	15.2

From the reported nature of the movement, it may be safely concluded that its sustenance was largely derived from the cultivators and agricultural labourers. The low incidence of agricultural labourers suggests that the slogan of "land to the tillers" is unlikely to sustain a militant peasant movement for long.

It will be unwise, however, to ignore altogether the significance of agricultural labour. The census data reveal the peculiar intermingling of role-structures—a relatively high proportion of cultivators double up as agricultural labourers, and similarly, a significant proportion of agricultural labour too declare "cultivation" as their major secondary occupation.

Besides, no idea can be more mistaken than that the cultivators constitute a homogeneous group. There are discernible distributions which mark them out into several groups, one such

17. *Darjeeling District Census Hand Book,* 1961, pp. 52-53.

being their relative degree of poverty or affluence. Although there is no absolute criterion for assuming this, one can yet choose to clarify the cultivators in terms of the size of the holdings they cultivate. For purposes of clarity the holding size of 5 acres or less is chosen here as the dividing line to mark out the poorest among the cultivators. Table IV[18] brings out clearly the proportion of cultivators possessing less than 5 acres of land in each police station under consideration.

TABLE IV
Proportion of cultivators possessing less than 5 acres of land

Police Stations	Percentage of the total
Naxalbari	68.3
Phansidewa	59.6
Kharibari	43.7

The table shows the high incidents of small cultivators, particularly in Naxalbari and Phansidewa. There is, however, another element to which it is necessary to draw attention. Not all the cultivators are owners of the holdings they cultivate, and a significant proportion cultivate on agency basis (bhagchash). Table V analyses the available data from this angle, and shows the incidence of three categories of holdings, viz., those which are directly held from the Government (owner-cultivators), those which are held from private persons on an agency basis, and those which are combinations of both. This table lays bare what the crux of the problem is in the disturbed areas : the extraordinarily high proportion of bhagchash arrangements.[19]

Table No. V shows that as high as 50% of the holdings are held through agencies both in Naxalbari and Phansidewa. It should, therefore, be crystal clear that any meaningful land reform must include measures of protective devices against the eviction of bhagchashis (share-croppers).

18. *Ibid.*, pp. 184-185.

19. *Ibid.* For an outstanding analysis of the agrarian problems in the three tracts of Naxalbari, Kharibari and Phansidewa see Chandra S. Chakravarti, "Naxalbari: Evidence and Inference", *Now* (a former Calcutta weekly), July 7, 1967, pp. 8-11.

TABLE V

Types of holdings as percentage of total holdings of each thana (police stations)

Police Stations	Holdings directly held	Holdings held through Agencies	Combination
Naxalbari	37.1	49.7	13.2
Phansidewa	39.4	49.1	11.5
Kharibari	45.9	33.9	20.2

The data presented in the above tables would lead one to the following conclusions :

1. A slogan for the distribution of vested lands to agricultural labourers is unlikely to command mass support because of the relatively low incidence of this class in the area;
2. The high incidence of small holdings implies that the slogan of "land to the tiller" any in reality mean a demand for more land for the poor cultivators, and
3. The incidence of bhagchashis in an extraordinarily high proportion suggests that the land-hunger of the mass of the peasantry would be satisfied only when the authorities agree to resist their eviction.

In short, the militant base of the peasant movement rests heavily on the plight of the bhagchasis in this area, and not on that of agricultural labourers or of the tribal population. Some further details are furnished below for clarification. In table VI the holders of less than 5 acres of land have been grouped in terms of the three types of holdings referred to in Table V.[20]

It shows that the poorer cultivators are primarily agency holders. Table VII[21], on the other hand, enumerates the proportion of cultivators holding less than 5 acres of land in the total number of cultivators holding the different categories of farm in each tract.

20. *Ibid.*
21. *Ibid.*

TABLE VI

Incidence of three types of holdings as % of the total holdings of less than 5 acres of land for each tract

Police Stations	Owner-cultivators	Bhagchashis	Both
Naxalbari	33.2	60.1	6.7
Phansidewa	27.1	65.0	7.5
Kharibari	38.8	50.1	11.2

TABLE VII

Police Stations	Owner-cultivators	Agency-cultivators	Combined
Naxalbari	60.9	82.4	34.8
Phansidewa	41.4	80.3	33.5
Kharibari	37.7	66.4	26.8

The two tables taken together indicate that it is the class of bhagchashis which alone satisfied the criterion of homogeneity so necessary for the conduct of a militant peasant movement and it is in this setting that the well-organized happenings of 1967 took place.

Of course, the Naxalbari incidents should not be mistaken on stray unconnected events, since this was not the first warning. There were similar flareups in this area in the past, notably in 1939 when Khwaja Nazimuddin was Chief Minister of the undivided Bengal. Then, again in 1959 during the Chief Ministership of Dr B. C. Roy the same thing happened. The struggles related to the grievances of the share-croppers, mainly Rajbanshis (Bahes) and the tribals from Bihar, imported into the area as indentured tea garden labour about fifty years ago. These incidents foreshadowed some sort of a serious upheaval in this area. The pattern of struggles in the spring of 1967, therefore, bears striking uniformity with the previous incidents.

It should be noted that the immediate cause of the so-called "Kisan movement" could be attributed to the anomalies of the land policies of the Congress Government, thus providing a direct inducement to the local Communist elements to hatch and execute a plan on political basis. It has been revealed in an empirical study of rural radicalism[22], that the peasant most susceptible to radical movements lives in an area where the tenancy law is irregular; the old rural elite has been weakened, has had his traditional value system modified by political education, literacy, entry into the market, closeness to towns, accessibility to communications, etc., is a share-cropper, agricultural labourer, or dwarf (i.e., holding under one acre) found in certain crop areas such as rice and plantation which are labour intensive or one-crop areas susceptible to market fluctuations rather than areas with multiple crops. This analysis suggests, in so far as Naxalbari is concerned, that serious grievances of the peasants were there and this was carefully fanned by the propaganda of the local CPI(M) dominated Kishan Sabha into a series of irruptions in the spring of 1967.

A Revolutionary Tradition

It is interesting to note in this context that the North Bengal peasants had a long tradition of militant struggles against all sorts of oppression and injustice perpetrated by the landlords. Prior to the Naxalbari peasant uprising of 1967, the peasants of North Bengal had fought on many occasions against oppressive tenancy laws and other illegal exactions by the local landlords. They were inspired in their militant movements mainly by the peasants of the 24-Parganas district of Bengal. Apart from the historic Tebhaga Movement (movement for three-fourths share of the crops) of 1946, the storm-centre of which was the southern part of the 24-Parganas, other important movements launched by the North Bengal peasants are those against the eviction of the adhiars (share-croppers) and against "hat tola" and "mela tola" which began simultaneously in Rangpur, Dinajpur, Malda, Mymensingh.

In several districts of Bengal, the local landlords, talukdars, and their paid agents amassed vast fortunes by illegal exaction from the periodical markets or "haats". The poor peasants who used to sell their commodities in those market places owned by the landlords had to pay various kinds of fees, both in cash and kind. Although this practice had started much earlier, the

22. Donald S. Zagoria, "The Social Bases of Indian Communism", in Richard Lowenthal (ed.), *Issues in the Future of Asia,* New York, Frederick A. Praeger, 1969, p. 99.

peasants could not check it and their sporadic clashes with the sentries of the zamindars led to further oppression.

With the beginning of the Tebhaga struggle in the 24-Parganas in 1946, the militancy of the North Bengal peasants reached further heights. In North Bengal, the districts which had been worst affected by this movement were Dinajpur, Malda, Mymensingh and Rangpur (the last two now being in Bangladesh). Thousands of peasants who had been suffering from the "Tanka", "Nankar" and "Bhowal" systems, raise the slogan of "Tebhaga" and revolted against the landlords and the money-lenders under the leadership of the CPI sponsored BPKS (Bangiya Pradeshik Krishak Sabha). From 1946 to 1950 these districts in North Bengal remained hotbeds of a violent mass upsurge.[23]

Though the "Tebhaga" struggle proved abortive, they left a lasting impress in the minds of the Bengal peasants, and the first ideological basis of their simmering discontent was provided by a highly secret Communist Party document known as the "Tactical Line," circulated to the members of the Central Committee of the CPI at the time of the Third Congress of the Party held at Madurai in December, 1955[24].

The central thesis of the document is that in India imperialism and feudalism constitute the common enemies of all classes of people except the feudal landlords. To liquidate these enemies it is essential that "a broad-based nationwide united front of all anti-imperialist classes (including the national bourgeoisie)" should be evolved. The existing state was characterized as "upholding the imperialist feudal order", and "has to be replaced by a People's Democratic State." It was, therefore, necessary to mobilise the masses to fight for the liberation of the country. For this the key task was to build the alliance

23. For detailed information of these movements, see Sunil Sen, *Agrarian Struggle in Bengal*. 1946-47, New Delhi, People's Publishing House, 1972. Satyen Sen, *Gram Banglar Pathe Pathe*, Muktadhara Publications, Calcutta, 1955, and Asim Mukhopadhyaya, "Peasants of the Parganas", *Frontier*, January 3, 1970.

24. The document was prepared in Moscow when a committee consisting of S. A. Dange, A. K. Ghosh, Rajeswar Rao and N. Basavapunniah was called there in order to settle the differences that had cropped up in the Party circle. For the full text of the document, see *Indian Communist Party Documents*, 1930-1956, compiled by the Democratic Research Service, Bombay, 1957, pp. 71-78.

of the working class and the peasantry with the former playing the role of leadership. It was absolutely essential to combine two basic factors: the partisan war of the peasants and workers' uprisings in the cities.

As regards the scope of the partisan warfare of peasants the document announced that "the agrarian crisis is maturing rapidly" and in order to make the agrarian revolution successful it called for :

> a network of peasant and agricultural workers' organisations with underground units in villages as their leading and guiding centres. Volunteer squads of the most militant and conscious sections of the peasants have to be formed to defend the peasant movement against the attack of the enemy squads; that will form nuclei of the partisan squads as the movement will develop and reaches the stage of seizure of land and partisan warfare.[25]

While the "Tactical Line" was reticent as regards the question whether the stage of "seizure of land and partisan warfare" had been reached, it was answered in the affirmative after a long interval, when the Central Committee of the CPI(M), meeting at Nurmahal in October 1966, laid down the "Tasks on the Kisan Front."

In criticising the error of the undivided CPI, the CPI(M) document says that "the extremely poor state" of the Kisan movement is "due mainly to the deep-rooted reformist understanding prevalent in the Party regarding the role of the kisan movement in the anti-imperialist, anti-feudal struggle." The "Right deviation" expressed itself:

> in placing undue reliance on the middle and rich peasant sections is virtually distorting the correct concept, of all in peasant unity in the struggle against feudal land-lordism and building that unity based upon the middle and rich peasantry instead of building it around the rural labour...... To put it sharply, the Party had failed in giving the correct class orientation to the work on the peasant front.[26]

Demanding a "sharp break" with this organizational pattern, the resolution directs the Party to "undertake the political

25. *Ibid*. p. 77.

26. *Tasks on the Kishan Front,* Resolution of the Central Committee, Communist Party of India (Marxist), 1966, pp. 5-6.

task of formulating the concrete demands and slogans of the peasant and agricultural labour movement as well as the organizational tasks of throwing the entire party cadre in the rural areas into the job of building mass organizations of poor peasants and agricultural labourers" in order to make them "the militant vanguard of the anti-imperialist, anti-feudal revolution."[27]

In view of the later developments in the spring of 1967, it should be clearly borne in mind that the CPI(M) Central Committee's criticism in 1966 of the agrarian policy of the CPI for its "reformist orientation directed to parliamentary work in the main rather than to mass work on correct class lines" bounced back like a boomerang on the leadership of the CPI(M) itself when the dissidents went "rabid" for the smart drift of their party to "respectable parliamentarism" by bringing its tactical line in tune with that of the "revisionist" CPI through a motley combination with the CPI and other "bourgeois reactionary" parties like Bangla Congress after the 1967 General Elections both in West Bengal and Kerala.

Secondly, while in its resolution on "Tasks on the Kisan Front" the Central Committee of the CPI(M) mainly confined itself to the slogan of "seizure of land" as the key to the anti-feudal revolution, the extremist leaders in the CPI(M) who had engineered the Naxalbari Peasant struggle in 1967, declared that their struggle was not for land, crops etc., but for "seizure of State Power."[28]

What, therefore, acted as a catalyst, thereby breaking the ice of "reformism" in both the CPI and the CPI(M), was the acceptance of Maoism by a section of the Indian Communists on the only valid strategy of revolution in India. And it may be further pointed out that the peasant uprising that burst upon the Darjeeling district was never planned in a hurry just after the installation of the U.F. regime in West Bengal in 1967. Rather the train had been very carefully laid during the early

27. *Ibid.*, pp. 25-27.

28. Charu Mazumdar, "One year of Naxalbari Struggle", *Liberation*, June, 1968, pp. 27-28. For the same observation see Kanu Sanyal, "Report on the Peasant Movement in the Terai Region", *Liberation* November, 1968, pp. 28-53.

60's and it exploded at a time when the pent-up excitement of the peasants gave way as the instigation came from within.[29]

Trouble Up North

Following the formal organizational split in the CPI in 1964, the highly activised cells of the party in the northern districts of West Bengal, particularly in Darjeeling were entirely captured by the militant Left Communists. Many of their leaders operating in the Terai region (locally called Norang) were too well-known for their political convictions which had little difference with Mao's philosophy of armed peasant revolution. Five[30] such important figures were Charu Mazumdar, Kanu Sanyal, Jangal Santhal, Khokan Mazumdar (alias Abdul Hamid) and Kamakshya Banerjee,[31] who had infiltrating, along with their followers, into the cells and mass organisations in the district from the very beginning of 1965. These hardliners, particularly Charu Mazumdar, started circulating leaflets on their political line often in open defiance of the party instructions. Other important leaders of the militant Left Communist Group in Naxalbari area were Shani Santhal (brother of Jangal Santhal), Kadam Mallik, Keshab Sarkar, Panchanan Sarker, Phani Das (alias "Phani Master"), Manglu Tameng, Karberi Thapa, Bansia Singh, Prahlad Singh, Mani Lal Singh, Shib Sharan Paharia and Mujibur Rahman. This "Siliguri Group" brought out as many as

29. Within a few days of the U.F. Government's assumption of power in West Bengal, the Land and Land Revenue Minister and a leading figure in the CPI(M)'s peasant front, Hare Krishna Konar announced both inside and outside the State Legislature that police would not interfere with share-croppers' disputes with landlords and no landlord could evict a bargadar, and further that the Government would redistribute vested lands among kisans equitably and speedily. This is the instigation that is being referred to. For further information, see *Amrita Bazar Patrika* (Calcutta Daily), June 10, 1967.

30. For biographical notes of important Maoist leaders in West Bengal, see Appendix.

31. Later it was alleged that in 1965 when Mazumdar had revolted against the West Bengal State Committee of the CPI(M) and started circulating his own views among the party cadres, he was subjected to "vilest slanders" by the party bosses. Even persons like Promode Das Gupta and Hare Krishna Konar doubted Mazumdar's sanity. See "Kanu Sanyal's Address at the May Day Rally", *Liberation,* May 1969, pp. 117-118.

six cyclostyled leaflets in 1965-66 calling for an instant armed peasant revolution. For example, on April 9, 1965, they published a secret document entitled, "What is the meaning of the Spontaneous Revolutionary Outburst in India?". A particular paragraph of the leaflet read : "It is necessary now to come forward powerfully and tell the people forcefully that capturing of power area-wise is our way." Again on August 30, 1966, another leaflet entitled "Main Task at Present Is To Build Real Revolutionary Party Through Uncompromising Struggle Against Revisionism", which declared:

> Party members should realise today that in the struggle against revisionism this leadership of the party is not our comrades, they are not even our fellow travellers.[32]

The document, it is striking to note, gave a call for partisan warfare within six months in the Terai region of the district. It may be pointed out that it was actually within six months that the Naxalbari peasant uprising flared up in the spring of 1967.

Apart from publishing leaflets inciting the party cadres to take up arms, these extremist leaders started working clandestinely to take over control of the Darjeeling District and local Committees of the CPI(M). By May 1966, a parallel party centre had started operating openly in the district. The meetings and the decisions of the elected District Committee of the party became formal and superficial. The extremist leaders of the parallel party centre used to call meetings of the party members and sympathisers of the different areas of the district and push forward their own decisions.

Quite a number of the local Bengali extremist leaders of the CPI(M) in the area had picked up the local dialects and got easily mixed up with the tribes. This naturally gave them a good hold over the plantation workers and poor landless peasants. They infiltrated the remotest corner of the villages in the Siliguri sub-division and organized party cells. Usually a cell consisted of a member of the party's local committee, acting as

32. For further details of these inner-party documents, see "Situation in Naxalbari Area: Siliguri Local Committee's Report" in *On Left Deviation*, Calcutta, Communist Party of India (Marxist), 1967, pp. 25-44.

Also see, *Naxalbarir Shiksha* (Lessons of Naxalbari), a Bengali booklet published by the West Bengal State Committee of the Communist Party of India (Marxist-Leninist), 1970.

leader-cum-instructor and four persons from among the locality. Lessons, both theoretical and practical, on guerrilla warfare were given by experienced cadres.[33] These cells were regularly used to give shelter and protection to underground workers.

Because of its contiguous international borders with India, Nepal had always been of vital importance to the extremists of the Terai region in the Darjeeling district. The Nepalese extremists maintained a strong base in Eastern Nepal, which was easily accessible from Naxalbari. Elaborate arrangements for training in the use of fire-arms were there and the Nepalese extremists were always ready to cooperate with their Indian counter-parts across the border. It is no secret now that the Nepalese Maoists kept themselves in close touch with the extremist group in Siliguri and it is quite possible that in the last few years preceding the Naxalbari peasant revolt, they had helped the latter considerably to remain in with the Chinese leaders.[34]

Brisk preparations had been made throughout 1966 for a big offensive against the Government. It was then reported by the Darjeeling District Administration that the Kisan cells had collected a huge armoury of bows and arrows and a few rifles as well. The West Bengal State Kisan Conference of the CPI(M) which had held its session at Satgachia[35] of Burdwan district in

33. In fact, ever since the India-China border war in 1962 the Central Intelligence became very active in the Terai region because the Government had apprehended that any largescale Communist violence in the eastern region would be launched in that area. The shifting of the CPI(M)'s headquarters from New Delhi to Calcutta in 1964 strengthened the suspicion and the State Government was taken by surprise when it was reported that the Left extremists had been taking full advantage of the guerilla training being imparted by the Central Government under the Special Border Security Scheme, and as a result, screening of sorts was immediately introduced. But by then, quite a number of Communists and their sympathizers had received full training in guerilla tactics. It may be noted that most of these trained guerillas actively participated in triggering off the trouble at Naxalbari.

34. It may be pointed out that immediately after the Naxalbari flare-up many extremist leaders including Kanu Sanyal slipped into the Jhapa district of Nepal, which adjoins the Naxalbari tract of Siliguri sub-division. These fugitive extremists were given shelter at Jhapa by the Nepalese extremist leader, Gopal Parshai.

35. West Bengal State Kisan Conference, 17th Session, Satgachia, District Burdwan, October 1966.

October 1966, was attended by eight delegates of Siliguri Sub-division Kisan Conference.

Not quite satisfied with the resolutions of the Conference, these delegates, on their return to Siliguri, organized a Revolutionary Kisan Convention with the motive that a People's Democratic revolution in India would have to be spear-headed by the rural proletariat. The Convention gave a call to the local peasants to (i) establish the authorities of the peasant committees in all matters of the villages, (ii) get organized and be armed in order to crush the resistance of jotedars and rural reactionaries, and (iii) smash the jotedars' monopoly of ownership of land and re-distribution of the land through the peasant committees. The Convention also raised the slogan—"Share-croppers shall never give paddy to the land-owners."

The ultimate objective, however, of the extremist peasant leaders was to smash once for all the village feudal set-up and to create revolutionary peasant bases for the final "seizure of State Power." And whatever the extremists at Siliguri were doing for their ultimate objective was fully endorsed and encouraged by the party's West Bengal State Secretariat as it was evident from the fact that towards the end of 1966 several top leaders of the CPI(M) like Promode Das Gupta, Secretary, West Bengal State unit of the party, Hare Krishna Konar, Secretary of the CPI(M)-led West Bengal Provincial Kisan Conference (and later Land Revenue Minister in the United Front Government formed after the 1967 General Elections) and Ganesh Ghosh (later a CPI(M) Member of Parliament, but lost in 1970) paid regular visits to Siliguri to help the extremists in their work.[36] It was then decided that the agitation would be launched immediately after the

36. See *Times of India* (Bombay), September 6, 1967. Also see C. N. Chitta Ranjan, "Left CP and the Adventurists", *Mainstream* July 1, 1967, pp. 10-12. The subsequent condemnation of the Naxalbari Movement by the CPI(M) Central Committee as "Left adventurist," however, came like a bland self-deception insofar as the party's alleged complicity in the movement was concerned. The Central Committee held: "The organizational line of the left opportunists demands that the Party be reduced to a federation of autonomous groups each having complete liberty to advocate and practise its line. Proof of this is seen in what they did in Naxalbari. See "On Left Deviation", Revolution of the Central Committee, Communist Party of India (Marxist), Madurai, August 18 to 27, 1967, p. 15.

General Elections, due in March 1967, when the new Ministry would be sworn in (and as the party's calculation ran at that time, it would be the Congress Ministry once again back to power!). Thus, before March 1967 the peasant cells, organized by the extremists in the whole Siliguri sub-division, were just on the spring-board and a pent-up excitement gripped the whole area.[37] Immediately before the elections reports from Darjeeling started pouring into Writers' Building, Calcutta, suggesting that serious disturbances might take place in the district if the Congress were returned to power.[38]

What had gone wrong in the CPI(M) leadership's calculation and thrown it into a jolt was the fact that the Congress failed to secure an absolute majority in West Bengal in the 1967 General Elections. The CPI(M) leaders had assumed that the Congress would be returned to power, though with a depleted strength, and a peasant movement at Naxalbari would be a handy tool with the party to harass, and if possible, to topple the new government. They could not possibly foresee that the CPI(M) would be the leading partner of a non-Congress coalition government that would take office in West Bengal after the elections.[39]

37. Later giving an account of the scale of preparations made by the Siliguri sub-division Peasant Convention, Kanu Sanyal, "hero" of the Naxalbari Peasant Uprising, observed:

.... The call of the Sub-divisional Peasant Convention (Siliguri) instantly created a stir among the revolutionary peasant masses. Almost all the villages got organized during the period from the end of March to the end of April 1967. About 15 to 20 thousand peasants began to do whole-time work and built up peasant committees in villages .... With the speed of a storm the revolutionary peasants, in the course of about one and a half months, formed peasant committees through hundreds of group meetings and turned these committees into armed village defence groups. In a word, they organized about 90% of the village population ..... Kanu Sanyal, "Report on the Peasant Movement in the Terai", *op. cit.*, p. 33.

38. For this report, see *Amrita Bazar Patrika* (Calcutta), June 10, 1967.

39. Following is the break-up of seats won by different political parties and independents in the West Bengal Legislative Assembly in the 1967 General Elections:

Parties	Seats Won	Total number of seats
1. Congress	127	
2. Bangla Congress	34	
3. C.P.I.	16	

On February 25, 1967, leaders of the two left fronts, the United Left Front (ULF), represented by CPI(M), R.S.P., S.S.P., S.U.C., Workers' Party, R.C.P.I. and the Marxist Forward Block, and the People's United Leftist Front (PULF) consisting of the CPI, the Bangla Congress, the Forward Bloc and the Bolshevik Party, met in a conference in Calcutta and formed the United Democratic Front of 14 constituent parties (including some independents) with Shri Ajoy Kumar Mukherjee of the Bangla Congress as their leader. On March 2, the United Front Ministry was sworn in.

Commanding a strength of 151 seats in a House of 280, the Front represented the relative strength of the 14 parties in the Assembly and in the Ministry as per the table in page 72.

Those UDF parties which did not have representation either in the Assembly or in the Ministry had, however, a voice in formulating the basic policies of the government. For this purpose a "Super Cabinet" called the United Front Committee was formed.

With the installation of the UF Ministry, the CPI(M) leaders suddenly found themselves pitchforked into a quandry. The excitement of the Naxalbari extremists had reached such a pitch that the party leaders were absolutely helpless to contain these elements and the State Secretariat of the CPI(M) had adopted quite an ambivalent attitude at that critical stage. It did not overtly lend its support to the idea of launching such a violent agitation, nor did it advise the party cadres at Siliguri to refrain from such an adventure. It was thus staking and toying with a very explosive situation. Perhaps the leaders had thought that the United Front Government would not last more than a few weeks or perhaps they had anticipated an immediate Central Government intervention to eject a ministry having the CPI(M) as the leading partner. In either event, a peasant movement in Terai region

4.	C.P.I. (M)	43	
5.	Forward Block	13	
6.	P.S.P.	7	
7.	S.S.P.	7	
8.	Swatantra	1	
9.	Jan Sangh	1	
10.	Independents & others	31	
	Total:	280	280

Parties in the UDF	No. of seats in the Assembly	No. of Ministers representing each party
A. P.U.L.F. :		
Bangla Congress	34	3
C.P.I.	16	2
Forward Bloc	13	2
P.S.P.	7	1
Lok Sevak Sangha	5	1
Gorkha League	2	1
Bolshevik Party	—	—
B. U. L. F.:		
C.P.I.(M)	43	3
S.S.P.	7	1
R.S.P.	6	1
S.U.C.	4	1
Workers' Party	2	1
Forward Block (Marxist)	1	—
R.C.P.I.	—	—
Independents	10	1
	251	18

would have been useful for the party. Whatever the colour of a government might be, as long as the CPI(M) was not one of its constituents, such an agitation could fit in well with the party's policy and programme. Moreover, this type of militant move ment was an immediate necessity as it would just feed the revolutionary "fire" of a large section of militant cadre of the party, who had not seen any action (excepting the 1966 food movement in West Bengal) ever since the party's birth in 1964.

A belated attempt to persuade the Naxalbari extremists to give up the plan of a violent agitation was, however, made by the CPI(M) State Committee leaders only after it had become apparent that the Congress Government at the Centre had no intention whatsoever to intervene in West Bengal simply because the CPI(M) was in the Cabinet. But by then, the extremists had developed a strong feeling of indignation against the State Committee leaders for having "betrayed" them, and they most unceremoniously dismissed the leadership's overtures for a rapprochment. On the other hand, they continued to work in the name of the party and to use the party flag in open defiance of the directives of the State Committee.

Thus understood, the catalyst for the open revolt of the Maoist faction in the CPI(M) came when the party leaders had decided to toe the line of the "revisionist" CPI by entering into ministerial coalitions in West Bengal and Kerala through a motley combination with the CPI and other "bourgeois reactionary" parties like Bangla Congress after the 1967 General Elections[40] The CPI(M) leaders were greatly overwhelmed by the unexpected Congress rout at the polls and the emergence of non-Congress coalition governments in as many as eight Indian states.[41]

CPI(M)'s "Strange" Rationalisation

At the height of its election the CPI(M) Central Committee saw in the defeat of the Congress "a qualitative change" in India's political situation, which was readily characterised on "the beginning of a political crisis." It further held that "the

40. It might be of some interest to note here that with a view to confronting the Congress with straight fights in the 1967 General Elections, the CPI(M), the CPI, the Bangla Congress and a dozen of other parties planned to forge a single united front of all the opposition parties. The negotiations, however, failed due to the mounting intra-party ideological crisis in the CPI(M). The "Five Flags" circular of the Albanian Labour Party (the only Communist Party owing allegiance to the CPC) which had been smuggled into India during this period, urged the Communists to uphold the purity of the Marxist-Leninist ideology and to give up the path of expediency. The radical CPI(M) members accordingly demanded that the party should not at all participate in the parliamentary democracy. Finally, a compromise was, however, struck that the CPI(M) would collaborate only with the like-minded parties and would ensure that it would not only be the largest single party in the alliance but would also be larger than all the other partners taken together. These conditions could hardly be acceptable to the Bangla Congress or even to the CPI. The negotiations, therefore, failed.

For an interesting analysis of this development in West Bengal politics before the 1967 General Elections, see Kedar Ghosh, "How the Left CPI wrecked the ULF in West Bengal." *Statesman* (Calcutta), November 25, 1966.

41. The eight states in which the Congress lost in 1967 elections were Bihar, Kerala, Madras (Tamil Nadu), Orissa, Punjab, Rajasthan, U.P. and West Bengal.

maturing economic crisis, as the post-election political scene evidently demonstrates, has passed into the political sphere, ushering in a political crisis", which was directly connected with the deepening crisis of world capitalism. "Our party, as the Marxist-Leninist party of the Indian working class, can ill-afford to be oblivious to this changed situation if it is to play its vanguard role in shaping the events and leading the struggle."[42] The CPI(M) thought that its key role in forming non-Congress governments in Kerala and West Bengal was of "special political significance" because the party could set the tone for other non-Congress ministries and force a new alignment of democratic forces on a higher political plane. In order to justify this further, the Central Committee stretched its imagination to observe:

> In clear class terms, our party's participation in such governments is one specific form of struggle to win more and more people and more and more allies for the proletariat and its allies in the struggle for the cause of People's Democracy.[43]

Carried to its logical extreme, this statement signified that running those coalition governments in West Bengal and Kerala became the sole pre-occupation and the singular form of struggle of the party, on which the party's whole future was staked. The Central Committee spelled out its strategy in clearest terms:

> Since the fortunes of the entire party at the present stage of development are closely linked with the successful running of these ministries and the role our party plays in them, the whole party throughout the country will have to be mobilised to back the agreed programmes of these two non-Congress ministries and to see that they are earnestly implemented. [44]

The Maoist Challenge From Within

Thus understood, the CPI(M) leadership, by a strange rationalisation of the imminence of a fancied "political crisis"

42. *New Situation and Party's Tasks,* Communist Party of India (Marxist), Calcutta, 1967 (Political Report Adopted by the Central Committee in April 1967), pp. 4-6.
43. *Ibid., p.* 70.
44. *Ibid.,* p. 67.

complacently settled down for peaceful parliamentarism as a short-cut to power, thereby aligning and identifying itself, for all practical purposes, with the "revisionist" CPI. This sudden *volte face* by the leadership created frustration and confusion among a large section of the party membership. The quick shift to parliamentarism from extra-parliamentary struggle based on mass actions was construed by the extremists in the party as "stark betrayal."[45] They started vilifying the party leaders for their "neo-revisionist" attitudes and for practising "Dange revisionism without Dange". They further charged that "the bond that binds the neo-revisionist champions of people's cause to other reactionaries in the U.F. is the common urge to oppose revolution and people's revolutionary struggles".[46] It was contended that as a partner of the United Front governments in West Bengal and Kerala, the CPI(M) was caught in a pathetic paradox, clogged as it was by constitutional and legal inhibitions. Since it had accepted the premises of the bourgeois state-order, constitutional limits, parliamentary procedures etc. to wrest power, it was well-nigh impossible for the party to by-pass them to bring about any radical change in favour of the people.

The dissidents' attack on the CPI(M) leaders was spear-headed by the "Antar Party Sodhanbad Birodhi Sangram Committee"[47] ("Committee to Fight Inner-Party Revisionism"),

45. This phenomenon did not remain confined only in West Bengal, but similar extremist groups quickly mushroomed in Andhra, Kerala, Punjab, Bihar, Uttar Pradesh, Bombay and Jammu and Kashmir. In Bombay, for instance, the Maoists brought out their own newsletter the "Red Flag" which criticised the CPI(M)'s choice of peaceful parliamentary path.

They concluded that the CPI(M), like the "Dangeite revisionists" of the Right CPI, had succumbed to the temptations of "bourgeois parliamentarism" and that this "class collaborationist policies pursued by the leadership of the party only strengthen the bourgeois reaction and its imperialist allies."

For further report, see *The Times of India* (Bombay), August 13, 1967.

46. For a resume of the views of the dissidents in the CPI(M) in West Bengal, see, An Indian Communist, "Marxist Leaders in Their True Colours", *Liberation* (Miscellany No. 1), 1967,pp. 72-73.

47. This Committee included prominent extremist leaders in the CPI(M) like Sushital Ray Chowdhury, Asit Sen, Saroj Datta, Promode Sengupta, Suniti Ghosh, Promode Das Gupta and others.

which was organized by the Maoists in Calcutta just after the 1967 elections. Immediately after the formation of the U.F. government in March, this Committee brought out two letters entitled "Letters To the Politbureau, Nos. I and II". In the first issue the dissidents put forth their general ideological-tactical line and in the second, they attacked the party's decision to be a constituent of the U.F. governments in West Bengal and Kerala. Originally written in Bengali, these letters were subsequently rendered into English for the Politbureau members of the party.

Directing its fire of criticism against the Politbureau members, the Committee argued that "The Indian Parliamentary democracy, it can be said, is an expanded edition of what was introduced by British imperialism". It further observed:

> Marx taught us that 'force is the mid-wife of every old society pregnant with a new one'. And Comrade Mao Tse-tung teaches us that 'Political power grows out of the barrel of a gun'. But are you not teaching us the path of 'peaceful transition' to the New Democratic State by the parliamentary means through actual practice of forming electoral blocs and alliances with bourgeois social reformists, with the serious intention of forming coalition governments at state levels in West Bengal, Kerala and other states?[48]

Denouncing the united front tactics adopted by the party's central leadership, the Committee wrote :

> The present leadership of the party is pursuing the same political line though they are using apparently revolutionary language. It is an extremely difficult task to eradicate the tradition of parliamentary opportunism, which has struck deep roots inside different sections of the leadership. An opportunist coterie of seekers of seats in Parliament and the Assembly has firmly entrenched itself in the Party and as a very strong group is influencing this party in numerous ways. The party leadership is nursing these people, because the root of this kind of politics and outlook is seen in the political slogans like "Government of Democratic Unity" the "Kerala Way" (after the formation of our government there) etc. and activities corresponding to these slogans.[49]

48. "Letter to the Politbureau, No. II" (Typescript). Also see "On Left Deviation", *op. cit.*, p. 6.

49. *Ibid.*

In the other letter to the Politbureau the Committee totally rejected the party's programme as "new-revisionist" and laid down its own tactical line. It observed:

> ..... bourgeois democracy can no longer flourish as it did in the nineteenth century. So in connection with elections we should pay special attention to this aspect and it should also be marked that from their experience of the way Parliament and Assembly etc. have functioned and have been run for the last twenty years under Congress rule, the illusion of the masses for the said institutions has worn off comparatively....So it would have been possible to persuade the masses to boycott the elections if conscious efforts were made to bring to its natural culmination the form which the mass movements displayed in the different states, especially in West Bengal, and to raise the movement to a higher stage.... So to remain bogged at the level of mass consciousness on the pretext that the masses are thinking on this line, instead of actively carrying forward this struggle is nothing but opportunism.[50]

Apart from the letters written to the Politbureau, the dissidents in the CPI(M) brought out a number of journals in order to carry on their campaign more vigorously and systematically These journals included *Commune, Bidroha* (Rebellion), *Santras* (Terror), *Dakshin Desh* (The Southern Country), *Chhatra Fouz* (Students' Army), *Kalpurush* and a host of others. The *Chhatra Fouz* the most militant of the lot, carried in its columns slogans like "Down with Revisionism", "Long Live the Teaching of Mao Tse-tung" etc.[51] Editorial extracts from these journals also made interesting reading and gave the idea of the way things were moving in these quarters. The May 1, 1967 issue of the *Commune* came out with an editorial bearing the title "Snatch the Red Flag From the Hand of the Bourgeois-Fad Socialists." The editorial categorically mentioned Ranadive, Sundarayya, Ramamurthy, Basavapunniah, Gopalan, Namboodiripad, Jyoti Basu, Promode Das Gupta and Hare Krishna Konar by name to say that they were as much "revisionists" as the Right Communists whom, particularly Dange, they had fully supported in the past.

50. "Letter to the Politbureau, No. 1", *Ibid.*

51. For further details, see *The Times of India* (Bombay), August 13, 1967.

The failure of those people to criticise their own past also came under fire. Continuing the attack, the editorial held that "these aristocratic Marxists were found caught in two minds during the Indian aggression on China."

The May 16 issue of the *Dakshin Desh* carried an editorial, "United Front and Left Leadership" in which the CPI(M) leaders were bitterly criticised. They are attacked for having set as their only task the preservation of the coalition governments. The editorial contended that while it was the task of a Marxist party to lead the people in their struggle against the bourgeois political setup and on to the path of revolution, the CPI(M) was worried only with giving some immediate relief, to the people; this was stated to be an attempt by the party leadership to create an illusion in the minds of the people regarding the character of the bourgeois society and the bourgeois state machinery.

In the absence of any opportunity for criticism in the CPI(M) organization, which is essential in a Marxist-Leninist party, the extremists believed that the journals would help in maintaining ideological purity and thereby safeguarding and advancing the cause of Indian Communist movement.[52]

"Instigation" From The CPC

In their relentless ideological struggle against the "neo-revisionist" CPI(M) leadership, the Maoist revolutionaries in the party were soon reinforced by the ideologues of the Communist Party of China. In the very first review of the post-election scene in India, the CPC did not regard the United Front governments of West Bengal and Kerala even as "instruments of struggle" as viewed by the CPI(M) Central Committee, and denounced the participation of the CPI(M) in these governments as a gross "revisionist" act identified hitherto only with the pro-Moscow C.P.I. The CPI(M) was content to see signs of a "maturing political crisis" in Indian politics, but the CPC saw "sparks of revolt glowing". The February elections, in the CPC's view, fur-

52. The publication of so many journals should not, however, necessarily give one the impression that there were so many groups in the party as there were journals. Those running the journals belonged to the same group which believed in doctrinaire and militant Marxism-Leninism, identified with the Chinese line.

ther sharpened Indian class contradictions and made the classes increasingly antagonistic to one another. It brought at the Centre a Government "more reactionary than ever" and "still more subservient to U.S. imperialism and Soviet revisionism", but its great significance was that in several states it broke the "monopoly of local power" of the Congress Party and made it "ineffective in the face of people's resistance".[53] However, the CPC held, it was entirely wrong to think that the non-Congress governments were in any way progressive and that substantial advances in the interests of the people could be achieved peacefully, through the parliamentary road. The formation of non-Congress governments in several states merely indicated the "decay and decline of the Congress party." Those who had assumed powers in the non-Congress states were "from top to bottom the local feudal-Comprador forces" and, therefore, "no different" from the Congress government. In Kerala and West Bengal where the Indian Communists were partners in the coalitions, the CPC held that even these two governments were "component parts of the state apparatus of India's big landlords and big bourgeoisie under the direct control of the Central Government; they were completely unable to either introduce any reforms in substance or shake the foundations of the capitalists and feudal relations of production."[54] The elections has left India "littered with dry faggots" but there were dangerous possibilities of the rising revolution being betrayed, and the greatest danger came from the revisionists in the Indian Communist movement, "certainly not confined to the Dange clique" only.[55]

Thus the CPC's disapproval of the CPI(M)'s participation in the parliamentary system as a whole came in no uncertain terms. And this was subsequently followed up by an indirect call for people's war:

> These facts prove that without a people's revolution, without the seizure of political power by force and without the smashing of the old state apparatus there can be no change in the social system, in the nature of the political regime

53. "After the Indian Elections: A Still More Reactionary Government", *Peking Review,* March 24, 1967.

54. "Dange's Plot to Sabotage Indian People's Revolution Will Surely Fail", *Peking Review,* June 9, 1967.

55. *Ibid.*

and there can be no real social reform. There is no precedent in history, nor will there by any in the future.[56]

The First Spark

But before the CPC's directive for a people's revolution could be seriously taken into account by the CPI(M) leadership, a violent peasant uprising sparked off in the Naxalbari, Kharibari and Phansidewa police stations in the Darjeeling district of West Bengal. Surely convinced of the class character of the United Front Government in West Bengal by the CPC's intensified propaganda, the extremist leaders of the Siliguri Sub-division Peasant Convention held a meeting on March 18 and declared that the United Front Government was not in a position to solve the land problems and the new Government could at the best give some relief to the working Class.[57] They issued a call for immediate seizure of land and setting up liberated base areas.

Describing the proceedings of the Kisan Convention to the correspondent of a New Delhi Weekly a delegate wrote:

> There were 500 delegates at the conference and some observers. Many came with bows and arrows. A discussion began on the tactics of the movement and its objectives ..... The discussion at the Kisan Conference was very lively. One of the leaders—Kamakshya Banerjee—said that land could never belong to anyone who was not a peasant. A delegate —Jatin Singh—said that Marxism taught there must be worker-peasant unity. A delegate brushed aside the idea. "We must go ahead with peasant revolution. We must organize an armed uprising and set up a free zone in the area." Jatin challenged this understanding and said that revolution could not be achieved in a handful of villages of

56. *Ibid.*

57. Later commenting on the "true nature" of the CPI(M)-dominated U.F. Government in West Bengal in 1969, a *Liberation* Editorial observed:

"..... the United Front Government are pledged to maintain the old relations of production. The experience of the 'United Front' governments has once again demonstrated that without smashing the state machinery of the big landlords and the big bourgeoisie and without destroying feudalism in the countryside, no benefit can be rendered to the masses and the talk of 'relief' or reformist pure deception". "The Real Face of the U.F.", *Liberation,* June 1969, p. 6.

Siliguri Sub-division. "We must take into consideration the objective situation obtaining in the whole of West Bengal and the country." Delegates Thomas, Sarkar, Mujibur Rahman and some others took a similar line. But the discussion was abruptly concluded by Kanu Sanyal. He said: "Everything will depend upon our committee. It will decide to whom to give and to whom not to give land. We shall not give the smallest piece of land to those who are not with us." His eloquent summing up in the pithy local dialect settled the issue. Secretary of the Siliguri Kisan Sabha, Malik said, "The decision has been taken. We must all go to implement it." Jangal Santhal who presided over the meeting did not speak.[58]

As a last-ditch attempt to restrain the extremists, Hare Krishna Konar, the then CPI(M) Land Revenue Minister of the U.F. Government and Secretary, West Bengal State Peasants' Conference led by the CPI(M), hurriedly announced the new land policy of the Government, which *inter alia* included:

1. Quick distribution of surplus lands among the peasants with the active cooperation of the People's Committee to be set up for that purpose;
2. No eviction of adhiars or share-croppers in future;
3. Permanent right of the share-croppers to cultivate land on hereditary basis; and
4. Land reforms at the earliest opportunity in favour of the poor landless peasant.[59]

This policy, however, was not to satisfy the extremists who had already reached the point of no return. But they were intelligent and tactical enough to grasp the implications of these measures, and taking full advantage of this land policy of the Government, they quickly started organizing People's (Kisan) Committees to strengthen their operational strategy.

And this signalled the eruption of the trouble at Naxalbari. What had happened in the meanwhile was that Kanu Sanyal and Jangal Santhal went on a whirlwind propaganda spree to convince the poor landless peasants of the Siliguri subdivision that all lands

58. "The Naxalbari Story", *Link,* August 15, 1967. Also see "What should the Peasants Do?", *Deshabrati,* December 7, 1967.
59. *Amrita Bazar Patrika* (Calcutta), June 10, 1967.

belonging to jotedars would be available for the peasants only if they immediately enrolled themselves as members of the Kisan Committee of the CPI(M). A nominal subscription of 20 paise only for membership was fixed and the extremist leaders, with the help of their cadre, started intimidating and even coercing the unwilling peasants into joining the Kisan Committees. The peasants were told not to worry about police actions against them, because the U.F. Government had pledged not to suppress "the democratic and legitimate struggle" of the landless peasants against the jotedars as foreshadowed in the 18-point Programme of the Front.

From early March till July 5 the extremists let loose a systematic campaign of terror and violence in the Naxalbari areas. First, processions and demonstrations were organized by the Kisan Committee members, dressed in red and black and carrying the red flag of the party to intimidate the local rich. They also carried lathis, spears, bows and arrows. Slogans like "Mao Tse-tung Zindabad" (Long Live Mao Tse-tung), "Take the Path of armed peasant revolution" etc. were frequently rending the skies of Naxalbari.

The first spark which had set the powderkeg of Naxalbari ablaze was apparently a very minor incident with nothing much unusual in the daily life of the Naxalbari peasants. In early March one Bigul Kisan, a local share-cropper, was severely beaten and evicted by the armed agents of one Buddhiman Tirki, a local jotedar.[60] This was not, however, an isolated incident, clashes between jotedars' men and the share-croppers being quite frequent in the area. But this incident took place at a moment when the militancy of the armed Peasant Committee members was at its peak. Soon, a wave of violent clashes swept the whole tract, followed by forcible seizure of land and looting of food grains by armed bands of the Kisan Committee members.[61] The

60. For further information regarding the beginning of the trouble at Naxalbari, see *Deshhitaishi* (Bengali weekly) organ of the West Bengal State Committee of the CPI(M) May 28, 1967.

61. On February 6, 1967 the author joined the Political Science Department of University of North Bengal as a Lecturer. Naxalbari, it may be pointed out, is only about 1 miles from the University campus at Raja Rammohanpur (locally known as Atharakhai). So, when the Naxalbari peasant movement was raging in early March, the author was almost on the scene.

penalty for resistance was loot, arson and murder. Between March 9 and May 22, as many as one hundred such incidents were reported to the police authorities, who, while wanting to intervene, were hamstrung by their political bosses at the Rotunda of the Writers' Building in Calcutta.

Towards the end of May the situation went completely out of control and the clamour for intervention by the State Government became too insistent. The Government, however, was reluctant and vacillating. Constituted as it was, it could hardly have been otherwise. So the leaders at Calcutta first tried persuasion, and Hare Krishna Konar was sent by the CPI(M) State Secretariat to have a tete-a-tete with the extremist leaders at Siliguri.[62] He succeeded in bringing Kanu Sanyal at the Sukhna Forest Rest House for a talk. Sanyal came on the specific understanding that he would not be arrested. He was not, although the Superintendent of Police, Darjeeling District, Mr A. P. Mukherjee was present at the table.

The decisions reached at the meeting were that lawless activities should be suspended forthwith; all distribution of lands should take place through official agencies, advised by local People's Committees; dehoarding of stocks should be done by the police on the basis of information supplied by People's Committee, and lastly, all the persons wanted by the police including Kanu Sanyal himself and Jangal Santhal would surrender at an early date. It was further decided that within two days the S.P. would submit a list of wanted persons to Sanyal at a far-off place called Hathighisa, a stronghold of the extremists.[63] The S.P. accordingly went with a list to the place at the appointed hour, but none of the local CPI(M) extremist leaders or their emissaries contacted him throughout the day.

As it transpired later, at the instruction of Kanu Sanyal the local membership of the Peasant Committee had decided to ignore

62. When Konar reached Siliguri on May 17, he was "greeted" with a huge poster, hung up by the extremists in the town, which read: "This movement can succeed only by the armed struggle and resistance of the working class. Resistance is meaningless without guns—let the working class collect guns and be vanguard in the struggle of the Kisans". This very clearly revealed the militant attitude of the extremists towards the CPI(M)-led United Front Government in West Bengal.

63. See *Amrita Bazar Patrika* (Calcutta), June 10, 1967.

the decisions of the Sukhna meeting and stepped up their preparation for a violent uprising. The district police authorities which waited for another couple of days, had meanwhile received permission from the Home Department under the CPI(M) leader, Mr Jyoti Basu to apprehend those persons wanted in connection with specific charges. On May 25, an armed police party led by Inspector Sonam Wangdi went to Jharugaon, a sparsely populated hamlet under Naxalbari police station to round up the wanted miscreants. The police passe was ambushed by a large violent crowd of tribal men and women, and Wangdi was killed in the encounter. The murder of Wangdi marked a turning point in the chain of events as it was the first open and violent confrontation between the Naxalbari extremists and the police.

The police had anticipated in the meanwhile that the next target of the rebels would be the Naxalbari police station. On May 25, two police parties—one, led by the S.D.O. Siliguri subdivision and the other, by the S.D.P.O. proceeded towards Naxalbari from different directions. At the junction of Prosadjote and Dakunjote they were encircled by a big riotous mob, the vanguard of which consisted of women and children, while the extremist leaders took cover at the rear. As the situation turned out to be too desperate, the S.D.O. Mr Dipak Ghose felt that the police party might be overpowered. Thereupon he ordered some quick rounds of effective fire upon the mob. This resulted in the death of 10 persons, mostly women and children.

The police firing at Naxalbari created tremendous tension in the U.F. cabinet. The CPI(M) members in the ministry were particularly sore at the attitude of the Chief Minister, Mr Ajoy Kumar Mukherjee on this issue. They alleged that the police firing was just the result of a "conspiracy" of the Central Government. The CPI(M) State Secretariat which met on May 30, declared that the dispute had arisen out of the agitation for possession of lands which had been vested in the government but were under the illegal occupation of the jotedars. Mr Hare Krishna Konar, Land Revenue Minister of the U.F. Government, it was claimed by the Secretariat, had arranged for a settlement of the whole issue when he visited Naxalbari in the middle of May, but the police firing marked the chance of a settlement.[64]

64. *Deshahitaishi* (Bengali weekly organ of the West Bengal State Unit of the CPI(M), June 2, 1967).

Cabinet Mission

The views of the CPI(M) ministers and the Chief Minister on the issue of the Naxalbari police firing appeared to be diametrically opposed to each other. However, the course adopted by the CPI(M) to settle their accounts with the Chief Minister was to ask their ministers to fight and protest against the police "excesses" at Naxalbari in the Cabinet meetings and, if necessary, lead demonstrations outside without resigning from the Cabinet. Finally, the Chief Minister had to bow to the pressure of the CPI(M) and on June 11, in a telephone communication to the Deputy Commissioner of Darjeeling district he personally gave a distinct and express order that the police should keep off the disturbed area as far as practicable and that there must be no police action. When the district police authorities pleaded that inaction would only mean submission to intimidation and violence, what the Chief Minister was able to offer was that a Cabinet Mission of six ministers would visit the disturbed area in order to make an on-the-spot inquiry.[65]

When the Cabinet Mission reached Naxalbari on June 12, it was greeted with a series of violent incidents of loot, arson and murder. Throughout the month of June as many as 66 such cases were reported from the three police stations of Naxalbari, Kharibari and Phansidewa. The most disquieting development at this stage was that instead of bows and arrows, the extremists were

65. The Cabinet Mission consisted of the following six ministers representing some of the major constituent parties of the United Front Government in West Bengal.

Name	Party	Portfolio
1. Mr. Harekrishna Konar	CPI(M)	Land & Land Revenue
2. Mr. Biswanath Mukherjee	CPI	Irrigation & Waterways
3. Mr. Sushil Dhara	Bangla Congress	Commerce & Industry, and Community Development
4. Mr. Nani Bhattacharyya	RSP	Health
5. Mr. Amar Chakravarti	Forward Bloc	Law & Excise
6. Mr. Deoprakash Rai	Gurkha League	Tribal Welfare

using firearms and also laying greater stress on snatching arms and ammunition during their raids on the houses of the local landlords. When questioned by the press reporters, the Chief Minister Mr Ajoy Mukherjee denied that the rebels had established a "parallel government"[66] of their own in the area but confirmed that their insurrectionary activities had assumed a serious proportion. Later on, however, it transpired that the Naxalbari rebels had established "People's Court". In the judgment of a "People's Court" in which Kanu Sanyal himself had presided, one Nagendra Ray Chowdhury, a jotedar of Badarsuli village under Naxalbari police station, was sentenced to death, and the order was duly carried out.

Speaking at the Lok Sabha on June 13 after a heated debate on the Naxalbari situation, Union Home Minister Mr Y. B. Chavan agreed that a state of "serious lawlessness" prevailed in the three tracts Naxalbari, Kharibari and Phanisdewa.[67] On June 16, the Naxalbari affair acquired a new dimension when the local people took to arms to resist the raiders. Some political parties including the S.S.P., Forward Bloc, Bangla Congress and the Gurkha League organized armed resistance groups in their respective areas of influence to settle accounts with the extremist rebels. Several pitched battles between the rebels and the resistance groups were reported. In a memorandum submitted by the General Secretary of the Darjeeling District Committee of the Bangla Congress it was observed:

> Judging the facts chronologically, we are satisfied to remark that these acts have no ties whatsoever with Kisan Move-

66. Messrs. Bijoyananda Chatterjee (killed by CPI(M-L) guerilla action squad at Howrah in 1971), Hansadhwaj Dhara and Chapala Kanta Bhattacharyya, M.P., who, on behalf of the West Bengal Pradesh Congress Committee, visited the three disturbed tracts, declared in a joint statement that there had been a total breakdown of law and order in those areas. They observed that as in Nagaland, Mijo Hills and South Vietnam, "parallel government" had been functioning at the Naxalbari-Kharibari-Phansidewa belt. Mr. Bhattacharyya, who had represented the area in Parliament as a Congress candidate in the 1967 General Elections likened the geographical position of the region to the "neck" of India and held that he who controlled the "neck", would be able, sooner or later, to bring the entire country to his knees. And that was the singular objective behind the peasant struggle. See *Amrita Bazar Patrika*, (Calcutta), June 11, 1967.

67. See *Statesman* (Calcutta), June 14, 1967.

ment. The real intricacies of land disputes of these areas have completely been overridden and it is nothing but simple defiance of Law and Order. We shall, therefore, request the Hon'ble Ministers on the basis of the foregoing facts and circumstances to tackle the entire situation from the point of Law and Order . . . .[68]

Next, the Mission was surrounded and detained for four hours by an irate crowd of SSP demonstrators at Siliguri. In a memoranda to the Cabinet Mission the Darjeeling District Committee of the SSP argued:

Murder, attempt to murder, abduction, continued looting of paddy, rice and money, snatching of guns and catridges, rioting, ... by organized groups, ... cannot and should not be called (Kisan Movement) in any case . . . . It is the consensus of opinion of all the villagers that the West Bengal U.F. Government is playing the role of silent spectators and has left the peace loving villagers at the mercy of criminals notably belonging to the CPI(M) banner.[69]

On the insistence of the demonstrators that immediate police action should be taken against the offenders in order to restore law and order, the Mission was on the spot constrained to authorise the police to open fire to stop lawlessness and to maintain a round-the-clock vigil in Naxalbari and the adjoining tracts. Simultaneously, the Cabinet Mission issued an appeal to the rebels to give up the path of violence and to end their "misguided" movement by June 21, failing which hard measures would follow.[70]

On June 17, the ministers suggested arrangement of police patrolling in the disturbed villages, sealing of borders with East Pakistan and Nepal and provision of police protection on receipt of complaints. By June 19, the West Bengal borders with Pakistan and Nepal were sealed. Later, on July 4, the government decided to follow a policy of "isolating the extremists", to speed up land reform and to intensify police action in the area. The U.F. government set up Thana Land Reform Committees for

68. Quoted in Biswanath Mukherjee, "Two Faces of Naxalbari", *Link,* August 2 , 1967.

69. *Ibid.*

70. The deadline for the surrender was extended twice at the request of the CPI(M) ministers. The ultimatum finally expired on July 4. Only five persons, none of them on the wanted list, had surrendered by that date.

each of the police stations in the Siliguri subdivision of Darjeeling district, namely, Siliguri, Phansidewa, Naxalbari and Kharibari for the purpose of full implementation of land reforms measures as provided for by the law and for the expeditious redress of the legitimate grievances of the various sections of agricultural population of the area.

The Committees were to deal with the following subjects of vital importance:

1. *Prima facie* cases of *malafide* transfers of lands between May 5, 1953 and the date of vesting, requiring enquiries and action under section 5A of the West Bengal Estate Acquisition Act, 1953.
2. Matters relating to lands which have vested in government under the West Bengal Estates Acquisition Act.
3. Distribution of khas and vested land for agricultural purposes.
4. Cases of illegal eviction of bargadars or adhiars (share-croppers), cases needing enquiry and action for the restoration of possession under Section 19B of the West Bengal Land Reform Act, 1956, cases needing prosecution under Section 19A(1) of the said Act.
5. The Thana Land Reforms Committees were also to maintain contacts with all sections of the agricultural population within the thana—raiyats, bargadars, adhiars and agricultural workers, and assist in educating them in their rights and obligations under the law.
6. The Thana Land Reforms Committees would also keep watch on the agrarian situation within the thana (police Station).

Each of the four Thana Land Reforms Committees was to consist of Special Officer, Land Reforms, Darjeeling as Chairman, Bloc Development Officer, Siliguri as Vice-Chairman, Subdivisional Land Reforms Officer, Siliguri and one representative each from the Communist Party of India (Marxist), the Communist Party of India, the Bangla Congress, the Gorkha League, the Forward Bloc, the Revolutionary Socialist Party and the undivided Congress.

Besides, the State Government had also set up a high power sub-division Land Reforms Committee for Siliguri with the Additional Deputy Commissioner of Darjeeling district as Chairman and the Junior Land Revenue Officials and representatives of the political parties as members. The functions of the Sub-divisional Land Reforms Committee were to coordinate the works of the Thana Committees and to keep a watch over the programmes of their works to give directives to the Thana Committees on important questions of principle, particularly as regards matters in respect of which there might be difference of views between two Thana Committees or a division of opinion within the same Thana Committee; to keep a watch on the agrarian situation in the subdivision and to advise the local administration on measures which might be necessary to expedite the programmes of work.[71] By July 22, the Naxalbari uprising was effectively quashed by police and the number of arrests rose to 562, with the rest of the extremists on the run. Finally, with the arrest of Jangal Santhal complete lull descended over the whole area.

After the tactical retreat of the movement, little was done to restore confidence among the local population. Farming had already come to a dead stop. Most of the able-bodied peasants had left their homes for forest hide-outs; they appeared in small groups in the evening, and held meetings before melting away into darkness. The movement was thus by no means over.

NAXALBARI : A BALANCE-SHEET

Many false notions have been cast about the Naxalbari peasant agitation, which, on the face of it, was fundamentally an armed agrarian struggle against forced evictions from vested land, and for its redistribution. But the issue assumed a rather chameleon like complexion because of a host of self-contradictory statements made, not infrequently, by those who engineered the uprising.

One of the figures of the Naxalbari movement and President of the Siliguri Subdivision Peasant Convention, Jangal Santhal, openly declared in his statement on May 20, 1967, that the Naxalbari peasant revolt was a focus of resistance against the illegal occupation by jotedars of vested land tilled by the peasantry for

71. For further details on the working of the Committees, see, *The Agrarian Problems and the Naxalbari Peasant Uprising*, a 36-page document published in Bengali by Socialist Unity Centre of India, Calcutta, August 15, 1967.

years and that it was openly organized under the leadership of the Siliguri Sub-division Kisan Samiti. He further observed :

> In the Terai areas whenever the peasant started protesting against the reactionary clique of landlords built up during the Congress rule, reactionary cliques in order to hold on by force their benami, illegal rights (possession) over land acquired through the cooperation of Settlement Amins and police and government officials, attempted to throttle the peasants' demand for social justice by launching widespread offensives. In order to create such an opportunity this hue and cry about anarchy has been raised . . . .[72]

Later, when Jangal Santhal was in police custody at Siliguri, his views were reported to be the same by a fellow extremist prisoner who had been released on bail. Once again he described the struggle in Naxalbari as purely a spontaneous agrarian movement against "the age-old domination and exploitation of the feudal gentry".[73] It may be interesting to note that the very first issue of *Deshabrati* categorically described the uprising as "the legitimate struggle of the Terai peasants for land; the peasants' class struggle against the landlords."[74] With the intensification of the oppression by the landlords, it observed, the peasantry started resisting more resolutely and gradually the whole movement assumed political colour.

Soon, however, Naxalbari underwent a drastic transformation in the imagination of those who had engineered the revolt. For example, Charu Mazumdar, whose brain-child was the Naxalbari agitation, definitively dubbed it as a struggle "not for land or crops but for political power,"[75] and that it should be regarded "not only as a national but an international struggle against capitalism, and imperialism".[76]

Then, at a May Day rally in Calcutta in 1969, the "hero" of

72. Quoted in Biswanath Mukherjee, "Two Faces of Naxalbari", *op. cit.*

73. *Deshabrati* (a Bengali weekly, first started by the supporters of the Naxalbari movement, subsequently transformed into the weekly organ of the West Bengal State Unit of the CPI(M-L), November 2, 1967.

74. *Deshabrati,* July 6, 1967.

75. Charu Mazumdar, "One Year of Naxalbari", *Liberation,* June, 1968, p. 28.

76. *Deshabrati,* May 29, 1968.

the Naxalbari drama, Kanu Sanyal spoke in accents, quite identical with those of his mentor. Addressing the mass rally to mark the foundation of the CPI(M-L), Kanu Sanyal hailed Naxalbari as the "Chinkang Mountain of India,"[77] and armed uprising against imperialism, feudalism, comprador capital, and old and new revisionism.[78] While giving an exhaustive account of the peasant struggle in Naxalbari in the spirit of Mao Tse-tung's Human Report,[79] Sanyal was also talking in the same breath, though his report was marked with the most confusing assessment of the whole event.

Starting with a poser as to why the peasant movement in the Terai region proved to be an event having more far-reaching consequences than even an earth-quake, Sanyal sets about giving the answer. He says:

> Ours is a semi-colonial and semi-feudal country, 80% of whose population live in the villages. The contradiction between the people of our country and feudalism is the principal contradiction .... So the peasants are the basis and main force of the anti-imperialist and anti-feudal struggle. Unless the peasants are liberated it is impossible to achieve the liberation of all other oppressed classes.... These heroic peasants dealt merciless blows to the obsolete and rotten feudal elements—the jotedars, landlords and usurers. The State apparatus of the comprador-bureaucrat bourgeoisie... is preserving the feudal system by force and carrying on armed rule. Inspired by Chairman Mao's teaching—'Political power grows out of the barrel of a gun', the heroic peasants opposed this armed rule with armed revolt .... That is why the Naxalbari struggle has shown the path for liberation of India's oppressed classes .... The struggle of the Terai peasants acted as a midwife in the revolutionary situation pre-

77. Mao Tse-tung had submitted a report to the Central Committee of the CPC on the struggle in the Chinkang Mountains on November 25, 1928. For details of the struggle, see *Selected Military Writings of Mao Tse-tung,* Current Book Depot, Kanpur, 1969, pp. 21-49.

78. *Liberation,* May 1969, p. 118.

79. "Report on the Investigations of the Peasant Movement in Hunan, March, 1927", *Selected Writings of Mao Tse-tung,* National Book Agency, Calcutta, 1967, Vol. II, pp. 438-470. In 1927 the Hunan Province was the centre of the peasant movement in China.

vailing in India. That is why a single spark of the Naxalbari struggle is kindling widespread forest fire everywhere.[80]

Again, quite in line with Mao's call,—"Get Organized" in the Hunan Report, Sanyal has also detailed the history of the peasant organizations in Naxalbari under the caption, 'Establish the peasant committees and get organized." He writes:

> With the speed of a storm the revolutionary peasants, in the course of about one and half months, formed peasant committees through hundreds of group meetings and turned these committees into armed village defence groups. In a word, they organized about 90% of the village population . . .[81] Finally, Sanyal enumerates "ten great deeds" carried out in Naxalbari—virtually a conscious echo of the "Fourteen Great Achievements"[82] as laid down in Mao's Human Report:
>
> 1. A blow was dealt at the political, economic and social structure in the villages based on monopoly land-ownership....The old feudal structure that had existed for centuries was thus smashed through this action of the peasants.
> 2. The peasants seized all the legal deeds and documents relating to land which had been used to chest them. They held meetings and burned all the receipts, acknowledgements, plans, deeds and documents.
> 3. The jotedars and moneylenders, taking advantage of the party of the rural folk, got them committed to unequal agreements relating to the mortgage of land and bullocks. The peasants declared all such agreements as well as the huge burden of interest imposed on them null and void.
> 4. The hoarded rice which is used as capital for carrying on usurious and feudal exploitation was confiscated by the peasants and distributed among themselves . . . .

80. Kanu Sanyal, "Report on the Peasant Movement in the Terai Region", *Liberation,* November 1968, pp. 29-32.

81. Mao Tse-tung, "Get Organized" in Report on Investigations of the Peasant Movement in Hunan, March 1927, *op. cit.* Vol. II, p. 439.

82. Kanu Sanyal, *op. cit.,* p. 33. Here the claims of Sanyal appear to have been modest compared to what had been done on the organizational level by the Hunan peasants as laid down by Mao Tse-tung. *op. cit.,* p. 439.

5. All jotedars in the villages who were known for a long time as oppressors and those who tried to oppose the peasant struggle were all subjected to open trial and sentenced to death.
6. The wicked, ruffian elements and flankeys who are used to preserve the political, economic and social authority of the jotedars in the villages and those who cooperated with the police were all brought to open trial. In some cases, death sentence was given, in others the followers were paraded through the village streets with shoes strung around their necks and with fool's caps on their heads, so that they would not dare commit crimes in future.
7. Realising that their struggle against the jotedars, the landlords and the moneylenders would be subjected to armed repression by the state apparatus, they armed themselves with their traditional weapons like bows and arrows and spears as well as with guns forcibly taken away from the jotedars, and organized their own armed groups.
8. Lest the general administration of the villages should suffer, they arranged for night watch and shouldered the responsibility of running the schools in a smooth way.....
9. In every area they created regional and central revolutionary committees and established the peasants' political power.
10. They declared the existent bourgeois law and law courts null and void in the villages. The decisions of the regional and central revolutionary committees were declared to be the law.....The leadership of this struggle was naturally, in the hands of the landless peasantry. The reason why these revolutionary actions could become so far-reaching and so vast in their sweep is that the leadership of the struggle was in the hands of the poor landless peasants, who constitute 70% of the peasantry.[83]

It is self contradictory that while Sanyal declared in his report that the leadership of the Naxalbari struggle was in the hands of the poor landless peasants, later in the same document

83. Kanu Sanyal, "Terai Report", *op. cit.*, pp. 34-36.

he has come out with disarming frankness in admitting that "we, the petty-bourgeois leadership imposed ourselves on the people...." And this petty-bourgeois leadership, with no stretch of imagination would be classified as landless peasants; strikingly enough, most of these leaders are reported to have their own large holdings. The land settlement records of the Siliguri sub-division, compiled immediately after the Naxalbari struggle reveal interesting facts. Excluding the lone exception, Kanu Sanyal who does not belong to the area and holds no land there, every other extremist leaders owns some land. Khokan Mazumdar whose bonafides as an Indian citizen are very much doubted, also owns some land in the area. Great secrecy prevails as to the exact nature and size of Charu Mazumdar's land holdings, because it was alleged most of the holdings were transferred *malafide* to the names of his relatives in 1953, just before the Estate Acquisition Act was passed. Of the twenty others in the second and third rank leadership, two have land in excess of the ceiling, two hold the full 75 bighas allowed under the Estate Acquisition Act, 1953, and the rest hold between twelve and seventy-five bighas apiece. Not one in the leadership is a landless labourer. The table in the next page gives an idea about the different sizes of holdings owned by the leaders of the Naxalbari peasant struggle.[84]

It should not, however, be understood from the foregoing analysis that since the bulk of the leading kisan activists of the Naxalbari agitation came from the rich and middle peasant families, the landless peasantry did not participate in the movement. Rather these people acted as the vanguard of uprising.

What may be immediately discerned from the report of Sanyal is that most of the "ten great deeds" of the Naxalbari peasants exclusively constituted what is called an agrarian movement for land and crops. But soon he is caught into the meshes of self-contradiction by his strange observation that "the struggle

84. For further information, see *Jugantar* (Calcutta) July 29, 1967. According to a report, the Government of West Bengal took over in 1970 from Charu Mazumdar 63.56 acres of agricultural land and 17 acres of non-agricultural land. The Settlement Officer of North Bengal informed that Mazumdar had owned over 88.56 acres of agricultural land including a holding of nearly 23 acres in his own name. Under the present law of the State a person cannot possess more than 25 acres of land. For this report, see *Amrita Bazar Patrika* (Calcutta), September 1, 1970.

	Name	Size of holding
1.	Panchanan Sarkar	51 acres
2.	Jibon Santhal	42 bighas
3.	Jangal Santhal's family	25 acres
4.	Majbur Rahman	25 acres
5.	Lata Kison	25 bighas
6.	Machchru Oraon	36 bighas
7.	Jupra Oraon	20 bighas
8.	Rupna Oraon	22 bighas
9.	Batai Munda	18 bighas
10.	Dharani Barman	14 bighas
11.	Taope Naik	15 bighas
12.	Mathura Oraon	15 bighas
13.	Balaram Singh	12 bighas
14.	Tutul Kisan	14 bighas
15.	Subhas Karmakar	14 bighas
16	Krishna Bahadur	12 bighas
17.	Lukha Oraon	20 bighas
18.	Suklal Oraon	15 bighas
19.	Vakru Oraon	20 bighas
20.	Kadam Mallik	75 acres

of the Terai peasants is an armed struggle—*not for land, but for State power*. This is a fundamental question, and the revisionist thinking, which has been prevailing in the present movement for the last few decades, can only be combated by solving this question .... We all know that every class struggle is a political struggle and that the aim of political struggles is to seize state power."[85]

Again, guided by the teaching imparted by his mentor, Charu Mazumdar, that "the struggle for land amounts to economism, because possession of land merely converts the poor into the rich peasantry" and "the agrarian revolution must await the smashing of state power"[86], Sanyal gives a highly confused picture about the true nature of the Naxalbari agitation as he writes:

Without this consciousness, any struggle for land, no matter

85. Kanu Sanyal, *op. cit.*, p. 39.

86. Charu Mazumdar, "March Forward by Summing the Experience of Revolutionary Peasant Struggles of India", *Deshabrati*, December 4, 1969.

> how militant it may be, is militant economism. Such militant struggle for land generates opportunism in the peasant movement and demoralises the majority of the fighting section as happened during the struggle for seizing the benami lands. Such militant economic movement leads one into the blind alley of revisionism.

Such a logic of Sanyal seems to be most confounded as he does not see any difference between economism and struggle for economic demands. Any militant struggle for land does not necessarily generate opportunism. If that struggle is led by opportunists, then only it degenerates into economism pure and simple. And the correct assessment of the Naxalbari peasant uprising is that though at the initial stages it was just an agrarian movement for land and crops, it gradually developed into a political movement.

Then, again, Sanyal's worst confusion is sadly revealed over the question of leadership in the Naxalbari struggle. For instance, he describes, first of all, the movement as being led by "the poor landless peasants" who constitute 70% of the peasantry and "in every area they created regional and central revolutionary committees and established the peasants' political power". At the same time he finds that the agitation was surging forth under the leadership of the tea gardens workers as he writes:

> An important aspect of the struggle of the heroic peasants of Terai is its success in gaining the support of the tea garden workers and other toiling people and thus, intensifying the struggle still further by building united front in the anti-feudal struggle. This is the most important task. The struggle of the heroic peasants of Terai has solved this problem .... The struggle of the Terai peasants helped the tea garden workers to come out of the mire of trade unionism and economism. This happened in spite of the fact that the so-called Communist trade union leaders were opposing the struggle there grew up a genuine workers-peasant alliance *under the leadership of the tea garden workers*.[87]

And finally, the anti-climax of the Naxalbari drama is reached when Sanyal writes "we, the petty-bourgeois leadership improved ourselves on the people .... we, of the petty-bourgeois

87. Kanu Sanyal, *Ibid.*, pp. 42-43, emphasis added.

origin opposed them".[88] This is really a baffling position of a loquacious revolutionary when he finds an agrarian movement is led by the poor landless peasants, the tea-plantation labour and then, by the petty-bourgeois leadership—all at a time.[89] And it is this predicament which ultimately caught the Maoists in India in the wrong foot and set in motion the quick process of endless splinterisation among their leadership.

Kanu Sanyal, however, never appears to be more disarming than when he goes into retrospection on the line of retreat of the Naxalbari agitation. He has almost openly admitted that the leadership failed, though temporarily, to advance the struggle of the heroic peasants of Terai. The reasons for its failure, according to Sanyal, are: "Lack of strong party organization, failure to rely whole-heartedly on the masses and to build a powerful mass, ignorant of military affairs, thinking on old lines and a formal attitude towards the establishment of political power and the work of revolutionary land reform".[90] It is rather interesting to note in this context that though he has enumerated these reasons for the failure of the Naxalbari peasant struggle, whatever sectarian errors had been committed during the agitation were not reviewed and corrected when it collapsed. On the other hand, Sanyal and his party went on merrily glorifying these errors in their subsequent actions and policies. For example, the primary reason for the failure of the Naxalbari peasant movement was the lack of a strong party organization. But it was Naxalbari which offered a real chance to the Maoists in India to build a party of their own. And this chance was later wasted by the extreme left faction in West Bengal under Charu Mazumdar's leadership as it could not consolidate all the other Maoist factions under the banner of the CPI(M) that was subsequently founded in the May Day, 1969. Thus the Third Communist

88. Kanu Sanyal, *Ibid.*, pp. 47-48.

89. Charu Mazumdar, however, contradicted Sanyal's analysis of the question of leadership in the Naxalbari agitation of a year later by oversimplifying the whole problem as he wrote: "The Naxalbari struggle has taught us that the peasantry was not all dependent on others for leading the movement, it fought by solely relying on its own struggle". See Charu Mazumdar, "March Forward by Summing Up The Experience of the Revolutionary Peasant Struggles in India", *op. cit.*

90. Kanu Sanyal, "Terai Report", *op. cit.*, p. 15.

Party of India was 'imposed from the above' by some persons who had taken off from the CPI(M) just as the "32" rebels had organized themselves into India's Second Communist Party after leaving the CPI.[91]

Secondly, as regards the Naxalbari leadership's failure to build a powerful mass base, Sanyal admits with somewhat disarming naivete:

> We were unable to raise the struggle firmly to a higher stage because we failed to rely wholly on the people and to build a powerful mass base. The reason is, we did not understand, nor did we ever try to understand, the actions of the masses. On the contrary, under the influence of old revisionist habits we artificially set limits on how far they should go.

And the ultimate result of this failure was that the "the masses scattered before widespread terror, the struggle lost its edge," and "the escapist mood deepened"[92] and that the whole course of the movement quickly slid from "strategic retreat" to "retreat into inaction". Mr Sanyal's excuse for the failure to build up strong mass base is a glaring exposure of the petty-bourgeois revolutionary character of the Naxalbari leadership. To have confidence in the masses is not just too subjective an affair. It can be carried through only by intensified mass organization, through day-to-day contacts with the masses. But even after the failure of the Naxalbari agitation there was hardly any visible sign that this tactical error would be corrected. On the other hand, the mass-line of action that was subsequently propounded[93] by the party theoretician, Mr Charu Mazumdar was just "an infantile delirium of negative petty-bourgeois revolutionism" as was subsequently denounced by his critics. Mao Tse-tung wrote

91. For a detailed analysis of this charge of the imposition of the Maoist party from above, see Mohan Ram, *Maoism in India,* Vikas Publications, New Delhi, 1971, pp. 99-103.

92. Kanu Sanyal, *Ibid.,* pp. 47-48.

93. This line of action included a cluster of 4 "Don'ts"; (1) No mass movement for economic demands; (2) no trade unionism; (3) No peasant organization and (4) No union activities for student-cadres. For the details of these slogans, see Charu Mazumdar, "To my Comrades", *Liberation,* October, 1968, pp. 14-15 and "A Few Words to the Revolutionary Students and Youths", *Liberation,* March 1970, pp. 13-14.

in 1936 that "the important thing is to be good at learning" and "to learn is no easy matter and to apply what one has learned is even harder".[94] But the Indian Maoists would not learn anything new, but forget everything old. Their subjective thinking ultimately landed them in a serious predicament and completed the process of their disintegration.

Thirdly, ignorance of military affairs and thinking on old lines forced a quick retreat upon the movement. In the initial stages, according to Sanyal, the leadership underestimated the enemy's strength and later over-estimated it. It had a wrong understanding of the Mao Tse-tung's teaching in that it helplessly turned from "the strategic retreat to the retreat into inaction". Most damaging of all is the muddled statement of Sanyal obscuring the line between fact and fancy in the leadership's use of guerrilla terminology:

> We assumed that with the arming of the people, and with the jotedars, vested interests and other bad elements leaving the villages, a liberated area had come into being. We looked on the armed people on an actual army—hoped that guerrila units would emerge from the spontaneous uprisings of the broad masses. Often we would recruit vagabond elements with some revolutionary leaning as captains who would organize the armed bands.[95]

It is absolutely clear from Sanyal's own words that the rebels hopelessly minimized the repressive power of the State. There was no preparation to face a ruthless military force. The Naxalbari extremists did not even have an occasion of facing the army. Police action, and that too a rather half-hearted one (because of the prevailing differences among the U.F. partners) was more than enough to force the peasant movement into a whispering collapse. The operations of the Naxalbari peasants were marred by a queer blend of naivets and ingenousness. Their reveris of conquering State power with bows and arrows amounted to a rollicking caricature of the Hunan drama.

A fundamental reason, according to Sanyal, for the defeat of the Naxalbari struggle can be traced to the twin failure in

94. Mao Tse-tung "Problems of Strategy in China's Revolutionary War", *op. cit.,* Vol. I, pp.179-88.

95. Kanu Sanyal, "Terai Report", *op. cit.,* pp. 47-48.

establishing revolutionary political power and in carrying out the land reforms programmes. He writes:

> Our failure in establishing the revolutionary political power and in carrying out revolutionary land reforms blunted the edge of the class struggle both during and after the struggle. The revolutionary peasants accomplished two tasks through mass mobilization. They are: formation of central and local revolutionary peasant committees and distribution of land. And we turned exactly these two things into a most formal affair. Our petty-bourgeois day-dreaming was at the root of it. We never seriously considered how deeply significant were these two tasks.[96]

It may be easily discerned from the observation of Kanu Sanyal that at the most critical stage of the Naxalbari movement the leadership lost contacts with the masses of the peasantry because of their "negative petty-bourgeois adventurism". They never thought of consolidating the "successes" achieved by the peasants. With their initial obsession with the Naxalbari peasant struggle as a "struggle for State power", the leader blurred off the qualitative differences between revolutionary economic struggle and economism as understood in the Marxist-Leninist and Maoist political thinking.[97] But in their bid to fight "revisionism" in the Indian Communist movement, they got themselves bogged down in the mire of "sectarianism" by neglecting the vital job of carrying out revolutionary land reforms in the Naxalbari-Phansidewa-Kharibari belt during the struggle.

Sanyal drew some interesting lessons from the experience of the Terai peasant struggle:

> Mao Tse-tung's political and military theories need deeper study; armed group formed after arousing the villages and arming them will become the village defence groups; knowledge of guerrilla warfare should be acquired by arming the peasants with conventional weapons and organizing assaults on class enemies; liberated zones will have to be built gra-

96. Kanu Sanyal "Terai Report" *Ibid.,* p. 52.

97. For an exhaustive analysis of the deviations of the Indian Maoists from Mao's teachings and of the similarities of their action-patterns with the Latin American guerrillas, the author has undertaken a further comprehensive work on "The Political Theory of the New Left—India and Latin America".

dually by forming peasant guerrilla groups. But without persevering in building liberated zones, formation of guerrilla groups or their functioning would be difficult. The guerrilla groups are to be the nucleus of the people's armed force.

But these lessons had been drawn only to be forgotten by the Maoists as was revealed from their subsequent action patterns which spelled anything but Maoism in Indian Communism.

In the final analysis it would be very pertinent to note that Naxalbari was neither the first peasant armed struggle nor the first revolutionary base area in India and was by no means the beginning of the Chinese style revolution in India. It is at the height of his "petty-bourgeois snobbery", as the leader of a rival Maoist group derisively put it[98], that Charu Mazumdar writes "Naxalbari is the first instance of successful application of Maoism in India. It is for the first time in the Naxalbari when the peasantry launched an armed struggle for state power".[99] But it was at Telengana of Andhra Pradesh that the first successful application of Maoist strategy of people's war was made outside China in 1946-51. Even the ideologues of the Communist Party of China unhesitatingly recognized Telengana as the first "Red Area" in India. In all its reviews following the Naxalbari peasant uprising the CPC gave the pride of place to the Telengana movement. The Chinese ideologues just saw in the miniscular peasant revolt at Naxalbari the resurrection of the Telengana movement. It observed:

> The armed struggle in Telengana had been betrayed and put down. But in a dozen or more years, the peasants in Darjeeling have risen and set up a Red area for carrying on armed struggle.[100]

Then, again, it should be noted that Naxalbari is not the first peasant armed struggle after Telengana, because the struggle in the 800 square-mile tribal belt in the Srikakulam district of Andhra Pradesh, launched in 1959 had grown into mass actions by November 1967.[101] The Srikakulam peasant struggle did not re-

98. For this and similar remarks, see Promode Sengupta, *Biplab Kon Pathe*? (Which Road to Revolution?), Calcutta, 1970.

99. *Deshabrati*, September 4, 1969.

100. Commentator, "Historical Lessons of Telengana Uprising", *People's Daily*, August 3, 1967; *Peking Review*, August 11, 1967.

101. For details of the Srikakulum peasant struggle, see Andhra Pra-

ceive so much publicity because of the fact that the Naxalbari uprising took place in West Bengal, then ruled by the United Front Government with the CPI(M) as the strongest partner in it, and, therefore, assumed a special significance for the CPC which was symbolically challenging the strategy of "peaceful transition to socialism", thereby totally discrediting the CPI(M) for its participation in India's parliamentary system.

desh Revolutionary Communist Committee "On Srikakulum Girijan Armed Struggle", Mimeographed, and Narayanamurthi, "The Srikakulum Story I & II," *Frontier,* (Calcutta weekly), September 13 & 20, 1968.

CHAPTER III

NAXALBARI II: BATTLEGROUND OF THE CPC

THE NAXALBARI peasant struggle had to beat up a hasty retreat in the face of stern police action taken by the United Front Government of which the CPI(M) was the leading partner. Naxalbari, which came to be reckoned as a symbolism for a definite ideology and readily identified with the much talked-of Hunan Peasant Uprising in China in 1926-1927, threw an open challenge to the State CPI(M) leaders either to opt for a "class-collaborationist" policy by declaring their final choice for peaceful parliamentarism or to go in for armed struggle as the sole tactic of the Indian People's Democratic revolution. The situation was made still worse for the CPI(M) leaders by the Communist Party of China which came to intervene persistently in favour of the Naxalbari extremist leaders, since Naxalbari provided to the CPC not only an instant opportunity to implement the strategy of shifting its world-wide "crusade" against the American "imperialists" and the Soviet "revisionists" to the "Third World", in particular, by intensifying revolutionary struggles in the area but also an occasion for exploding the "myth" of "peaceful transition to socialism" through parliamentary democracy and for spelling out the Maoist line for the Indian revolutionaries.[1]

THE CPC APPLAUDS THE INDIAN MAOISTS

The first ever expression of the Chinese support for the Naxalbari peasant uprising came in the shape of a Radio Peking plaudit on June 28, 1967. It declared with a bit of ecstasy:

> A phase of peasants' armed struggle led by the revolutionaries of the Indian Communist Party has been set up in the countryside in Darjeeling District of West Bengal State of India. This is the front paw of the revolutionary armed struggle launched by the Indian people under the guidance

1. For an exhaustive analysis of the motivation pattern behind China's "Third World" strategy, see, see Chapter I.

of Mao Tse-tung's teachings. This represents the general orientation of the Indian revolution at the present times.[2]

Further, upholding the Maoist line for India the broadcast declared:

> Like pre-liberation China, India is a semi-colonial and semi-feudal country. The Congress Government, representing the Indian big landlords and big bourgeoisie, has always pursued a foreign policy of surrendering to imperialism and a domestic policy of brutality suppressing and exploiting the broad masses of the labouring people, thus driving hundreds of millions of people to the brink of starvation and death. Under this counter-revolutionary rule, the workers, peasants and other labouring people throughout the country are in a desperate situation. Only through revolution by violence can they maintain their existence. The Indian people, in order to liberate themselves, must proceed along the path pointed out by Comrade Mao, the path carved out by the Chinese people under the leadership of Chairman Mao in overwhelming the reactionary rule and winning victory in the revolution; this is the road of armed revolution to oppose armed counter-revolution, the establishment of rural bases, the concentration of forces in the villages, using the villages to encircle the cities and then finally, the taking over of cities.

Within a week of this Radio Peking broadcast an article was published in People's Daily which hailed the Naxalbari peasant uprising as "the prelude to a violent revolution by hundreds of millions of people throughout India." Naxalbari, the article observed, was the result of the militant action of the "revolutionaries" in the Indian Communist Party, who deserted the United Front Government in West Bengal because it had "served as a tool of the Indian reactionaries.[3]

The Chinese press linked up the Naxalbari peasant uprising with the Telengana peasant struggle of the late 1940s. Naxalbari was the rekindling of "the torch of armed revolution once lit by

2. Radio Peking, June 28, 1967. For full text of the broadcast, see *Mainstream* (New Delhi) weekly, July 8, 1967.

3. "The Darjeeling Peasant Armed Struggle", *People's Daily*, July 5, 1967; *Peking Review*, July 14, 1967.

the peasants of Telengana." But in the Chinese assessment, compared with Telengana, Naxalbari presented better strategic advantages necessary for a protracted guerrilla struggle, since the Terai tract "is only 4 miles from Nepal, 30 miles from Sikkim, 14 miles from East Pakistan and 60 miles from China's Tibet".[4]

The implication was clear enough that an expanded armed revolutionary base could in certain circumstances be fed from a rear base and a sanctuary; the Chinese probably had in mind an argument advanced by some of the CPI leaders in 1951 justifying the abrupt suspension of the peasant struggle in Telengana because it did not have such a firm contiguous rear base as the Chinese People's Liberation Army was said to have had in the contiguous Soviet territory.[5]

In an even more strikingly captioned article, "Spring Thunder Over India", the *People's Daily* laid down in absolutely unambiguous terms the Maoist line as the only valid strategy for armed revolution in India. With a warm applause for the Naxalbari extremists the article observed:

> A peal of spring thunder has crashed over the land of India. Revolutionary peasants in the Darjeeling area have risen in rebellion. Under the leadership of a revolutionary group of the Indian Communist Party, a red area of rural revolutionary armed struggle has been established in India .... The Chinese people joyfully applaud this revolutionary storm of the Indian peasants in the Darjeeling area as do all the Marxist-Leninists and revolutionary peoples of the whole world ....[6]

4. *Ibid.*
5. For an account of the CPI policy in 1951 vis-a-vis the Telengana peasant movement see Kautsky, J. H., Moscow and the *Communist Party of India,* Cambridge: The M.I.T. Press, 1956, Chapter 3. The onetime highly secret inner-party document of the CPI entitled, "Tactical Line", which had been allegedly prepared in Moscow and circulated among the members of the Central Committee of the party at the time of its Third Congress held in Madurai in December 1953, clearly reflects this position.

   For the full text of the document, "Tactical Line", see *Indian Communist Party Documents,* 1930-1956,published by the Democratic Research Service, Bombay and the Institute of Pacific Relations, New York, 1957, pp. 71-85.
6. "Spring Thunder Over India", *People's Daily,* July 5, 1967; *Peking Review,* July 14, 1967.

Addressing itself to the central question as to what road was to be followed by the Indian revolutionaries, the Chinese ideologue prescribed that the revolutionary process in India

> must take the road of relying on the peasants, establishing base areas in the countryside, persisting in protracted armed struggle and using the countryside to encircle and finally capture the cities. This is Mao Tse-tung's road, the road that had led the Chinese revolution to victory and the only road to victory for the revolutions of all oppressed nations and people .....[7]

Discarding the Zhdanovist prescription of the city-based action strategy of the Indian Communists, the article put an acute accent on the peasant question because the peasants constitute

> the main force in the national-democratic revolution against imperialism and its lackeys; they are the most reliable and numerous allies of the proletariat. India is a vast semi-colonial and semi-feudal country with a population of 500 million, the absolute majority of which, the peasantry, once aroused, will become the inevitable force of the Indian revolution.....

According to the CPC theoretician, the specific feature of the Indian revolution, like that of the Chinese revolution, was "armed revolution fighting against armed counter-revolution." Armed struggle was the only correct road for the Indian revolution; there was no other road whatsoever. "Such trash as Gandhism, parliamentary road and the like are opium used by the Indian ruling classes to paralyse the Indian people. Only by relying on violent revolution and taking the road of armed struggle can India be saved, and the Indian people achieve complete liberation."

Since the reactionary forces were "temporarily stronger than the revolutionary forces," the Indian revolutionaries must use the "whole set of the flexible strategy and tactics of people's war" and preserve in protracted armed struggle. The armed struggle must begin in the countryside "where the reactionary rule is weak", and where "the revolutionaries can manoeuvre freely". It mattered little if the beginning was modest and if the peasants

7. *Ibid.*

had to fight at first with bows and arrows. So long as the Communists adhered to the revolutionary line of Marxism-Leninism and Mao Tse-tung's thought and relied on the peasants "it is entirely possible for them to advance from one revolutionary rural base to another in the huge backward rural areas and build a people's army of a new type," and the article concludes with the observation that "although the course of the Indian revolutionary struggle will be long and tortuous, the Indian revolution, guided by great Marxism-Leninism and Mao Tse-tung's Thought will certainly triumph."[8] And in order to give further incentive to the Naxalbari extremists, the CPC began to see "dozens of Naxalbaris" appearing "in all parts of the Indian countryside".[9]

As regards the tactics of armed struggle to be followed by the revolutionaries the CPC's prescription was that they must "adhere to mobile and flexible guerrilla tactics" in order to smash one enemy "encirclement and suppression campaign" after another. The Commentator held in another article:

> So long as these revolutionary forces are good at employing the tactics of 'the enemy advances, we retreat; the enemy camps, we harass; the enemy tires, we attack; the enemy retreats, we pursue ....,' they will be able to gather strength and exhaust the enemy's effectives .... To gain a firm footing and to stick to long-term armed struggle, the revolutionary peasant armed forces must set up and expand their base away in the countryside. This is an important task for the present Indian revolution.
>
> In their struggle against the reactionary troops and police, the armed peasant forces in Naxalbari have withstood the first test. This shows that the revolutionary forces in the countryside have ample space to manoeuvre in and are quite capable of growing and expanding from small to big in the course of struggle.
>
> The Chinese revolution from the very beginning was tasted in battles by repeated "encirclement and suppression" and "counter-encirclement and suppression" campaigns. It was only through a protracted struggle that a powerful people's army and vast rural base areas were established and final

8. *Ibid.*
9. "Dozens of Naxalbaris", *Peking Review,* July 28, 1967.

victory was won. The Indian revolution will naturally do the same.[10]

The CPC Debunks The CPI(M)

Almost synchronising with the open support[11] for the Naxalbari revolutionaries, the CPC mounted a very sharp attack on the "revisionist" policies of the two older Indian Communist parties. To the Chinese mind the real threat to the Naxalbari peasant struggle came not so much from the Indian "reactionaries" as from the revisionists in the Communist movement, who had betrayed the Telengana uprising and who were about to betray Naxalbari revolutionaries as well. In a major article in the *People's Daily* a CPC ideologue observed:

> Since the end of World War II there has been a constant sharp and complicated struggle in the Indian Communist Party between these two diametrically opposed lines. On the one side is the revolutionary line of Marxism-Leninism, Mao Tse-tung's thought, followed by the revolutionaries in the Party . . . The other is the revisionist line pursued by Dange, Namboodiripad and their like. They preach the theory of India being an "exception" and maintain that the parliamentary road of "peaceful transition" should be followed. They oppose violent revolution and want the revolutionary people who have taken up arms to lay them down and abandon their struggle. This is an out and out capitulationist line, a counter-revolutionary line.[11]

10. Commentator, "Let the Red Flag of Naxalbari Fly Still Higher", *Peking Review,* August 11, 1967.

11. The CPC's support to the Naxalbari uprising without directly attacking the CPI(M) leadership but attacking the West Bengal United Front Government was calculated to pressurise the Party into quitting the United Front. But finding the CPI(M)'s reaction very much lukewarm the CPC sharpened its attack through Radio Peking by specifically mentioning that it was "those revisionist leaders of the Indian Communist Party who serve as Deputy Chief Minister or Ministers in the State Government for perpetuating the "fraud" of land reforms, and when it failed, agreeing to use of police force on the peasantry, and disowning the revolutionaries as "ultra-left elements" and "adventurists". These revisionists, according to Radio Peking, were no better than those of "renegade Dange clique".

Analysing the Telengana "sell out" by the Indian revisionists the Commentator wrote:

> The peasants' armed struggle in Telengana from 1946 to 1951 was the result of the triumph of the revolutionary line of Marxism-Leninism, Mao Tse-tung's thought .... However, this excellent situation for the Indian revolution was undermined and finally put an end to by the revisionist line enforced by Dange and his followers.[12]

Against this "foul play" by the Indian revisionists the article warned the Indian revolutionaries by asking them to draw clear line between themselves and the revisionist line politically, ideologically and organisationally and to wage "a resolute struggle against modern revisionism centred on Soviet revisionist clique." The Commentator concluded with a clarion call that "the revolutionaries in the Indian Communist Party will surely enhance their stength in the struggle and build a genuinely revolutionary Party of Marxism-Leninism, Mao Tse-tung's thought".[13]

In the later issues of the Peking Review, Peking's denunciation of the CPI(M) leadership became more strident. E. M. S. Namboodiripad, the then Chief Minister of Kerala was a special target of this vehement attack. Namboodiripad and his colleagues were "faithfully adhering to the Congress-ruled Central Government". They had "babbled" much about the 'parliamentary road' and 'peaceful transition,' but in fact, stood "firm against the peasant armed struggle," worse still, "they hanker after high office .... and sick to have themselves elected". There were "many facts to show that the Kerala State Government which enforces the fascist rule of the Central Government is part of the state machine operating in the interests of the landlords and the bureaucratic-comprador bourgeoisie" . Namboodiripad "acts as an apologist and protector of the international agents of U.S. imperialism".[14]

12. Observer, "Historical Lessons of Telengana Uprising", *Peking Review,* August 11, 1967.

13. *Ibid.*

14. "Indian Revisionists in Kerala: Serving the Reactionaries", *Peking Review,* September 8, 1967. Also see, "Indian Revisionists Are Quacks", *Peking Review,* September 22, 1967.

In January 1968, the CPC ideologues derived some broad conclusions about the revolutionary situation in India. First, an Indian revolution had become a significant factor for the triumph of Maoist strategy of revolution in South and South-East Asia in so far as India "occupies an extremely important strategic position in the world proletariat revolution". The second major conclusion was that 1967 had been a "turning point" for India not simply because of the outbreak of a Maoist revolution in Naxalbari, but also because "the struggle between the two lines and the two roads" was intensified and carried a step further. Thirdly, the CPC concluded that the CPI(M)'s policy of peaceful transition had proved "bankrupt" and "gone up in smoke". And finally, Peking laid down in clear, unmistakable terms the Maoist line as the only valid strategy for Indian revolution:

> .... to make a specific analysis of India's objective conditions in accordance with the brilliant thought of Mao Tse-tung: to formulate the programme and tactics of the Indian revolution on this basis; and to give impetus to the peasant revolutionary struggle and develop Naxalbari-type movements.[15]

In-fighting in West Bengal

It is striking to point out that "a peal of spring thunder" which had crashed over Naxalbari, instantly sent the West Bengal State leadership of the CPI(M) dithering. The first visible reaction of the city-bred extremists of the CPI(M) could be witnessed on June 14, when the muffled rumbling of their discontent over the police repression at Naxalbari found vocal expression at a meeting of the ultra-left group held at the Rammohun Library Hall, Calcutta. Different speakers belonging to this group attack with all vehemence the CPI(M) leaders for toeing a "revisionist" line, and threatened to pull them down if they did not mend their ways. They further contended that socialism could never be achieved without armed insurrection, and those who thought of peaceful transition to socialism were, in fact, social democrats. The speakers also charged the CPI(M) leaders

15. "Historic Turning Point in the Indian Revolution", *Peking Review*, January 12, 1968.

with giving lip service to the fight against revisionism while they themselves were being guided by that "abhorable tendency".[16]

Significantly enough, the holding of this meeting just on the eve of the session of the CPI(M) Politbureau (which was to be held from the 15th to the 18th of June), was a direct way of putting pressure for clarifying the party's hitherto undefined ideological position.

The first serious trial of strength between the CPI(M) supporters and the pro-Naxalbari elements in the party took place on June 28, 1967 over the possession of the office of *Deshahitaishi,* the Bengali weekly organ of the CPI(M)'s West Bengal State Unit. In the violent clash that followed the incident, the extremist group which had been on the Editorial Board of the paper was forcibly ousted from the office premises at Dharmatolla Street, Calcutta by the CPI(M) supporters.[17]

The ouster of the pro-Naxalbari elements in the CPI(M) from the *Deshahitaishi* office further intensified the intra-party squabble, which assumed a new dimension when the extremist leadership brought out a new Bengali weekly, *Deshabrati* on July 6 under the editorship of Sushital Ray Chowdhury and

16. For further details, see *Amrita Bazar Patrika* (Calcutta) June 15, 1967.

17. The June 29, 1967 issue of the *Statesman* (Calcutta) which carried a detailed report of the incident, informed that in the evening of June 28, a group of persons headed by Sudhanshu Dasgupta, Editor of the *Deshahitaishi,* entered the office of the journal and asked Niranjan Bose, Manager of the weekly, to hand over charge of the office to the former. They showed Bose a letter written by Promode Dasgupta, Secretary of the Party's West Bengal State Unit, to that effect. When Bose challenged their authority, he was assaulted by the Dasgupta's man. Thereupon some supporters of the extremist group rushed into the office and chased away the intruders.

In the same evening a general meeting of the members of the CPI(M) was being held at the Muslim Institute Hall, when the news of the occupation of the *Deshahitaishi* office by the extremists reached there. Incited by Promode Dasgupta, who was addressing the meeting, the CPI(M) cadres stormed into the journal's office and ousted the extremists.

Later in the evening, Promode Dasgupta said in a press statement that "an anti-party group" led by Saroj Dutta, Niranjan Bose and Sushital Ray Chowdhury, had "conspired to capture the *Deshahitaishi* office and struggle own writings into the paper. But the loyal members of the party foiled the conspiracy".

described it as the "forum of the new struggle". The publication of the new weekly was indicative of the extremists' determination to run a parallel party centre, beside the CPI(M), with the declared objective of winning over the party's rank and file and isolating the "new-revisionist" leadership.

The *Deshahitaishi* affair and certain other stray incidents which took place in quick succession made one thing absolutely clear that though the Naxalbari agitation quickly petered out, it had dealt a stunning blow to the CPI(M) leadership. The party had ceased to be a monolith, and the leadership was not in a position to enforce its will on ordinary members, a phenomenon unheard of in a Communist Party.

It may be pointed out that in the pre-1967 election period the total membership of the Party's West Bengal State unit was about 13,000. A large number of young men who had worked for the Party during the election were later given Party membership and this swelled the figure to around 22,000. And by the end of June it was estimated over 40 per cent of the members were sorely critical of the Party leadership over the Party's "betrayal" of the Naxalbari peasant struggle. Any drastic action against them would instantly split the Party into two. Moreover, the younger section of the Party membership and especially, the students had developed a special sympathy for the Naxalbari agitation, and if they went out, the loss would be pretty heavy for the Party. The elections of the students' unions in different colleges under Calcutta University gave a sufficient indication of the popularity of the extremists. Contesting on the basis of support to the Naxalbari line the extremists succeded in securing many more seats than those who favoured the official line of the CPI(M). The most striking example of the success of the extremist students was the overwhelming victory of the Presidency College Students' Consolidation in the 1967-1968 Union election. The PCSC which had broken off from the CPI(M)-led BPSF under the leadership of Ashim Chatterjee, an undergraduate student in Economics in that college, captured 25 of the total 42 seats, while the remaining seats were shared by the BPSF (Left) and BPSF (Right). The extremist Students' Union in the Calcutta University, the CUSF, won two major Calcutta University Union elections held during that time. Following are the results of these elections:

C.U. Economics Department
(Baranagar) : Total Seats: 6

Name of Unions	Seats Won
C.U.S.F.	4
BPSF (R)	1
BPSF (L)	1

Ballygunj Science College : Total Seats : 40

Name of Unions	Seats Won
C.U.S.F.	27
BPSF (R) & Others	13

It is interesting to note that throughout the period between 1969 and 1971 Presidency College and the Hindu Hostel had been the hub of Naxalite activities, and this College had produced some of the best Maoist student leaders including Ashim Chatterjee. Throughout 1968 and 1969 the students' wing of the CPI(M-L)—the Progressive Students' Coordination Committee (PSCC) which infiltrated and captured almost all the student organisations of different academic institutions in and around Calcutta, and later following Charu Mazumdar's call for boycott of elections successfully foiled all the elections held therein. Subsequently, again following Mazumdar's line of replacing all open mass organisations and mass actions by guerrilla warfare, both urban and rural, the PSCC was dissolved at a convention held in December 1969. But as personal and ideological differences had already cropped up in the PSCC leadership, a breakaway "renegade group" in the Ballygunj Post-Graduate Science College, the PGSF, maintained its own organisation.

Although at the initial states the pro-Naxalbari extremists were not functioning as a homogeneous group and they had their differences over tactics and strategy of revolution, the only common bond which held them together was their admiration for Mao Tse-tung. And the policy of the extremists was not to split away immediately from the CPI(M) and form a third Communist Party or to grab power for themselves, but to launch a pitched struggle against the "neo-revisionism" of the CPI(M) leadership and coordinate their own forces so as to be able to present a consolidated front when conditions would demand it. And the process of coming together had already started with the founding of the "Committee for the Assistance of the Naxalbari Peasant Struggle", with Promode Sengupta,[18] a leading extremist figure at Calcutta as its President. This Committee represented a formidable opposition and a positive threat to the CPI(M) leadership in West Bengal.

THE CPI(M) RESPONDS

As a result of all these inner-party crises, the CPI(M) leaders found themselves badly caught in a cleft stick. Unless the Party could check the excesses of the Maoists within the rank and file, the whole United Front concept was bound to crumble down, as was evident from the stern disapproval of the tactics of terror and insurgency registered by other constituents of the 14-party coalition government in West Bengal. But the stronger the action would be against the extremists, the more vulnerable the CPI(M) leadership would become to charges of "neo-revisionism" by virtue of its partnership in the government.

Thus understood, the seriousness of the pitched inner-party ideological struggle could not be easily by-passed; it would have to be squarely met. And in order to face it, the party leadership would have to place before the ranks the objective political situation in India devoid of an untenable revolutionary gloss. On the other hand, Maoism would have to be exposed as a manifestation of "ultra-left, self-destructive disorder". The necessity for a phase by phase development of democracy must be explained to the rank and file; not even an absolute CPI(M) majority in one or two State Assemblies could possibly usher in the brand of people's democracy that the Party had been advocating.

Unless the capacity of the Indian masses for democratic advance was fully explained to party cadres, any electoral move by the CPI(M) leadership would cause only confusion and resentment. The persistent and raucous anti-Soviet-cum-pro-China stand in international affairs and the non-stop, violent attacks on

18. For information on the Committee and its President see Promode Sengupta, *Biplab Kon Pathe* ? (Which Road to Revolution), Calcutta, 1970.

the CPI as a "revisionist" party on the ground of its admission of the possibility of a peaceful transition to socialism, had made a large section of the CPI(M) rank and file utterly sceptical of orderly democratic advance through legitimate constitutional pro cesses. They came to look upon armed struggle as the only instrument of political progress, even if that armed struggle was as isolated and adventurist as the Naxalbari peasant revolt. This made them susceptible to the extremely romantic, but equally vocal, propaganda of extremists regarding the "revolutionary ardour and preparedness" of the Indian people.

The CPI(M) leadership, however, showed at this stage a lack of political acumen and organizational skill as it chose a negative way to counter the extremists by cracking down over them on the organizational front. The official measures of the party to get rid of the ultra-left elements took two different forms. One was the dissolution of the defiant party committees in the districts and subdivisions and expulsion of those members who had taken to the "adventurist" course of action in support of the Naxalbari agitation in open defiances of the Party policies and discipline. The other way of tackling the extremist took the form of isolating those members of the Party by deprecating them as "agent provocateurs."

The first official action taken by the West Bengal State Secretariat of the CPI(M) was the dissolution of the party's Darjeeling District Committee and Siliguri subdivisional Committee in the middle of June. Ratanlal Brahman was nominated Convenor of the Darjeeling District Committee and Biren Bose was made Secretary of the Siliguri Sub-divisional Committee. This action was simultaneously followed up with the expulsion of prominent members of these two committees like Charu Mazumdar, Sourin Bose and P. K. Bharadwaj.

Immediately after their expulsion from the Darjeeling District Committee, Charu Mazumdar and Sourin Bose charged in a jointly addressed letter to all the members of the Party that the real reason for the dissolution of these party units in Darjeeling was not the organizational irregularity as had been alleged by the Party Secretariat but the fact that the leadership of these committees was absolutely in the hands of the tea plantation labourers and poor peasants who had been engaged in militant mass movements during the past few years, some times even in open defiance of the "neo-revisionist" party leadership as in the case of the Naxalbari peasant struggle. It was further contended in the letter of Mazumdar and Bose that in the Darjeeling District Committee of the party 15 out of the 25 members were tea-garden workers and landless peasants, while only 9 were drawn from the middle class. In the Siliguri local Committee out of the total 21 members, 12 were represented by the plantation labour and landless peasants and only 9 by the middle class. These Party units in the Darjeeling District, it was alleged, struck terror in the "petty-bourgeois new-revisionist" leadership of the party. And the suspension of these two committees just exposed the most "brazen-faced mockery" of Marxism-Leninism by the party bosses.[19]

Very soon about 40 members from different district committees of the Party were expelled. Most prominent among them were Sushital Ray Chowdhury, a State Committee member, Parimal Dasgupta, a member of the Calcutta District Committee, Asit Sen, Promode Sengupta, Suniti Ghosh, Saroj Dutta, Niranjan Bose, all Calcutta District Committee members, Dilip Bagchi of the Murshidabad District Committee and Mahadeb Mukherjee of the Asansol Local Committee. Two prominent leaders of the CPI(M) student front, Asim Chatterjee and Nirmal Brahmachari were also expelled. All these dissenters, who had been officially charge-sheeted by the State Secretariat of the Party, were expelled even without having any chance to defend themselves.

Along with expulsion, the CPI(M) leadership adopted a queer method of repudiation of the extremists by branding them as "left-opportunists" and "agent provocateurs". In a press communique issued on June 21 following the expulsion of the extremist group, Promode Dasgupta, Secretary of the CPI(M) West Bengal State Committee, declared that "certain agent provocateurs have also penetrated into these groups. The activities of these group are no doubt helping the reactionary vested interests and the Central Government in their nefarious plan for

19. For details of the charges, see "Resist the Arbitrary Actions of the Party Leadership"—a letter addressed to all CPI(M) members by the expelled members of the Darjeeling District Committee, dated, June 16, 1967. *Deshabrati* (Weekly), July 13, 1967.

attacking our party".[20] Perhaps the motive in circulating these invocatives was to isolate and to break the hold of the extremist section in the party by making it suspect. This move, however, did not work at all. For one thing, the extremists were well-entrenched in different party units, particularly, Darjeeling, Nadia, Murshidabad and Calcutta districts. For another, Peking propaganda extolling these "revolutionaries" had already given them an added stature. Thus nothing much was gained by the party in expelling the extremists. On the other hand, this action set in motion of steady exodus of militant party cadre who went to swell the ranks of the extremist group. Moreover, when the CPI(M) relaxed inner-party discipline considerably in order to prevent further defections to the extremist camp, many CPI(M) members started collaborating with the ultra-left group clandestinely, while retaining their membership in the CPI(M).[21]

The CPI(M) Ideologues on the Defensive

The failure of the CPI(M) leadership to contain the Maoists on the organization front forced the Editor of *People's Democracy,* the Central English Organ of the CPI(M), B. T. Ranadive and a senior member of the Politbureau, M. Basavpunniah to come out with a series of articles in the columns of the weekly in order to clarify the party's position vis-a-vis the pro-Naxalbari extremists.

Through his writings Basavpunniah mounted a counter

20. *Hindusthan Standard* (Calcutta), June 22, 1967.

What had, in fact, prompted Promode Dasgupta to call the extremists "agent provocateurs" and "CIA agents" was the fact that many of the supporters of the Naxalbari movement, primarily drawn from among college students and the disillusioned middle class, had their education in the United States. For full information, see "The Growth of Adventurism in West Bengal, Central Committee Information Document" in *On Left Deviation,* Communist Party of India (Marxist), Calcutta, 1967, p. 24.

21. This kind of double-dealing by a section of the CPI(M) members in West Bengal was responsible for the steady erosion of party discipline and growing confusion in the rank and file. Some posters which came out leaving the name of the CPI(M) Local Committees in parts of North Calcutta, Baranagar and Dum Dum in 1970-1971 read—"Down with Promode—Jyoti—Hare Krishna clique". "Go Ahead CPI(M-L) Comrades, We Are With You" etc.

attack on the extremists. Dismissing these elements as "Left adventurists" and "Left opportunists" he declared that these people, in an organized manner, were:

> .... working as a party within our own Party, with a view to subverting the accepted Party Programme and political line and foisting their alternative pseudo-revolutionary line on the Party.[22]

In another article Basavpunniah denounced the extremists as "agent provocateurs" by holding that "we have every reason to believe and enough facts to prove that there is much deeper game of the vested interests behind it, that the ruling classes have succeeded in planting certain agent-provocateurs inside the Party to mislead the honest militants of the Party and to disrupt it from within, and it is a well-planned conspiracy of the big bourgeois-landlord government to isolate and destroy the CPI(M) and thus behead the rising democratic and revolutionary people's movement".

Declaring that these "left adventurists and anarchists are outside the pale of our Party", he wrote:

> It is so because the political objectives set for the Naxalbari Kishan Struggle have absolutely no relation to the realities of class alignments obtaining either in the State of West Bengal or the country as a whole, and the slogan of boycott of the parliamentary institutions they are raising is nothing but left-sectarian and adventurists;. . . .it is so because the forms of struggle and organization these leaders are advocating and practising are subjectively deduced and arbitrarily imposed upon the fighting kisans rather than based on the concrete study of the entire situation.[23]

Finally, he appealed to "the honest and militant rank and file Party members" to rise and unite as one "to carry on a determined fight in defence of the Party's unity, its programme and political line and rebuff this infantile insanity".[24] In ano-

22. M. Basavpunniah, "Rebels Come out in Their True Colours", *People's Democracy,* English Weekly organ of the CPI(M), July 16, 1967.

23. M. Basavpunniah, "Our Party's Stand on Naxalbari", *People's Democracy,* July 9, 1967.

24. M. Basavpunniah, *Rebels Come Out In Their True Colours, op. cit.*

ther signed article published in the *People's Democracy* on July 23, 1967, Basavpunniah came out with a candid confession about his party's failure to formulate a more militant line for the rank and file members. He said:

> We are quite aware that we have not yet succeeded in liquidating all the hated legacies of reformism and revisionism, we also so realize that in the process of fighting Right reformism certain Left errors are liable to occur and certain individuals or groups might become victims of dogmatism and adventurism because of their elemental hatred against and aversion to revisionism; and above all we are not oblivious of the fact that ours is a society with a predominantly petty-bourgeois class composition, that is still politically backward with an extremely low level of class consciousness, that the proletarian and semi-proletarian element is weak in the composition of the Party, that Marxist-Leninist education is far from satisfactory and it will have to travel yet a long and difficult path before it becomes a real mass revolutionary proletarian party capable of fulfilling its historic role ....[25]

Ranadive's line of reflection came in the form of an open admission of the party's numerical and organizational weakness, of the superior strength of the bourgeoisie, and of the party's plan to use the parliamentary way to increase its influences. Ranadive argued that the Indian national bourgeoisie element was much stronger than the forces ready to line up with the proletariat; wide section of the masses were still under the influence of "parties not hostile to the State". He held that being revolutionary to the core, the CPI(M) could not go in for "summary revolution"; it had to make a realistic assessment of this strength of its opponents and of its own strength. It was because of the weakness of the Communist movement in India that 'partial' and 'auxiliary' struggles still had revolutionary potentialities; they could provide "immediate recruiting ground for drawing the masses into the revolutionary struggle". He further contended that the facts of contesting elections and joining the coalitions in West Bengal and Kerala did not necessarily mean that the

25. M. Basavpunniah, "Revisionist Approvers of Criminal Conspiracy", *People's Democracy*, July 23, 1967.

CPI(M) had degenerated into a 'revisionist' party. On the contrary, this strategy was absolutely necessary for "the isolation of the main party of the bourgeoisie, advancement of the ideology of the Party and increasing people's confidence in themselves as against the bourgeois landlord government led by the big bourgeoisie". The very fact that "the ruling Congress gentry" saw the main danger to its hegemony arising from the left coalition governments was evidence of their revolutionary potential. The Left coalition ministries must function parallel to "constant pressure of the mass movement from below"; the "strategic position of the ministry" could be used to "deliver a blow at the vested interests". Ranadive claimed that in West Bengal "the struggle around the ministry has become the symbol of the class struggle among contending forces".[26]

Notwithstanding the mass expulsion of the extremists and the Basavpunniah-Ranadive polemics against them, they were in no mood to relent. On the other hand, the CPI(M) continued to face converging attacks on its programme and tactical line from the Maoists within and the CPC without.[27]

The Madurai Monologue

In view of this twin challenge, the Central Committee of the CPI(M) held its meeting at Madurai in Madras from August 18 to 27, 1967. Two separate documents were adopted at the

26. B. T. Ranadive, "CPI(M) Follows Leninist Path", *People's Democracy,* July 14, 1967.

27. That the Radio Peking broadcasts against the CPI(M) leadership created a good deal of uneasiness was clear enough from the observations of three CPI(M) stalwarts in West Bengal,—Muzaffar Ahmad, Promode Das Gupta and Hare Krishna Konar. Muzaffar Ahmad tried initially to attribute the Peking broadcasts to some inimical pirate radio station. But he admitted later that "if the reported broadcasts actually happen to be from Peking, then it is very regrettable indeed. It is based on totally wrong facts. If this kind of broadcast continue then the people in our country will lose all respect for Peking Radio". Promode Das Gupta, on the other hand, observed with a pinch of sarcasm that Radio Peking had even hailed the anti-cow-slaughter demonstration in New Delhi as a "revolutionary upsurge", while Harekrishna Konar quipped, "One is no necessarily a good Marxist by virtue of being born in Moscow or Peking." For details, see *Statesman* (Calcutta), July 26, 1967.

meeting. The first resolution "On Left Deviation or Left Opportunism" endorsed the line elaborated in the party's different documents and tactics about elections and participation in the United Front ministries and rejected the formulations of the "Left opportunists", which challenged the entire party line, "its basic programmatic assumptions, its organizational principles and substitute in its place a federation of autonomous groups each having the right to advocate and start any form of struggle when it limes".[28]

Attacking the Maoists in the Party, the document held :

> The Left opportunists attack the Programme as revisionist as mainly because, in their opinion, the State in India is a neo-colonial State, a State of neo-colonial powers, the government is a puppet and stooge government .... It is no wonder that with this wrong understanding of the class realities and the present situation in India they make no distinction between parliamentary institutions and fascism ... Using parliamentary institutions, according to them, is remaining bogged at the level of mass consciousness; class war i.e., direct revolutionary struggle is the only weapon to complete the education of the masses. The added argument is that parliaments are obsolete and hence participation in them is no good. Thus in the name of a revolutionary struggle this important forum is rejected in principle. This is nothing but an anarchist deviation which underestimates the fight against the State on the concrete ...[29]

Justifying the party's participation in parliamentary politics, the document observed in the same breath that "while participating in legislatures the Party must be vigilant about the objectives and not get into opportunist errors. The Party has to make a revolutionary use of legislatures. The boycott of bourgeois legislatures, as a matter of principle, is anti-Leninist and deprives the party of this form to organise its class, the masses and expose bourgeois democracy.[30]

At the same time, this document admitted that many militant, honest, young members in the party were be-

28. *On Left Deviation*, CPI(M) Central Committee Resolution adopted at Madurai, 18-27 August, 1967, p. 16.

29. *Ibid.*, pp. 4-10.

30. *Ibid.*, p. 6.

ing drawn towards the "pseudo-revolutionary line" because it appeared to be militant. However, the main cause of attraction, according to this document, was that due to the growing economic crises and desperation, impatience and frustration and also due to the fact mass struggles as yet did not develop to the pitch when they could be seen as the effective means of fighting the present regime. Lack of Marxism-Leninism, failure of the party to transform the militancy into revolutionary fervour—all created a situation in which the appeal of "Left doctrinarism" remained.

The more important resolution adopted at the Madurai meeting of the Central Committee was the one on "Divergent Views between Our Party and the CPC on Certain Fundamental Issues of Programme and Policy", which revealed serious differences between the CPI(M) and the CPC on a number of issues connected with the Indian revolution.[31]

The Central Committee held that the Chinese Communist Party had practically concluded:

> (a) that our Party is fundamentally wrong in certain vital aspects; (b) that the entire assessment of the country's political situation made by our Party and the political-tactical line worked out accordingly is wrong and reformist; (c) that our Party is not a genuine Communist Party, while the extremist rebels who are expelled by our Party and those who rally round them are the real revolutionaries; and (d) that our Party's political line is to be publicly denounced through their press and radio as reformist and revisionist.[32]

The difference between the CPI(M) and the CPC centred round three distinct issues:

> .... the first is regarding the programmatic aspect i.e., the class character of the present Indian State and Government, the character and the role of the different sections of the Indian bourgeoisie and its attitude to imperialism etc. The

31. "Divergent Views between Our Party and the CPC on Certain Fundamental Issues of Programme and Policy", Resolution adopted by the Central Committee of the CPI(M) at its Madurai session from August 18 to 27, 1967. *People's Democracy Supplement,* September 10, 1967, p. 1.

32. *Ibid.*

second concerns with the actual assessment of the economic-political situation in the country, the degree of development of the class contradictions and mass consciousness among the proletariat and toiling peasantry and the concrete tactics and forms of struggle adopted to the requirement of the mass struggles. The third category falls in the matter of political-organisational principles governing the fraternal relations between two Communist Parties, i.e. Our Party and the CPC.[33]

The Central Committee further held that "Our analysis of the Indian bourgeoisie, its divisions into different categories, the class character of the new Indian State and Government, and the stage and strategy of the revolution worked out accordingly in the Party Programme do not tally with the analysis and assessment of the CPC comrades. Our study of concrete conditions of the Indian situation compels us to differ with them and arrive at different conclusions of our own in the matter".[34]

According to the Central Committee, the CPC thought the Indian bourgeoisie was a parasitic class fostered by the British Imperialism and represented the comprador, bureaucratic capital in India and the Congress government was the Chief instrument and mouthpiece of this comprador, bureaucratic monopoly capitalist class. For some time after independence, Nehru had to a degree acted on behalf of the non-comprador, non-bureaucratic and non-monopolistic sections but of late had gone over to imperialism as a result of the sharpening of internal class contradictions, as Chiang Kai-shek had done in 1927. This suggested that the revolution in India should be aimed principally against the British and American imperialism though the struggle against feudal landlordism was fundamental.

But the Central Committee contended that contemporary Indian capitalism and the Indian bourgeoisie were very different from the pre-liberation capitalist development in China and the Chinese bourgeoisie. Secondly, the place and the role of the comprador bourgeoisie and its bureaucratic capital in pre-liberation China were different from the place and role of the big bourgeoisie in present day India. Bureaucratic capital was

33. *Ibid.*, p. 2.
34. *Ibid.*

a specific characteristic of the Chiang Kai-shek regime "dominated by the notorious four big families of Soong, Keng, Chang and Lin." Though certain bureaucratic capitalist tendencies were present in the Indian situation, it was by no means the principal characteristic of the Indian big bourgeoisie.

The resolution defended the assessment made by the Party Programme—that the Indian government was a bourgeois-landlord government led by the big bourgeoisie which was compromising and collaborating with foreign monopoly capital, and that being by its very nature counter-revolutionary, the bourgeoisie had no place in the People's Democratic Front in spite of the occasional contradictions it had with foreign monopolies. Thus understood, the nature of India's people's democratic revolution would be "anti-feudal, anti-imperialist and anti-monopolist".[35]

Another significant point of difference in this context related to the appraisal of the Nehru Government prior to 1959, i.e., before the good relations between India and China were strained. The Central Committee did not agree with the Chinese view that the Congress Government represented the non-big Indian bourgeoisie till 1959 but became the instrument of the big monopolists subsequently.

The fourth point of divergence related to the forces making for the change in the Nehru government's foreign policy after 1969. The CPC's assessment was that "the Nehru Government which was till then representing the class interests of the non-big bourgeoisie and to that extent playing an oppositional role to imperialism, had, due to the extreme sharpening of internal contradictions, transformed itself into the representative of the anti-national big bourgeoisie and big landlords, and a lackey of imperialism".[36]

Totally rejecting the CPC's estimation of the Indian situation, the resolution upheld the CPI(M)'s own political line in the following words:

> Our own experience teaches that the Congress Party still holds considerable political influence among the people, that several bourgeois-landlord reactionary parties still command

35. *Ibid.*, p. 6.
36. *Ibid.*, p. 7.

certain mass following, that the character of many petty-bourgeois parties and groups still is not exposed to any appreciable extent, and that the proletariat and its revolutionary party are far from properly organized and built. In the face of such reality it would be a grave error to exaggerate this aspect of sharpening class contradictions to the point of suggesting that class revolution on the part of the masses has already become immediate and acute and menacing to the bourgeoisie as to make its capitulation to imperialism final and irrevocable .... Hence we do not find any valid reason for the present Indian Government which has a more wider social base when compared to most of its counterparts in several countries and which does not face the imminent threat of class revolution at home, opting to play the role of a 'puppet', 'stooge' and 'lackey' of imperialism.[37]

Thus understood, while the CPI(M)'s programme characterised the Indian State as one of the bourgeoisie and the landlords, led by the big bourgeoisie and pursuing a path of development in collaboration with foreign monopoly capital, the Communist Party of China thought it was a puppet government led by bureaucratic capitalism and run by it mainly in the interest of imperialism and reconciled to parasitic existence on the crumbs thrown by foreign masters.

The Central Committee also disagreed with the "highly exaggerated and subjective" CPC assessment of the current political situation in India. The resolution contended that "it is virtually negating our premise of a deepening economic crisis and the initial stages of a political crisis ; and in its place substitution of the premise of an already revolutionary situation and a revolutionary crisis, demanding the highest revolutionary forms of struggle".[38] Even if the objective conditions for revolution obtained in India, the equally important subjective conditions were absent. Particularly irritating to the CPI(M) leadership was the CPC's formulations attacking the non-Congress governments as the tool of the landlords and bourgeoisie.

Finally, the resolution protested against the "gross interference" of the CPC in the internal affairs of the CPI(M) and

37. *Ibid.*, p. 9.
38. *Ibid.*, p. 15.

accused it of "dictating to and imposing on us a programme and political line which they have worked out for our country and Party". The Central Committee considered it extraordinary that the Chinese "did not deem it their elementary duty to take up their differences with our Party on a party-to-party level before they openly comment in their Press and radio".[39] Further, the Central Committee took serious objections to the open support of the CPC to the expelled extremists of the Naxalbari movement. "Such support," the resolution held, "to the splinter group and the reliance placed on them for leading the Indian revolution cannot be justified in terms of any Marxist-Leninist organizational principles".[40]

Reaction of the "Rebels"

Later on, commenting on the Madurai documents, Charu Mazumdar, the doyen of the Naxalbari faction, observed that at its Madurai meeting "the CC has made declaration in favour of peaceful transition to socialism and has chosen the path of country's progress through Parliamentary democracy. Despite high fault in polemics on the international ideological disputes, it has, in fact, wholly rejected the ideological stand of the Chinese Party and the thought of Mao ; naturally the CC meeting at Madurai has dragged down the party to the level of a revisionist bourgeois party. Therefore, to the genuine Marxist-Leninists there remains open no alternative but to oppose this policy".[41] Sushital Ray Chowdhury, another senior member of the group was more bitter in his observations on the Madurai resolution when he contended that it was, in fact, "nothing but a patchwork of pieces of self-contradictory theoretical ventures. For a complete theory they would have to accept unequivocally either the general line of the CPC or that of the CPSU".[42]

It may be pointed out that despite the CPI(M) Central Committee's loud protest against the CPC's "gross interference"

39. *Ibid.*, p. 21.
40. *Ibid.*, p. 22.
41. Charu Mazumdar, "It Is Time To Build Up A Revolutionary Party", *Liberation Miscellany,* No. 1, 1967, pp. 62-63.
42. Sushital Ray Chowdhury, "Revisionists' Understanding of the Nature of Contradictions", *Ibid.*, p. 99.

in the internal affairs of a fraternal communist party, the CPC paid no heed to it and went ahead, as before, projecting the Maoist line to the Indian situation. In a lengthy article on India published in March 1968, the Commentator noted hilariously that the revolutionary situation was better than ever. "Growing in scale, the peasant struggle to seize land by force has assumed such proportions that, like thunder-claps and flashes of lightning breaking the dead silence of the overcast skies over India, it is shaking the reactionary rule of the Congress Government. An excellent situation, never seen before, has opened up for the Indian revolution. We warmly acclaim and cheer the revolutionary storm let loose by the Indian peasants".[43]

Detecting that the roots of the feudal exploitation in India lay "deep in the countryside" the Commentator held :

> Maharajahs, patriarchal landlords and the bureaucrat-comprador bourgeoisie are the main social foundation of imperialist rule in India. This foundation must be overthrown if the Indian peasant had to achieve liberation. Indian revolutionaries have gone into the countryside to propagate Mao's thought that political power grows out of the barrel of the gun.[44]

It is rather interesting to note in this context that the obvious motive behind the CPC's intervention in the Indian Communist movement through the policy of attack on the CPI(M)'s programme and policies, and applause for the Naxalbari revolutionaries in that party simultaneously, was the quick radicalisation of the CPI(M)'s political-tactical line at a moment when that party was smartly drifting towards constitutional Communism. As it was not instantly forthcoming, the CPC started inciting the "rebels" in the CPI(M) to break off from the "neo-revisionists".[45]

43. Commentator, "Let the Peasants Revolutionary Storm in India Strike Harder", *Peking Review*, March 1, 1968.

44. *Ibid.*

45. For an account of the series of events during 1968-1969 leading to the split, see Chapter IV.

CHAPTER—IV

TOWARDS INDIA'S THIRD COMMUNIST PARTY : BIRTH OF THE COMMUNIST PARTY OF INDIA (MARXIST-LENINIST) 1967-1969

THE FINAL ROUND

A. The Burdwan Plenum

By the end of 1967 it had become too obvious a fact that the CPI(M) was just a house divided against itself. The elation which had swayed the party bosses immediately after the overwhelming victory in the 1967 General Elections was fast evaporating. The membership strength of the party including candidate members had sharply dwindled from 1,19,000 at the time of the Seventh Party Congress in 1964 to 76,425 by the end of 1967.[1] And despite the bitter attacks of the CPC on the programme and the tactical line of the CPI(M), its inner contradictions and inconsistencies persisted. There was no serious effort whatsoever to clinch the ideological issues confronting the international communist movement. The Party leadership was still refusing to face this reality and frankly answer the question whether it accepted or rejected peaceful coexistence between differing social systems, peaceful transition to socialism through parliamentary path, and the Maoist strategy of revolution as already accepted by a section of the party membership. The Madurai resolution of the party's Central Committee on its differences with the CPC regarding certain fundamental issues of programme and policy made it more than clear that techni-

1. It may be pointed out that while in 1964 the primary members and the candidate members of the Party were, 1,06,313 and 12,370 respectively, in early 1968 the figures were 65,402 and 11,023 respectively. It means the Party lost pretty heavily from among its regular members as a result of the inner-party ideological crisis. For the membership figures of the CPI(M) during 1964 and early 1968, see *Political-Organizational Report* of the CPI(M) Central Committee to the Eighth Party Congress held at Cochin, December 23-29, 1968, p. 286.

cally even at the crucial stage the CPI(M) had not taken its stand on the ideological questions dividing the international Communist movement. But things were moving so fast against the party that it became too clear for the leadership that in immediate future, at any rate, the Party's propaganda posture and political practice must coincide, even at the risk of its being branded "revisionist" by a section of its own members. So the Central Committee which had adopted a draft document for ideological discussion at Madurai was constrained to release it for discussion and ultimately to present it at an extra-ordinary all-India plenum held at Burdwan in April 1968. The choice of the venue of the all-India plenum at Burdwan was rather significant. In normal circumstances, the plenum would have been held in Calcutta but the extremists had already made Calcutta too "hot" for the official leadership. As the 1967 election survey of the West Bengal unit showed, the Party had strong bases only in five of the sixteen districts in the State, e.g., Calcutta, Howrah, 24 Parganas, Hooghly and Burdwan. Since Calcutta appeared to have been already lost to the "ultra-left" faction, the next district unit was Burdwan where the Party had a strong base among peasants and workers.

It should be noted that organisational irregularities were reported to have preceded the plenum. The draft had been divulged to the press long before it was made available to different party units for discussion. State plenums to discuss the draft were held only in Andhra Pradesh, Punjab, Kerala, Tamil Nadu and Jammu and Kashmir. In West Bengal, in particular, only 9 of the 16 districts were allowed to hold district level plenums and the State-level plenum was not held possibly because the leaders had apprehended sure defeat at the hands of the extremists.

The CC document, it is interesting to point out, was nothing but "a poor show of strange ideological acrobatics" put up by the Central leadership of the party. It analysed in details the Soviet positions on all issues excepting one, but rejected them. The lone exception related to the slogan of "unity in action" where the Chinese case was examined and rejected. "In sum, it was anti-revisionism sans Maoism because the draft generally took positions which lay somewhere between the Soviet general line and the Chinese general line. But for a solitary exception, the Chinese positions were not examined at all. Examined from Soviet positions, the draft can be termed anti-revisionist but viewed from Chinese position, it might be revisionist".[2]

The draft claimed that the CPI(M) had demarcated itself "from the crassest class collaborationist and utterly revisionist line propounded by the Dangeites" on every issue relating to the stage and strategy of the Indian revolution.[3] It also suggested that the Party had no outside guidance in drawing up its programme and it was now projecting its "correct understanding" to the remaining ideological issues in debate and to arrive at its own conclusions. Following is a resume of the Central Committee draft's stand on sundry issues regarding international Communist movement.

New Epoch

"Ours is certainly a new epoch", observed the draft, "an epoch of transition from capitalism to socialism, an epoch when the international socialist system is becoming the decisive factor determining the course of world development, an epoch of national liberation and socialist revolutions, an epoch of rapid decay and disintegration of colonialism, an epoch of titanic class battles between forces of moribund capitalism and of socialism and national liberation revolutions, and an epoch of the collapse of world scale".[4] While admitting that imperialism had weakened on a world scale and the forces of revolution (including countries of the socialist system) were powerful enough to inflict defeat on imperialism and its allies, the document held that the process of mobilising and uniting these revolutionary forces involved "a revolutionary combination of socialist diplomacy, calculated to isolate the most reactionary imperialist groups, with the use of the armed might of the socialist camp against such reactionary powers as resort to aggression on peace-loving countries, or try to drown the national liberation movements in

2. Mohan Ram, *Maoism in India,* Vikas Publications, New Delhi, 1971, p. 78.

3. *Stand on Ideological Issues,* Communist Party of India (Marxist) Calcutta, 1969, p. 2.

4. *Ibid.,* p. 6.

blood". This also required "the ever-growing unity of the international Communist movement". Thus understood, the CPI(M) clearly demarcated its position from the Soviet general line which considered imperialism as no longer a serious danger.

On Contradictions :

The draft identified four fundamental social contradictions in the present era : "The contradiction between the camps of world socialism and capitalism ; the contradiction between the proletariat and the bourgeoisie in capitalist countries; the contradiction between the imperialist states and the oppressed countries ; and the contradiction among the different imperialist states and among monopoly capitalist groups". The draft also castigated the "modern revisionists" for their "un-Marxian and opportunist tendency to treat the contradiction between the socialist camp and imperialism as almost the only contradiction which determines the course of world development".

On the Issues of War and Peace and Lenin's Thesis on Imperialism :

The draft observed :

> ....Since the world capitalist and imperialist social order is still in existence over three-fourths of the globe's surface covering two-thirds of humanity....and since the capitalist encirclement of the socialist states is not yet replaced by the socialist encirclement of capitalist states, the thesis of Lenin on imperialism and war remains valid and to treat it as having become obsolete is to fundamentally depart from Marxism-Leninism.

Further, "the radically changed correlation of forces on a world plane in favour of socialism and against imperialism in the present epoch certainly has opened the possibilities of preventing, averting and postponing a particular war, or a war with particularly destructive technique and preserving the peace to the extent. But wars can be eliminated and lasting peace secured only when imperialism is eliminated ; as long as imperialism exists, there will be soil for wars and aggression".[5] In other

5. *Ibid.*, p. 15.

words, the CPI(M) mounted a severe attack on the Soviet position regarding the issue of war and peace.

On Disarmament and Banning of Nuclear Weapons :

The draft assailed the "pacifist, non-class and revisionist concept of disarmament" implied in the Soviet attitude to test-ban treaty, non-proliferation of nuclear weapons and banning of nuclear weapons, and the "perfidious" refusal of atomic know-how to China. Soviet leaders "risked a rift and even a split in the socialist camp over the issue". Soviet attitude was based "on the unwarranted premise that their collaboration with the Anglo-American imperialists" was a greater guarantee of peace than the unity of the socialist camp, its strength and its struggle against imperialism on every front.[6]

On Peaceful Coexistence :

> The interpretation of the concept of peaceful coexistence between the socialist and imperialist states is reduced by the revisionists to mean that the chief struggle between the two systems is in the main peaceful economic competition and thus conceal the truth that the struggle between the two systems comprises every field of economic, political, ideological and military nature.

Deprecating this interpretation the draft held :

> it seeks to conceal the constant imperialist aggression and to appease the aggressor, and it disarms the revolutionary proletariat of the world in its uncompromising fight against imperialist—economic, political, ideological and military.[7]

On the Forms of Transition to Socialism :

The draft gave a qualified support to the concept of peaceful transition to socialism in conceding that "there is no denying the fact that the proletariat would prefer to achieve the revolution and win power by peaceful means" and the CPI(M)'s programme had also incorporated it. But, according to the draft, the "modern revisionists" maintained that "in view of the changed correlation of forces on an international scale as well as in each country in favour of the proletariat and its cause of socia-

6. *Ibid.*, pp. 16-18.
7. *Ibid.*, p. 21.

lism, and in view of the ever-increasing grip of the ideas of socialism on the minds of wide masses of the people, the universal law of violent revolution as propounded by Marx, Engels, Lenin and Stalin, forced on the proletariat by the bourgeoisie, and as universally accepted by all the Marxist-Leninists has become outmoded and hence to be discarded. In its place, they argue, the law of peaceful transition and parliamentary path is to be substituted : they even expound the thesis that socialist transformation can be effected by a state of so-called National Democracy where the bourgeoisie and the proletariat hold joint hegemony of the National Democratic Revolution and the National Democratic state ; thus they seek to revise Marxism-Leninism on certain basic and fundamental issues of proletarian revolution, issues such as the Marxist-Leninist concept of state and revolution and the concept of proletarian hegemony in the revolutions of the present era".[8] The draft contended that "the enunciation and advocacy of this utterly revisionist thesis is nothing but giving encomiums to the bourgeoisie and ascribing to it a peace-loving and democratic character, intended to ideologically disarm and disorientate the revolutionary proletariat, and a downright betrayal of Marxist-Leninist teachings on the state and revolution".

The Concept of National Democracy and Non-Capitalist Path :

The draft rejected as "gross right-opportunist and class-collaborationist" the thesis of the so-called non-capitalist path and National Democracy being advocated and practised by "the modern revisionists" as a new transitional form of social revolution, a thesis that "negates the concept of proletarian hegemony and advocates joint hegemony along with the bourgeoisie to effect socialist transition, a thesis that distorts the Leninist concept regarding the new possibilities of skipping the stage of capitalist relations for backward countries, to reach socialism".[9]

On the Trio that Works Out Into A Full-Fledged Line of Class Collaboration :

The concepts of peaceful coexistence, and peaceful economic competition and peaceful transition as propounded by

8. *Ibid.*, p. 24.
9. *Ibid.*, p. 27.

> Khruschev at the 20th Congress of CPSU and as interpreted, elaborated and practised by the modern revisionists are, ...being rendered into a fully worked-out line of class conciliation and collaboration on a global plane....Today, this bankrupt revisionist line of the Soviet leaders has assumed such absurd proportions that it is glaringly seen and understood....as more and more a line of conciliation, compromise, and collaboration between the two great powers, the USSR and the USA, a line which objectively preserves and perpetuates the international status-quo and as a line which summarily abandons the revolutionary class struggles of the international proletariat....

"However", the draft observed, "our criticism of the compromising and collaborationist policies pursued by the revisionist leadership of the CPSU and the Soviet State does in no way imply the totally erroneous idea that Soviet Union has become an ally of U.S. imperialism or is working for sharing world hegemony with American imperialism and for the division of spheres of influence in the world as this is tantamount to nothing short of placing the Soviet Union outside the Socialist camp". Nevertheless, the draft concluded, this "right-opportunist line" has done the greatest damage to the cause of the working class and Communist movement in the world".[10]

On the Slogan of Unity in Action :

The draft observed that ruling out in principle the slogan of unity in action with political parties or states on the ground that parties or states question were headed by revisionists restricted the scope of unity with all those with whom it was possible to unite while singling out and isolating the most immediate and hated enemy. So the draft wanted the CPC to test the Soviet bonafides by agreeing to unity in action in Vietnam because "outright rejection of the slogan as unprincipled on the ground that it implies unity between revisionists and Marxist-Leninists is objectively tantamount to making a present of that State and its people to the revisionists instead of isolating the revisionists".[11]

10. *Ibid.,* pp. 30-31.
11. *Ibid.,* pp. 43-44.

On the Issue of Correct Relations Between Fraternal Communist Parties :

The draft expressed profound dissatisfaction at the tendency of the big Communist parties in power to subject other parties to the "reactionary slander" of being led by either Peking or Moscow, and to try to impose a political-tactical line on them. The "sound proletarian internationalist principle which should guide the relations between Parties is violated by big Parties, of course, either under pretext of some creative Marxism of theirs or under the totally erroneous notion that they alone can think, not only for themselves, but for all other Parties of the world....Our Party, while modest enough to learn from the achievements and mistakes of all other fraternal Parties of the world, should guard itself against any such outside interference and jealously defend its independence and its independent political line...."[12]

B. The Extremist Challenge

The reaction of the West Bengal extremists in the CPI(M) towards the Central Committee's stand on ideological issues could not be immediately ascertained because of the facts that the leading figures in the extremist faction had already been expelled from the Party. Secondly, the members of the delegation for the West Bengal State unit to the Central Plenum at Burdwan were chosen by the State Secretariat. The usual practice is that delegates attending a party congress or central plenum for considering vital documents on ideological issues are elected by the members at a state conference. But the state leadership was unwilling to face such an election, because it might land them in serious trouble. Thus with West Bengal extremists left out of the Burdwan plenum by the "crafty machination" of the State Secretariat, the plenum did not experience any attack from the West Bengal delegates.

However, the West Bengal State Co-ordination Committee, which had already been organized by the extremists attacked the CC Draft on Ideological Issues with all vehemence. One of the leaders of this Committee, Sushital Ray Chowdhury observed:[13]

12. *Ibid.*, pp. 46-47.

13. Sushital Ray Chowdhury, "Betrayal", *Liberation,* May 1968, pp. 7-11.

As expected, the so-called Plenum of the Central Committee of the CPI(M) held recently at Burdwan, has put the final seal of approval on an ideological and political line that is essentially revisionist. Some time ago, Chinese comrades said that those who were neutral on the issues facing the world communist movement would soon take the opportunist road and end by joining the counter-revolutionary camp. While the great ideological battle raged, the leaders of the CPI(M) pretended to remain neutral between Marxism-Leninism and revisionism, but their roads as well as deeds showed that they were pursuing a revisionist, counter-revolutionary line. . . . It is good that at Madurai and later at Burdwan, they had to define their stand on the ideological issue. But these wily, crafty men have tried their utmost to combine their sham loyalty to the Marxist-Leninist principles with their real suppport to revisionist theories and policies of the leading clique of the C.P.S.U. . . . .The 'Marxist' heroes are out to discover a new path for the Indian Revolution, which will be neither like Russian nor like the Chinese. . . Their Indian path, the path along which opportunists have been travelling, is actually the path of class collaboration and betrayal of the vital interests of the toiling people. That is why, they enter into alliance with the most reactionary and rabidly anti-Communist parties in order to form coalition ministries which act faithfully as the tools of imperialism, feudalism and comprador capital.

Another very sharp reaction against the Central Committee's Draft for Ideological Discussion came from Andhra Pradesh. The Andhra Pradesh State Plenum of the CPI(M), held in January 1968, rejected the official draft (by 158 votes to 52, eight remaining neutral), and demanded a new draft to be prepared by the Central Committee on the basis of the general line proposed by the CPC on June 14, 1963 and its nine comments on the Open Letter of 14 July 1963, and also on the basis of the two resolutions placed before the plenum by T. Nagi Reddy and C. Pulla Reddy, and Kolla Venkiah.

The Andhra Plenum challenged not only the ideological draft but, as the Central Committee noted later, was declaring its fundamental opposition to "a whole series of basic questions concerning the Indian revolutionary movement as well as the international Communist movement".[14]

The resolution of the Andhra Pradesh Plenum was based on a thorough examination of all the basic issues linked with the Indian revolution from the perspective of the general line laid down by the CPC ideologues. Assailing the Central Committee's draft, the resolution held that the draft had failed "to expose mercilessly the trecherous character of the Soviet revisionist leadership" which had weakened and disrupted the international communist movement and "has thus become a counter-revolutionary force".[15]

An important contribution of the Andhra Communists to the inner-party ideological debate was their thesis that the contradiction with Soviet revisionism was an antagonistic one and not only was unity between the Soviet and Chinese parties impossible, but at home no united front between the CPI(M) and the "revisionist" CPI was practicable. The Andhra Communists, thus understood, went beyond the ideological issues and virtually reopened the basic issues of the party Programme and tactical line.

The two other resolutions placed before Andhra Pradesh plenum by T. Nagi Reddi and Pulla Reddi, and by Kolla Venkiah also fully endorsed the CPC's stand on Indian situation and the path of People's War based on the application of the Chinese experiences :

> We feel that the rich experience of the Chinese revolution and the recent experience of the liberation struggles in the backward countries have shown that people's war, prolonged agrarian armed revolution is the only path left open to all backward countries for social emancipation. We feel that the path of people's war, taking our own particular objective conditions of our country into considerations is the only path of revolution.[16]

Despite their overwhelming defeat at the Central plenum at

14. "Letter to Andhra Comrades", Central Committee of the Communist Party of India (Marxist), Calcutta, 1968, p. 1.

15. *Andhra Plenum Rejects the New-Revisionist Ideological Draft*, Vijayawada, 1968, p. 3.

16. *Ibid.*, p. 59.

Burdwan, the Andhra Pradesh delegates who had carried on a pitched battle over the ideological issues, left their unmistakable mark on the party. The official draft could only be adopted in a considerably amended form with 162 votes in favour and 27 against, there being nine absentees. It is striking to note that as many as nine amendments were incorporated into the official draft just to strike a compromise with the dissidents. The amendments involved such vital issues as "the fundamental contradictions", on "Yugoslav revisionism" and on "unity of action". And the Central Committee even had to go out of its way to be conciliatory towards the opposition by sharpening the criticism of the Soviet leadership and hailing China's role in the fight against the Soviet "revisionism".

Even though both the alternative documents placed by Nagi Reddi and Pulla Reddi, and by Kolla Venkiah were defeated (22 votes for, 158 against, 13 neutral and 12 absent), an amendment of the official draft moved by the dissidents mobilised in its favour nearly a quarter of the delegates present.

The amendment said that "the revisionist leadership of the CPSU has totally repudiated Marxism-Leninism on all the basic national and international questions and its repudiation has been consolidated over the period of a decade with the result that we see revisionism in a concentrated form in all sections of the Soviet leadership, gravely endangering world revolution".[17] The amendment was rejected with 52 votes in favour, 145 votes against and no abstention.

In the wake of the Burdwan plenum one thing became crystal clear that the CPI(M) remained as openly divided as before. Whether the voting results correctly reflected the relative strength in the party as a whole or were determined by insufficient representation of dissident elements was difficult to ascertain immediately. However, it was clear from the voting patterns in the plenum that at least 25 per cent of the delegates voted with the opposition on some issues. This itself was a matter of grave concern for the leadership—hence possibly its concessions to extremist sentiment in the form of amendments to passages in the ideological documents relating to international developments. But this element of compromise, which was in any case insuffi-

17. See *Statesman* (Calcutta), April 12, 1968.

cient to win over the dissidents, only deepened the ideological confusion.

On the other hand, the ambivalence, noticeable in the Madurai document, persisted even after Burdwan and the leadership failed to chart out an independent course, to evolve an equidistant position,—equidistant both from Moscow and Peking. The General Secretary of the party, P. Sundarayya claimed at the Burdwan plenum that the Left Communist leaders had developed an ideological stand which was independent of both Moscow and Peking. This is, however, an absurd claim. In fact, they were only trying to blur ideological distinctions and to speak in two voices.

After the Burdwan plenum, the differences between the CPI(M) official line and that of the extremist dissidents became more acute. In West Bengal, Kerala and Tamil Nadu the Maoists had already mounted a severe attack on the party's ideological stand and finally, the open revolt of the Andhra Pradesh Maoists led by Tarimela Nagi Reddi struck deep at the root of the CPI(M) organisation.

In view of the serious organisational threat to the Party's unity in Andhra Pradesh, the Politbureau of the CPI(M) addressed a letter to the Party members in the State, charging the dissident leaders *inter-alia* with "sectarian and left-opportunist disruption" of the party's state unit. The "letter to Andhra Communists" held that the programme and the general political line of the party did not encounter any opposition from any party in it or any leading member till the time of releasing the Central Committee's ideological draft for discussion in the middle of August 1967. But the extremists in Andhra Pradesh sought to reverse the political line of the Party and substitute it with an alternative line, "which is neither born out of experience nor an outcome of reviewing the implementation of the accepted political line, but one broadcast by Peking radio and circulated by the Chinese Press".[18] The "grossly subjective and left infantile attack" on the Party's ideological-political line, according to the letter, was due to the fact that "some of our comrades, in their immense hatred of revisionism and innate urge for militant struggle against the exploit-

18. Politbureau, Letter to Andhra Comrades in *Stand on Ideological Issues,* Communist Party of India (Marxist), Calcutta, 1969, p. 35.

ers' rule, have lost their Marxist-Leninist bearing and slipped into petty-bourgeois revolutionism".[19]

While appealing to all Party members and units in Andhra Pradesh for unity, the Politbureau also left a note of warning that "no quarter should be given to the subversive and disruptive slogans of the Naxalbari leaders (and others who are wedded to the Naxalbari political-ideological line) who staged an open revolt against the Party and openly and shamelessly advocated the subversion of the CPI(M) wherever it is possible and disruption where such subversion is stalled. Such a conspiracy for building a factional party within the Party should be scotched....."[20]

Immediately after the release of the Politbureau's "Letter to Andhra Comrades", the Nagi Reddi group sought to parry it by circulating their "Open Letter to Party Members", in which they charged the CPI(M) leadership with making the false claim of a "simultaneous" fight against "revisionism" of the CPSU and "The adventurist political line" of the CPC. The "independent" political line was a mere "opportunist cover" for its "neo-revisionist line" of united front with the "CPSU revisionist leadership" and united front with "Dange revisionists and enmity towards Marxist-Leninists" and "love for the parliamentary path and opposition to militant struggles".[21]

With the publication of the "open Letter" the Andhra dissidents had reached the point of no-return in their ideological duel with the party's politbureau. The Central leadership, once again as in its dealings with the West Bengal Marxists, showed a lack of pragmatism by discarding the revolt of the Andhra extremists as having nothing more than "a nuisance value" and expelling Nagi Reddy, Venkateswara Rao, Pulla Reddy and Kolla Venkiah, who constituted the spearhead of revolt in the province. Commenting on the expulsion of Nagi Reddy and other prominent members from the Andhra Pradesh State unit of the CPI(M), the Party's General Secretary P. Sundaraya admitted that this would deal a heavy blow to the Communist movement in that State in particular, and elsewhere in general. Strongly defending the expulsions, he accused the expelled leaders of continued de-

19. *Ibid.*, p. 33.
20. *Ibid.*, p. 38-39.
21. T. Nagi Reddy and others, *Open Letter to Party Members*, Vijayawada, 1968, p. 23.

iance of the Party programme in spite of the Party's giving them several chances to retrace their steps. Sundarayya observed that of the 16,000 party members in Andhra, half would remain active, whether they joined the extremists or continued in the old Party. The other half would drop their membership because of the ideological confusion. Of the active members, he felt, not more than half would join the extremists. Dealing with the organizational repercussions of these ideological differences on various states, Sundarayya gave the following accounts of defections from the Party members:[22]

State	Total membership in 1967	No. of defections
Jammu & Kashmir	800	800
Punjab	600	100
Delhi	400	150
Bihar	2,600	300
Orissa	800	150
Maharashtra	2,300	150
West Bengal	16,300	500
Tamil Nadu	8,500	1,300

A more exhaustive account of the state of the CPI(M) organisation after the Naxalbari peasant uprising in 1967 is available in a document published by the Central Committee of the CPI(M) after its Eighth Congress held at Cochin on December 23-29, 1968. This account, however, widely varies from that of Sundarayya.:[23]

22. For this report, see *Statesman* (Calcutta), June 26, 1968.

23. Data compiled from the *Political Organizational Report* of the CPI(M) Central Committee to the Eighth Congress, Cochin, December 23-29, 1968, Table 1. Noting the state of party organisation in West Bengal, the same document held:

But even in West Bengal, if we analyse the district-wise Party membership and candidate membership, and its ratio, we find a not very happy state of affairs. For example, in 24-Parganas, in 1967, Primary members were 2,659 and candidates 1,195 total being 3,854. But by 1968 with all these candidates having become full members, party membership should have been 3,854. But it was only 3,398, i.e., a fall of 456 or

State of Party Organisation

	State	Total PMs and CMs—1967	8th Party Congress in 1968 : Total PMs and CMs
1.	Kerala	16,000	20,912
2.	Andhra Pradesh	16,456	9,428
3.	Tamil Nadu	10,209	10,017
4.	Karnataka	1,200	1,194
5.	Orissa	800	541
6.	West Bengal	16,393	16,066
7.	Tripura	2,100	2,092
8.	Assam	800	751
9.	Manipur	200	200
10.	Bihar	3,119	2,882
11.	Uttar Pradesh	4,056	3,095
12.	Madhya Pradesh	540	486
13.	Rajasthan	1,006	1,195
14.	Delhi	400	250
15.	Haryana	400	400
16.	Punjab	4,875	4,100
17.	Gujarat	250	250
18.	Maharashtra	3,166	2,316
19.	Goa	—	—
20.	Jammu & Kashmir	700	—

A New Communist Party Is Born

It may be remembered that in early August 1967 the CPC had asked the Indian revolutionaries "to draw a distinct line of

about 12 per cent. We do not know whether and how much of this was from the old membership. In Calcutta DC, it is 27 per cent, in Burdwan it is 19 per cent, in Howrah 21 per cent, in Hooghly 24 per cent, Midnapore 24 per cent, Jalpaiguri 34 per cent, Cooch Behar 34 per cent, Purulia 53 per cent, and for the whole state it is 19 per cent. Except in 24-Parganas, the other four major districts, Calcutta, Howrah, Hooghly and Burdwan show a drop of 20 to 25 per cent in renewal. It is a serious matter to be concerned with. *Ibid.*, p. 286.

demarcation with the revisionist line politically, ideologically, and organisationally", and to build "a genuinely revolutionary party of Marxism-Leninism, Mao Tse-tung's Thought."[24] Thus this call carried an overt directive for building a third Communist Party on the Maoist line even by splitting the CPI(M). And the initiative in this direction came from the breakaway West Bengal Maoists who had set up a state-level Coordination Committee of the Revolutionaries just before the CPI(M) Central Committee's meeing at Madurai in late August 1967. Several other coordination committees were formed in Bihar, Punjab, Maharashtra, U.P., Jammu and Kashmir and Kerala. The Andhra Pradesh extremists led by Nagi Reddi were the last group to form a co-ordination committee of their own in September, 1968, only after their formal expulsion from the CPI(M). Initially, the Andhra Committee, like other coordination committees had also, favoured the view of building a "truly revolutionary party" based on Marxism-Leninism and the Mao Tse-tung's thought.[25]

It was again on the initiative of the West Bengal Coordination Committee of the Communist Revolutionaries that the representatives of different State Coordination Committees had met in Calcutta in November, 1967 and resolved to form what came to be known as the All-India Coordination Committees of Revolutionaries. This Committee was to coordinate the activities of different Maoist groups and to go ahead, step by step, towards the formation of a revolutionary party based on Maoist thought. The Committee laid down its basic objectives to be:

1. Organization of class struggle at all levels, particularly the Naxalbari type of struggles in the countryside under the leadership of the working class;
2. Uncompromising ideological struggles against all brands of revisionist ideas and the extensive propagation of the thought of Mao Tse-tung to the people; and
3. Finally, coordination of the activities of all revolutionary elements inside and outside the party in order to build

24. For details, see *Observer*, "Historical Lessons of the Telengana Uprising", *op. cit.*

25. *Resolution of the Andhra Pradesh Coordination Committee of Communist Revolutionaries,* Vijayawada, 1968, pp. 24-25.

up a revolutionary party guided by Marxism-Leninism and the thought of Mao Tse-tung.[26]

Explaining its true nature, the Committee observed that a large number of Communist revolutionaries, guided by no leadership, had been waging sharp ideological struggles since 1962, and it was in 1964 when the Party was formally split that they consolidated themselves in the CPI(M). It was the urge to consolidate the revolutionary forces that led them to consolidate themselves within the CPI(M) at the initial stage. But even after the Seventh Congress of the Party inner-party struggles went on as before. Then came the Naxalbari peasant struggles which unleashed, on a wide scale, a mighty revolutionary force that overshadowed all sorts of group efforts for fighting ideological struggle within the Party. The party leadership was tested not on the basis of the political thinking of this or that group, but in the context of the Maoist tactics and strategy of revolution. This led to the widening and deepening of the ideological struggle. In the light of these events, the Committee held, the proposal that the problem of Party-building could be solved by the creation of a centre, representing various groups, was absolutely inadmissible. In that case, something would have been imposed on the revolutionaries. "That is why", the Committee pointed out, "the Coordination Committee did never assume the role of a group, and for that very reason did not evolve any formula for uniting with other groups. The emergence of a mighty revolutionary force, in the wake of the Naxalbari struggle, opened the eyes of many comrades and this led them to think that these forces must be consolidated; but as there was no party to do that it was through class struggles that this consolidation must be effected. Out of this consideration some comrades met in Calcutta and formed a Coordination Committee. Their object was to take the initiative of placing before the revolutionary comrades a proposal that a revolutionary party can only be built up by grasping revolutionary politics and sharpening class struggles ...."[27] Thus the committee "studiously avoided the mechanical process of convening a conference of the revolutionary comrades and forming a revolutionary party therefrom."

26. "The Coordination Committee—Its Nature and Objective", *Liberation,* May 1968, p. 18.

27. *Ibid.,* p. 24-25.

Almost a year after the formation of the All-India Coordination Committee of the Revolutionaries, the Andhra Pradesh Coordination Committee joined it in October, 1968. In May the All-India Coordination Committee which had met on the eve of the first anniversary of the Naxalbari peasant uprising reaffirmed in its declaration on the decision to form a "true Communist Party of India in the course of revolutionary struggle of Naxalbari type, for Revolution cannot be victorious without a revolutionary Party".[28] And in order to make itself a common platform of all the Indian Maoists, the Coordination Committee changed its name to All-India Coordination Committee of Communist Revolutionaries (AICCCR). In the same meeting the AICCCR also called for boycott of elections, and this negative slogan was to be followed up by positive action to mobilise and organise the people in revolutionary class struggles "under the banner of Chairman Mao's thought" and try to build a Naxalbari-type movement leading a people's democratic revolution.[29]

Despite the initial understanding among sundry Maoist groups and formations in the country on the stage and strategy of the Indian revolution and the need for a Maoist Party, the AICCCR slipped into the jabbing gloves of the State Coordination Committees of West Bengal and Andhra Pradesh. The differences between these two groups related to a host of issues including the questions of tactics and leadership. The West Bengal Coordination Committee which was in control of the AICCCR had these charges against the Andhra Coordination Committee to the Communist Party of China. It was contended that Nagi Reddi and his group had denounced the armed raids on two police posts in Kerala in November 1968 by the extremists as the handiwork of agent provocateur. They did not revise this view or withdraw it even after the CPC had hailed these raids as revolutionary guerrilla actions. The second charge was the Andhra Coordination Committee's "lukeworm" reference to the

28. "Declaration of Communist Revolutionaries", *Liberation*, June 1968, pp. 7-10.

29. "Resolution on Elections" *Liberation*, June 1968, pp. 29-30. For further details of the activities of the AICCR, see O. P. Sangal, "Alphabet of Mao: AICCR" The *Citizen and Weekend Review* (New Delhi), Vol. I, No. 5, May 10, 1969, pp. 21-23.

Srikakulam struggle instead of "owning and glorifying" it. The third charge related to boycott of elections. It was contended that Nagi Reddi had not resigned his membership of the State Assembly before October, 1968 as directed by the AICCCR. Finally, personality differences between the Andhra Pradesh and West Bengal Coordination Committee leaders surfaced on a number of occasions, while considerable higgling for leadership positions was reported to have disrupted several AICCCR meetings. While the West Bengal Maoists persistently stuck to their demands of the top positions for Charu Mazumdar and Kanu Sanyal both in the AICCCR and the Party to be formed, this leadership was not acceptable to some groups, especially the Andhra Coordination, which demanded Nagi Reddi as the leading figure in the whole movement. At this stage the West Bengal State Coordination Committee of the Communist Revolutionaries was also split as Parimal Dasgupta and his compatriots left the Committee on a host of tactical differences with it and formed a rival coordination committee.

In the first week of February 1969 the AICCCR adopted two resolutions noted "basic differences" between itself and the Andhra Committee. Therefore, it was decided to treat the Andhra Maoists "as friends and comrades" outside the AICCCR. Their relations would be "non-antagonistic."

In the second resolution it was declared that last one year's experience of fast developing revolutionary struggle had confirmed the growing need for a revolutionary party, because "without a revolutionary Party, there can be no revolutionary discipline and without revolutionary discipline the struggle cannot be raised to a higher level".[30]

In order to justify this decision, which was contrary to the earlier stand of the Committee against the immediate formation of a new party, the AICCCR had a queer line of reasoning. It observed:

> Idealist deviations on the question of party building arises as a result of the refusal to recognize the struggle that must be waged within the Party. The idea that the Party should

30. "Resolution of the AICCCR", *Liberation*, March, 1969, p. 6.

be formed only after all opportunist tendencies, alien class trends and undesirable elements have been purged through class struggles is nothing but subjective idealism. To conceive of a Party without contradictions, without the struggle between the opposites, that is to think of a pure and faultless party is indulging in mere idealist fantasy.[31]

Almost simultaneously, a sharp criticism was made of those groups which had broken off from the AICCCR (especially the Andhra Coordination Committee) by branding all of them as "counter revolutionaries". In an editorial in the *Liberation,* Sushital Roy Chowdhury, Editor-in-Chief of the journal wrote:

> Today there are many petty-bourgeois groups which pay lip-service to Chairman Mao's thought and even to Naxalbari. The Party holds that many of these groups represent a counter-revolutionary current within the revolutionary movement. They preach the "historical inevitability of groupism at this state", "building the Party from below" and other anti-Marxist-Leninist ideas. Thus they try to leave the task of building the party to spontaneity and deliberately to seek to prevent the formation of a revolutionary Communist Party at a time when comrades leading armed struggles in different areas feel necessity for it.[32]

Charu Mazumdar, the principal ideologue of the Naxalbari sect also rationalised the importance of forming a third Communist Party through a self-denying theorisation in an article entitled, "Why Must We Form A Party Now?" in *Liberation,* March 1969. He held that the question was not of building a party through revolutionary struggles but forming a party first in order to intensify the struggles.

It was, therefore, in pursuance of the unanimous decision taken in the first week of February 1969 that the AICCCR met in a plenary session in Calcutta between April 19 and 22 and formed India's third Communist Party—the Communist Party of India (Marxist-Leninist), "based on the thought of Mao Tse-tung", on April 22, the one hundredth birthday of Lenin and also announced the dissolution of the Committee itself, after setting up a

31. *Ibid.,* pp. 6-7.
32. *Liberation,* May 1969, pp. 1-2.

Central Organising Committee to hold the first Congress of the Party at an appropriate time.[33] But the formal announcement regarding the formation of the party was made by Kanu Sanyal, the "hero" of the Naxalbari peasant struggle at a huge May Day rally at the foot of the Octerlony Monument (now Sahid Minar), presided over by Asit Sen, a prominent Maoist leader. Sanyal declared:

> With great pride and boundless joy I wish to announce today at this meeting that we have formed a genuine Communist Party—the Communist Party of India (Marxist-Leninist). When our Party was born the historic Ninth National Congress of the Great Communist Party of China was in session under the personal guidance of Chairman Mao Tse-tung. I feel proud that the task of making this historic announcement has been given to me. I firmly believe that the great Indian people will warmly welcome this event, will realise that the formation of this Party is an historic step forward for the Indian revolution, and will come forward to raise the struggle to a higher stage under the leadership of the Party.[34]

He further said that "a revolutionary situation necessitated revolutionary Party, the formation of which has been constructed in the past by revisionists within the communist movement." "But", he declared, "all the trickery and opposition of the traitorous leading clique of the communist movement could not prevent the victorious onward march of Chairman Mao Tse-tung's thought in India. Thus, the conditions for the emergence of a genuine Communist Party in India were created."

Quoting the declaration of the CPC to the effect that ". . . . by the year 2,000, that is, only 31 years from now, the people of the whole world will be liberated from all kinds of exploitation of man and will celebrate the world-wide victory of Marxism-Leninism, Mao Tse-tung's thought". In the words of Sanyal:

> This is no mere declaration, it is an historic directive. Through this the great Communist Party of China points to

33. "Communique of the All-India Coordination Committee of Communist Revolutionaries", *Liberation,* May 1969, p. 3.

34. "Kanu Sanyal's Address at the May Day Rally", *Liberation,* May 1969, p. 119. For the full text of the address, see pp. 110-122.

> the Communists of the whole world how excellent the world situation is for making revolution, and at the same time, directs all of them to march forward boldly .... The historic responsibility of carrying forward the Indian revolution has fallen on our shoulders.

In founding the Party in a plenary session of the AICCCR held in the third week of April, the CPI(M-L) leaders followed the same pattern of party-building set in 1964 by their parent party, the CPI(M). While the second Communist Party was founded at the Tenali Convention of July 1964, the Party had to wait for a programme and a constitution until November. Similarly the CPI(M-L) was formed without a programme or a constitution. At its inception the party claimed to place ideology and politics above everything else but had to wait a little longer than a year before it could give itself a programme. However, the "Political Resolution" adopted by the Central Committee of the CPI(M-L) laid down in no uncertain terms the party's strategy and tactics for a people's democratic revolution in India.[35]

Identifying the "principal contradiction" in today's India as "between feudalism and the masses of our peasantry", the political resolution held:

> The Indian revolution at this stage is the democratic revolution of the new type—the People's Democratic Revolution, the main content of which is the abolition of feudalism in the countryside. To destroy feudalism, one of the two main props (comprador-bureaucrat capitalism being the other) of imperialism in our country, the Indian people will have to wage a bitter, protracted struggle against U.S. imperialism and Soviet social-imperialism too. By liberating themselves from the yoke of feudalism the Indian people will liberate themselves also from the yoke of imperialism and comprador-

35. See "Political Resolution of the CPI(M-L)", *Liberation,* May 1969, pp. 4-16. The Central Committee of the CPI(M-L) also laid down a separate programme for the students and youths. See "Draft Political Programme for the Revolutionary Student and Youth Movement", *Liberation,* April, 1969, pp. 57-67. Since the programme of the CPI(M-L) has been exhaustively analysed in the following chapter only a brief reference to its Political Resolution is being made in the next few pages.

36. 'Political Resolution of the CPI(M-L)", *op. cit.,* pp. 5-6.

bureaucrat capital, because the struggle against feudalism is also a struggle against the other two enemies.[36]

As regards the class strategy of the people's democratic revolution in India the resolution laid down:

> If the poor and landless peasants, who constitute the majority of the peasantry, the firm ally of the working class, unite with the middle peasants, then the vast section of the people will be united and the democratic revolution will inevitably win victory. It is the responsibility of the working class as the leader of the revolution to advance with the peasantry—the main force of the revolution, towards seizure of power through armed struggle. It is on the basis of the worker-peasant alliance that a revolutionary united front of all classes will be built up.[37]

On tactics, the resolution commended Mao's theory of people's war as "the only means by which an apparently weak revolutionary force can wage successful struggles against an apparently powerful enemy and can win victory. The basic tactic of struggle of the revolutionary peasantry led by the working class is guerrilla warfare."[38]

Finally, highlighting the international significance of the Indian revolution, the resolution held:

> Great Lenin dreamt of the day when revolutionary India would unite with revolutionary China and bring about the collapse of the world imperialist system. That is why at the time of the formation of the Party the Indian revolutionaries must resolve that they shall unite with the great people of China and thus forge unity with the liberation struggles of the various countries, that they shall build up a revolutionary united front and destroy world imperialism and its chief accomplice, modern revisionism..."[39]

It seems quite obvious that the determination of the CPI(M-L) leadership to emulate the Chinese example of a Communist revolution based on peasant uprisings and the anxiety to "unite

37. *Ibid.*, p. 14.
38. *Ibid.*, p. 16.
39. *Ibid.*, p. 16.

with the great people of China prompted the CPC to confer its "recognition" of the CPI(M-L) by printing excerpts from the latter's Political Resolution in the *People's Daily* of July 2, 1969.[40]

40. On the same day Radio Peking's evening transmission also announced the formation of the CPI(M-L).

In summarizing the Political Resolution of the CPI(M-L) Chinese media selected only those portions which reflected Maoist strategy and tactics. See *Peking Review,* July 11, 1969. Later in reporting armed peasant struggles, Maoist tactics and the Maoist essentials of such struggles were carefully selected. Ste reports in *Peking Review,* August 6, September 19, and October 31, 1969. See also, Shas Yung-hung, "Rising Revolutionary Storm of the Indian Peasants", *Peking Review,* September 9, 1969.

CHAPTER V

THE PROGRAMME AND THE ORGANISATION OF THE COMMUNIST PARTY OF INDIA (MARXIST-LENINIST)

I

General Programme : Almost after a year of its inception the CPI(M-L) held its foundation Congress at an undisclosed place in Calcutta on May 15 and 16, 1970. The Congress which was attended by delegates from all over India, unanimously adopted a Programme of People's Democratic Revolution and a constitution[1] as well.

Tracing the different stages of the Indian freedom movement the Programme holds:

British Imperialists conquered India and established their direct rule some two hundred years ago and since then the history of our country has been a history of ceaseless struggles between the heroic Indian peasantry and the British Imperialist aggressors. . . . The first war of Independence in 1857, a war fought by the peasantry and the rebel soldiers turned into a conflagration engulfing the whole of this country, inflicting many humiliating defeats on the imperialists and shattering the very foundations of the alien Imperialist Rule. This great uprising of the Indian people failed owing to the betrayals of India's feudal princes.

Since then, India has witnessed innumerable armed peasant revolts. However, these revolts failed as there was no scientific theory of revolutionary leadership capable of leading them to victory. The Great October Revolution brought the ideology of Marxism-Leninism to our country and the Communist Party of India was born. However, despite tremendous opportunities, the leadership of the working class could not be established over the national liberation struggle as the leadership of the party refused

1. A summary of the programme appeared in the *Hindusthan Standard* (Calcutta Daily) June 3, 1970. Also see, A. K. Roy, "India's Third Communist Party", *Institute of Defence Studies and Analyses Journal*, July-September 1974.

to fight Gandhism and the Gandhian leadership and to take the path of revolution ....

The smashing defeat of the Fascist powers at the hands of the world people led by the Soviet Union under the leadership of Great Stalin, and the world shaking victorious advance of the Great Chinese Liberation Struggle under the leadership of Chairman Mao, brought about a new alignment of forces the world over: Imperialism was immensely weakened and the National Liberation Struggle of the colonial people surged forward with a torrential force throughout Asia, Africa and Latin America, delivering staggering blows to Imperialism and its lackeys.

An unprecedented revolutionary situation overtook the Indian sub-continent too.... The country was partitioned amidst communal carnage and the Congress leadership representing the comprador bourgeoisie and the big landlords were installed into power while the British Imperialists remained in the background. The sham independence declared in 1947 was nothing but a replacement of the direct colonial rule of the British Imperialists with a semi-colonial rule over our country.

Analysing the post-Independence political scene of this country the Programme argues that "during these years of sham independence the Big Bourgeoisie and the Big landlord ruling classes have been serving their Imperialist Masters to the fullest extent. These lackeys of Imperialism are preserving the old British Imperialist exploitation of our country.... Thus instead of 2 mountains, British Imperialism and Feudalism, now the Indian people are breaking under the heavy weight of four huge mountains, namely U.S. Imperialism, Soviet Social-Imperialism, Feudalism and Comprador-Bureaucrat Capital."

Identifying the principal contradiction in the present phase of the country as "between feudalism and the broad masses of Indian people", the Programme holds that "as the obsolete semi-feudal society acts as the social base of U.S. Imperialism and as it facilitates also the plunder of our people by the Comprador-Bureaucrat Capitalism the problem of the peasantry becomes the basic problem of the Indian people." Therefore, the basic task of the Indian Revolution, according to the Programme, is to eliminate Feudalism, Bureaucrat-Capitalism and Imperialism. And this determines the stage of the Indian Revolution, which the Programme identifies as the "stage of a Democratic

Revolution, the essence of which is Agrarian Revolution. It is, however, not the old type of Democratic Revolution, as it forms a part of the World Socialist Revolution, ushered in by the Great October Revolution and as such can be successfully led by the working class alone and by no other class".

Elaborating the nature and the scope of the People's Democratic Revolution the Programme declares:

This Revolution will establish the Dictatorship of the worker-peasants, petti-bourgeoisie and even a section of the small middle bourgeoisie under the leadership of the working class who together with the peasantry constitute the overwhelming majority of the Indian people. It will be a State guaranteeing democracy for 90% of the people and enforcing dictatorship over a handful of enemies. That is why it is a people's democracy.

Outlining the class alliance of the People's Democratic Revolution the Programme prescribes that "the main force of the Democratic Revolution led by the working class is the peasantry. The working class absolutely relies on the landless and poor peasants, and firmly unites with the middle peasants and even wins a section of the rich peasants while neutralizing the rest. It will be only a tiny section of the rich peasants that finally joins the enemies of Revolution. The urban petty-bourgeoisie and the revolutionary intellectuals of our country are revolutionary force and overwhelming majority of them will be a reliable ally in the Revolution. Thus, in order to carry the Democratic Revolution through the end it is necessary that a Democratic Front of all these classes be built up under the leadership of the working class. This front, however, can only be built up when worker-peasant unity is achieved in the process of armed struggle and after Red political power is established at least in some parts of the country. It must be understood that the working class will exercise its leadership over the People's Democratic Revolution through its political Party, the Communist Party of India (Marxist-Leninist)."

As regards the tactics of the People's Democratic Revolution, the Programme holds that "the path of India's liberation as in the case of all colonial, semi-colonial and semi-feudal countries, is the path of People's War. As Chairman Mao has taught us, "The Revolutionary War is the war of the masses, it can be waged only by mobilizing the masses and relying on them".

Commending guerrilla warfare as "the basic form of struggle throughout the entire period of all Democratic Revolutions" the Programme holds:

As Comrade Lin Piao has pointed out: "Guerrilla warfare is the only way to mobilise and apply the entire strength of the people against the enemy". Guerrilla warfare alone can unleash the initiative and the creative genius of the Indian people to perform miracles, to function in various ways, effectively coordinate them and thus expand the small bases of armed struggle to mighter waves of people's army by which the reactionary rule of the four mountains will be overthrown from the countryside, the cities encircled and captured and people's democratic dictatorship established all over the country and resolutely carry it forward to socialism.

Paragraph 41 of the programme lays down the major tasks of the People's Democratic State to be established after the successful completion of the People's Democratic Revolution in India:

(a) Confiscation of all banks and enterprises of foreign capital and liquidation of all imperialist assets;

(b) Confiscation of all the enterprises of the comprador-bureaucrat capitalists;

(c) Confiscation of all lands belonging to the landlords and rich peasants on the principle of land to the tillers; cancellation of all debts of the peasantry and the other toiling people. All facilities necessary for the development of agriculture to be guaranteed;

(d) Enforce eight hours a day, increase wages, institute unemployment relief and social insurance, remove all inequalities on the basis of equal pay for equal work;

(e) Improve the living conditions of soldiers and give lands and jobs to ex-servicemen;

(f) Enforce better living conditions and remove unemployment from the people;

(g) Abolish caste system, remove all social inequalities and all discriminations on religious grounds and guarantee equality of status to Indian womanhood;

(h) Unify India and recognise the right of national self-determination;

(i) Abolish all exorbitant taxes and miscellaneous assessments and adopt a consolidated progressive tax system;

(j) Administration to be carried out by forming Revolutionary People's Committees at all levels;

(k) Alliance to be formed with the International Proletariat and the oppressed nations of the world under the leadership of the C.P.C."

Stressing the historical significance of the Indian revolution the Programme declares that "the Democratic Revolution in India is taking place in the era of Mao Tse-tung, when the Great Proletarian Cultural Revolution has consolidated socialism and the proletarian dictatorship in China and when China has emerged as the reliable base area of World Revolution. It is taking place at a time when the C.P.C., headed by Chairman Mao and Vice-Chairman Lin Piao, is leading the international proletariat to fulfil its historic mission of emancipating the whole mankind from imperialism and reaction and establishing Socialism and Communism on this earth. We are a contingent of this great army of International Proletariat."

II

The Constitution of the CPI (M-L) : Structure and function of the party

The organisational principles of the CPI(M-L) as laid down in its Constitution have been heavily borrowed from the Constitution of the Chinese Communist Party adopted at its Ninth Congress held in April 1969.

The Constitution of the CPI (M-L) itself leaves no room for ambiguity in this respect as Article 6 of the Constitution declares that "the CPI (M-L) regards the Communist Party of China as the leader of the international communist movement and recognise China as the centre and base of the World Revolution."

It is therefore, hardly surprising that most of the provisions of the CPI (M-L) Constitution have been grafted verbatim with a few minor modifications. The draft of the C.P.C. Constitution was first published in English translation in the *China Quarterly* (No. 37, 1969, pp. 169-173). The final text, which was passed at the Ninth Congress appeared in *Peking Review* (No. 18, 1969, pp. 36-40), and differs in minor points from the draft, placed the thought of Mao Tse-tung on a par with Marxism-Leninism. This equality entailed a change in the spelling of Mao's name in the English translation of the Constitution done in Peking. The hyphen between Tse and tung was dropped, and so the text in the *Peking Review* mentions "Marxism-Leninism-Mao Tse tung Thought."

The fact that the organisational plan of the Communist Party of India (Marxist-Leninist) is strikingly different from those of the CPI and the CPI(M) emanates from the programmatic differences of these parties. Thus while the two older parties operate openly within the constitutional framework of the country by setting "peaceful transition to socialism" as their avowed goal, the CPI (M-L) was meant to be a rural-based, secret and underground party committed to armed struggle against the state power. Even a casual reference to Articles 3 and 4 of the Constitution of the CPI (M-L) clearly reveals the party's operational strategy. Article 3 declares that "the basic programme of the CPI(M-L) is .... the establishment of the People's Democratic Dictatorship led by the proletariat in the place of the Dictatorship of the Bureaucratic Comprador Bourgeoisie and the Big Feudal Landlord classes. The ultimate aim of the Party is the realisation of Socialism and Communism." And to overthrow the rule of the enemies of the people, lays down Article 4, "the CPI (M-L) places the path of armed struggle before the Indian people. It rejects the parliamentary path for the whole of the strategic period. The people's war in semi-feudal and semi-colonial India is the peasants' war under the leadership of the working class. As pointed out by Comrade Lin Piao, our strategy of People's war is to rely on the peasants, build base areas, resort to persistent armed struggle and to use countryside to encircle and finally capture the cities."

It should be noted that India provides a unique case study of "competitive communism." In other words, each of the three Communist parties—the CPI, the CPI(M) and the CPI(M-L) —has its own model of revolution arising out of their divergent interpretations not only of the Indian State and the correlation of class forces, but also over strategy, tactics and techniques of mobilisation.

In their conflicting interpretations of the Indian State, the CPI saw the state as the "organ of class rule of the national bourgeoisie as a whole; while the CPI(M) saw it as controlled by the big bourgeoisie in alliance with the big landowners. Both viewed India as overtaken by the crisis of capitalist development which they saw reflected in the rising cost of living, food scarcity, hoarding and profiteering, corruption among politicians and civil servants, and the increasing misery of the masses.

These differing analysis of the balance of class forces resulted in divergent strategies for advancing the revolution in India. The CPI recognised the national bourgeois state of India to constitute a solid achievement towards independence and maintained that the next step should be its conversion into a "national democratic state" through a "national democratic front" *from above*. The CPI (M) on the other hand, considered the state, under the joint control of the big bourgeoisie and landlords, to be "anti-people" and aimed at replacing it with a "people's democracy" to be brought about through a "people's democratic front" *built from below* on the basis of mass struggles against the existing ruling forces. Neither party promised socialism in the immediate future, and both assured sections of the bourgeoisie and landlords a secure position in the new society they contemplated. The CPI excluded only the big bourgeoisie i.e., the monopolists—from its contemplated "national democratic front". Whereas both the upper bourgeoisie and the big landholders were to be excluded from the CPI(M)'s "people democratic front."

On the question of using violence to attain their objectives, neither the CPI nor the CPI(M) took a clear-cut and unequivocal position. The CPI did not raise the issue in any of the resolutions and documents adopted at its 1964 Bombay Congress, presumably because the party's explicit adherence to the parliamentary road to power ruled out any admission of the deliberate use of violence as a tactical weapon. The CPI(M)'s position on the use of non-peaceful methods, as laid down at its 1964 Calcutta Congress, was not made explicitly clear. It stressed the party's intention to strive for a peaceful transformation of the Indian society, but intimated that the revolutionary forces must be prepared for any contingency of the ruling classes violently resisting such change.[2]

The first ever document on the organisational line circulated shortly after the formation of the Party declared that the Party had to be a secret organisation, launching of mass or democratic struggles was ruled out. It said that "though the party should learn to utilise all possible legal opportunities for developing its revolutionary activities, it should under no circumstances function in the open".[3] The Party's first task, according to the document, would be for the kind of work through which the working class could be prepared for leadership of the revolution, rather than engage itself in economic struggles and cultural activities in the cities.

Thus understood, organisationally the new Party was to be (a) one of the armed revolution, totally rejecting the parliamentary path and therefore could not be built in isolation from armed struggle; (b) rural-based, to rouse the peasantry to wage guerrilla warfare, unfold agrarian revolution, build base areas in the villages, use countryside to encircle and finally to capture the cities; (c) secret and underground and by no means to function openly through front organisations; and (d) of a new style integrating theory with practice and forging close links with the masses and practising criticism and self-criticism, thereby raising the level of its understanding.

This organisational pattern was supposed to give priorities to ideological and political building over organisation and structure, training of party cadre in guerrilla action; building of revolutionary base areas in the countryside instead of working in the cities preparing the working class for leadership of the revolution instead of carrying on economic and cultural activities in the cities; and organising highly efficient cadre over mass enrolment of members. The principle of a compact organisation form in the shape of small units was to be generally followed in the party.

This analysis clearly shows that the CPI(M-L) leaders were

2. This analysis is based on the respective programmes of the CPI and the CPI(M) as adopted at their 1964 Bombay and Calcutta Congresses.

3. "Resolution on Party Organisation." Communist Party of India (Marxist-Leninist), circulated in April 1969.

going to pursue a Jugantar strategy rather than the Anushilan strategy largely taken up by the CPI and the CPI (M), a reference to the two old terrorist organisations operating in Bengal at the early stage of nationalist movement. Unlike the Anushilan Samity, which was organised in much the same manner as the present older Communist parties (with front groups and mass organisations), the *Jugantar* revolutionaries were a highly secretive underground organisation that used to surface only to carry out dramatic terrorist acts like raids, political assassinations[4] etc. Though the CPI (M-L) has nowhere openly acknowledged its adherence to a *Jugantar* style of revolutionary organisation, its leadership has always met secretly, shifted the party headquarters frequently and allowed the party units to surface only when revolutionary activities have demanded public acts. A highly underground organisation of this type obviously requires far more regimentation than either the CPI or the CPI (M) has been able to impose on their members, and must necessarily be even more elitist and centralised than either the CPI or the CPI (M).

With this basic understanding of the nature of the party organisation, an analysis may be made of the general organisational principles of the CPI (M-L).

The Communist Party of India (Marxist-Leninist) like all other Communist parties the world over assumes itself to be an exclusively fighting revolutionary organisation of the proletariat in its struggle for power, and as such it stands in constant confrontation with the bourgeois-capitalist state, which is the "most centralised force of violence and oppression." Unless the political party of the proletariat is organised, united and conducted on a highly centralised manner it cannot stand up against its most powerful class enemies and discharge its destined revolutionary tasks, and this can only be achieved by what has been universally accepted by all the Communist parties as the principle of "democratic centralism", that is, through leadership which is at once responsible to the members and has absolute authority over them.

"Democratic Centralism" in its slender core means centralised leadership based on inner-Party democracy and democracy

4. For an interesting study of the *Anushilan* and *Jugantar* orgazations, see Gobindalal Banerjee, *Dynamic of Revolutionary Movement in India* (Calcutta; Sudhir Kumar Ghosh, 1965), pp. 18-20.

under the guidance of the centralised leadership. As a theory of party organisation democratic centralism is based on two main principles: (1) all the leading policy-making organs of the party are elected by the party membership[5] and enjoy their confidence. They must report periodically to the membership as a whole; (2) the lower Party organisations must carry out the decisions and directives of the higher Party organs, the decisions of the majority shall be binding on the minority and the individual shall subordinate himself to the will of the collective. In theory, authority is built from the bottom up and is exercised from the top down. At the same time, the "democratic" basis of this centralisation must also be genuine; that is, authority must be based not on mere formal election but on a "living association" between leaders who must recognise the legitimacy of inner-Party leadership.

Democracy in the Party permits free and frank discussion within the Party units on all questions affecting the Party, its policy and work, and encourages criticism and self-criticism at all levels from top to bottom, especially criticism from below. But the expression of opinion is the right only of the individual, never of organised groups and factions. Factionalism and factional groupings inside the Party are impermissible in theory.[6]

5. The CPC Constitution as adopted at the Ninth Congress of the Party, contains a paragraph on democratic centralism, which is in clear contradiction to the Soviet principles of party organisation: "The organisational principle of the Party is democratic centralism. The leading bodies of the Party at all levels are elected through democratic consultation". (Article 5). It is not completely clear what this election through consultation means in practice. There are indications that the deputies to the Ninth Congress, after some consultation of the regional administration were in effect appointed by the party leaders in Peking and were neither directly nor indirectly elected. The only Congress of the Communist Party of China that consisted of more or less democratically elected deputies was the Eighth Congress held in 1956. The activities of many Central Committee members, who were elected at that very Congress, did not find favour in Mao Tse-tung's eyes. This may be one of the reasons why the idea of democratic elections was dropped. It may be pointed out that the Tenth Congress of the CPC held at Peking in August 1973, has also retained the principle of "democratic consultation" in the Constitution.

6. For an analysis of the general theory and practice of Communist Party organisation, see Philip Selznik, *The Organisational Weapon:*

The Constitution of the CPI (M-L) has incorporated "Democratic Centralism" as the main organisational principle of the Party. Article I of Chapter Three entitled, "Organisational Principle of the Party" declares that "the organisational Principle of the Party is Democratic Centralism. The democratic centralism means centralised leadership based on inner-party democracy and inner-party democracy under the guidance of centralised leadership."

In order to realise the principle of democratic centralism Article I lays down the following measures :

(a) All higher organs shall be elected except in exceptional circumstances;

(b) Individual is subordinate to the Party unit;

(c) Lower unit is subordinate to the higher unit;

(d) All units and members are subordinate to the Central Committee;

(e) Leading Committees are to give regular reports to their subordinate units and promptly convey their decisions;

(f) Leading committees shall take decisions only after full considerations and on the basis of thorough knowledge of the conditions of the people and lower units;

(g) Free and frank discussions within Party units on all questions regarding Party policy and work;

(h) Every unit is free to take full initiative in working out the methods of implementing the general line given by the leading organs;

(i) Every party member must belong to a party unit;

(j) Every member of a leading committee must be assigned a particular area of struggle to which he gives particular guidance and from which he gains direct experience. Exception to this rule may be made only in cases where it becomes necessary in the interest of some specific party work;

(k) Factionalism is incompatible with the principle of Democratic Centralism;

(l) Every party member is free to send his opinions, criticisms and appeal upto the Central Committee;

(m) When a party member violates discipline, the party

A Study of Bolshevik Strategy and Tactics (New York: McGraw-Hill, 1952), 350 pp.

organisation at the level concerned shall take disciplinary measures—warnings, serious warnings, removal from the posts of the party, placing on probation within the party."

Thus the Constitution of the CPI (M-L) provides for formal rules intended to create and maintain a high degree of centralisation as may be found in the Constitution of the CPC. But at the same time like the members of the CPC those of the CPI(M-L) enjoy the right to freely send their opinions, criticisms and appeal directly to the Central Committee.[7]

As regards the formal organisation of the CPI (M-L) it may be pointed out that as a corollary to the application of the principle of democratic centralism a hierarchical system has been introduced. Chapter Four of the Constitution lays down in details the structural plan of the Party, at the top of which is the All India Party Congress and at the bottom is the "Cell." (See the diagram: p. 164)

Article 1 of Chapter Four of the Constitution provides that "the highest organ of the party is the All-India Party Congress". The Party Congress, according to Article 2, "shall be convened every five years".[8]But under "special circumstances" it may be convened before it's due date or it may be postponed by the

7. Similarly, Article 5 of the Constitution of the Communist Party of China adopted by the Ninth National Congress of the Party in April, 1969 lays down that "if a Party member holds different views with regard to the decisions or directives of the Party organisations, he is allowed to reserve his views and has the right to bypass the immediate leadership and report directly to higher levels, upto and including the Central Committee and the Chairman of the Central Committee. It is essential to create a political situation in which there are both centralism and democracy, both discipline and freedom, both unity of will and personal ease of mind and liveliness."

8. The Constitution of the CPC requires the National Party Congress to meet every five years. But under special circumstances, it may be convened before its due date or postponed (Article 8). It may be pointed out that all the ten party congresses have been convened very irregularly. The congresses of the CPC have taken place as follows:

Founding Congress, Shanghai, June-July, 1921.

2nd, Shanghai, July, 1922.
3rd, Canton, June, 1923.
4th, Shanghai, January, 1925.
5th, Hankow, July, 1927.
6th, Moscow, July, 1928.
7th, Yenan, April, 1945.
8th, Peking, September, 1956.
9th, Peking, April, 1969.
10th, Peking, August, 1973.

Diagram of the CPI (M-L) Organization)

		Central Committee	———	All India Party Congress
		:		:
General Secretary	———	Politbureau		:
		:		:
State Secretary	———	State Committee	———	State Conference
		:		:
Regional Secretary	———	Regional Committee	———	Regional Conference
		:		:
Area Secretary	———	Area Committee	———	Area Conference
		:		
Cell Secretary	———	Cell		

——— .. Denotes line of responsibility

: .. Denotes line of authority

Central Committee. The main organisational duty of the All-India Party Congress, according to Article 3, will be to elect the Central Committee of the Party. Its regular political functions include reviewing the political situation and work of the Party, chalking out general line for the whole country and if necessary, changing or amending the Party Constitution, and even the Programme.

The Central Committee in its turn, is the highest authority of the Party between two All-India Party Congresses. It is responsible for enforcing the Party Constitution and carrying out the political line and decisions adopted by the Party Congress.

Its organisational duties include the election from among its members a Politbureau including the General Secretary and creation of other necessary standing committees. The Politbureau carries on the work of the Central Committee between its two sessions and has the right to take political and organisational decisions in between two meetings of the Central Committee. Later on, for smooth functioning of the party, the Central Committee set up four zonal bureaus with A. Kailashan as Secretary of south zone, R. P. Shroff, Secretary of north-west zone, S. K. Mishra of north central zone and Sourin Bose of north-east zone.

Like the All-India Party Congress electing the Central Committee (C.C.), at each lower level the Conference elects a Committee, e.g. the State Conference elects the State Committee, the Regional Conference elects the Regional Committee and the Area Conferences elect the Area Committees (See Articles 5-8).

The basic units of the Party, according to Article 9 of the Constitution, are the Cells. Since the Communist Party of India (Marxist-Leninist) is essentially an underground organisation waging guerrilla warfare, a cell is of absolute importance to the party organisation. An operational cell is usually composed of a leader and a few cell members operating directly as a unit. The leader or the Cell secretary assigns works and directives to the members of the Action Squads. Usually he is in contact with the leaders of the Actions Squads through couriers. (See Organisation Chart of an operational cell below).

Organisation Chart of an Operational Cell.

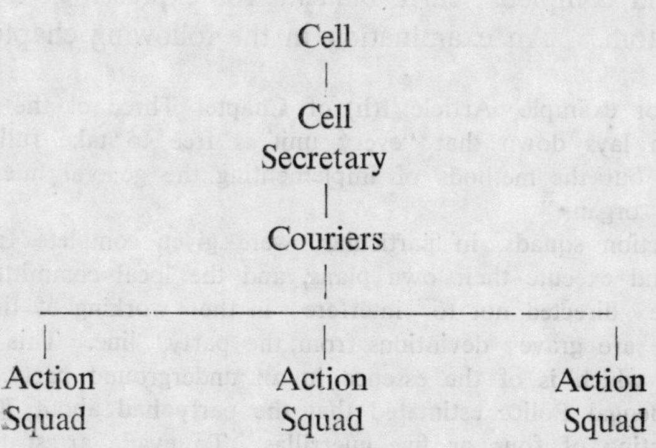

The size of an operational cell usually depends upon its assigned functions, but in difficult times the cell is kept as small as possible to reduce to the minimum the possibility of compromise. The cell may be compartmentalised in order to protect the underground organisation and to reduce the vulnerability of its members to capture. Compartmentalisation restricts the information any member has about the identity, background, or current residence of any other cell member. He knows individuals only by their aliases and the means by which they can be reached. This follows the underground "fail-safe" principle; if one element in the organisation fails, the consequences to the total organisation will be minimal. The cell is highly centralised, with directives flowing from a high command throughout the organisation; this tends to increase the efficiency of operations. On the other hand, the organisation is rather decentralised, with units in various parts of the country operating autonomously and it was found that during 1970-71 the whole organisation pattern had tended to be highly decentralised and the leadership had hailed every stray violent act as spontaneous outburst. These acts had never been planned or directed by the central organisation of the CPI(M-L). The foregoing analysis of the formal structure of the CPI(M-L) is of course only one aspect in the Party's whole operational pattern primarily based on the organisational principles as laid down in the Party constitution. Its behaviour, however, has frequently borne little resemblance to the model set in the Constitution. But so far as the Constitution bears any relation to the CPI(M-L)'s operation, it seems to suggest a combination of unusual centralisation of authority at the top and complete *carte blanche* for expression and action at the bottom.[9] An examination in the following chapter of the

9. For example, Article 1(h) of Chapter Three of the CPI(M-L) Constitution lays down that "every unit is free to take full initiative in working out the methods of implementing the general line given by the leading organs."

The action squads, in particular, were given complete freedom to draw up and execute their own plans, and the local committees of the party were directed not to interfere in the working of the squads unless there are grave deviations from the party line. This has made for secrecy which is of the essence in an underground party. In 1970 the West Bengal Police estimated that the party had about 700 squads, each consisting of four or five guerrillas. To evade arrest the squads

CPI(M-L)'s operation would show that these two paradoxical qualities were the most striking features of the Party in action.

Composition of the CPI (M-L) : Since the CPI(M-L) was never meant to be a mass party like the CPI or the CPI(M), its standards of admission to membership have been highly exclusive. In practice, however, the recruitment pattern largely deviated from the provision laid down in the Constitution.

Unlike the parent party, the CPI(M), the requirements for membership of the CPI (M-L) are rather stringent. Article IV (para 1) of the CPI(M) Constitution, adopted at the Eighth Congress in 1968, for example, provides that a member is one "residing in India, eighteen years of age or above who accepts the Programme and Constitution of the Party, agrees to work in one of the Party organisations, to pay regularly the Party membership dues (fee and levy as may be prescribed) and to carry out decisions of the Party, shall be eligible for Party membership." On the other hand, Article 3(a) of Chapter Two of the CPI (M-L) Constitution prescribes that any member of the working class, the toiling people, the peasantry, revolutionary middle class or any other revolutionary element who resides in India and has reached the age of eighteen years is eligible for membership of the Party, provided he accepts Marxism-Leninism-Mao Tse-tung Thought as the guide to action, accepts Programme and Constitution of the Party and pays regularly Party membership dues and levy as fixed by his unit according to his capacity and is ready to go to rural area for rousing peasant masses for agrarian revolution any moment when directed by the unit to do so." While Article 3(f) lays down that "members from the exploiting classes will not be allowed into the Party unless they relinquish their property at the disposal of the Party and have thoroughly integrated themselves with the

stopped operating in their own areas. Squads of one locality moved to another area of operation, where they could not be identified, to execute a programme. Even when the police were able to intercept a squad, they could not elicit much valuable information, for the squads always acted quite autonomously and independently of the party. If, however, this policy of decentralisation was of benefit for an action-oriented party like the CPI(M-L), the system proved rather fragile in the face of the party's deepening ideological crisis which almost synchronized with a heavier crackdown by the police.

masses." Article 3(g) bars "careerists, double-dealers, bad characters and enemy agents" from party membership.

Admission of the member would be on individual basis and generally through the basic unit (cell) of the party [Article (2c)] and an applicant for membership must be recommended by two Party members who know him well and provide the Party with all necessary information about him. While Article 3(a) of the CPI(M) Constitution provides for full one year's probation for any "candidate" member during which he has the duties of membership but no voting rights, Article 2(e) of the Constitution of the CPI (M-L) has laid down that "at least six months' period of work among the people for the applicants from the working class and poor peasantry, one year's record of work for applicants from middle class and middle peasant origin and two years record of work for others should be checked up before admitting one in the party. Membership fee would be 10 paisa annually. Levy can be fixed by the unit to which a member belongs after assessing the capacity of the member concerned [Article 2(b)]."

Following the letter and the spirit of the Constitution of Communist Party of China, the Constitution of the CPI (M-L) enjoins on party members duty to—

(a) Constantly study and apply Marxism-Leninism Mao-Tse-tung Thought in a living way and try to become the best disciples of Chairman Mao;
(b) Subordinate their personal interests to the interests of the people and the Party;
(c) Develop initiative;
(d) Be bold in making criticism and self-criticism;
(e) Be deft at uniting with the great majority including those who have wrongly opposed them but are sincerely correcting their mistakes.[10]

Any figure for Party membership must be treated roughly as an estimate, since everything regarding the party organisation is highly secretive. A Right CPI source which estimated an all-India membership of the CPI (M-L) in May 1969 as between 20,000 and 30,000[11] seems to be a bit inflated in view of

10. Article 4 of Chapter Two entitled "Name and Membership".
11. *Link* (a New Delhi Weekly), May 25, 1969. According to a

the highly stringent qualifications for membership prescribed in the party constitution. In West Bengal itself by the end of 1970 as many as 14,000 people were arrested of whom 4,000 were suspected "Naxalites." But all these 4,000 persons were not regular cardholding members of the CPI (M-L).[12] What, however, gave a sudden spurt to the increase in the CPI (M-L) activists was the package recruitment of the so-called lumpen-proletariat under instruction from the Party chief, Charu Mazumdar who wanted to gear up the party's "annihilation programme."[13]

Social composition of the leadership:

Because of the secrecy that has all the time pervaded CPI (M-L) affairs since its formation, accurate data on the social composition of the inner leadership of the Party is almost difficult to obtain. In fact, the social composition of the CPI (M-L) Central leadership does not differ in a significant way than those of the CPI and the CPI(M). The only difference however, is that where the CPI (M-L) leadership is mainly dominated by men of the generation of Kanu Sanyal, who had been recruited after independence, the Central Committee of both the CPI and CPI(M) are still led by essentially the same set of leadership which had joined the communist movement in the 1930's and 1940's. This leadership has always been intellectuals and elitist in character, because most of the important leaders were drawn from families of relatively high education and status.

One of the main factors which led to the dislocation of the Hindu gentry from their erstwhile power and position in the first quarter of this century and drove a larger section of its members

CPI(M) official source the number of defections was estimated at 7000 throughout India.

On the other hand, there were hardly any defections from the CPI. For these estimates see *Political Organisational Report,* presented by the Central Committee to the Eighth Congress of the Communist Party of India (Marxist), Cochin, December 23-29, 1968, pp. 287-88.

12. Sankar Ghosh, *The Disinherited State*: *A Study of West Bengal* 1967-70, Calcutta, Orient Longman, 1971, pp. XIV-XV.

13. For an exhaustive account of the "annihilation programme", chalked out by Charu Mazumdar, see Charu Mazumdar, "A Few Words About Guerrilla Actions," *Liberation*, February 1970, pp. 17-23.

to embrace communism was the complete alien pattern of political development in India and particularly in Bengal's institutional life. The introduction of the mass electoral system by the British Raj in the 1920's let loose a pattern of social mobilisation,[14] which completely cut off the Indian society from its traditional moorings by upsetting the hierarchical patterns of the Bengali society and by injecting competitiveness between men of different communities and castes. It may be pointed out that at the beginning of this century the Bengali high caste Hindu gentry or the "bhadralok" constituted a social privileged and consciously superior stratum of the society, economically dependent on land rents and professional employment. They maintained considerable distance from the masses by their acceptance of high-caste prescriptions and their command of education and showed a pride in their language, their literary culture and their history. They were maintaining their clan integration through a fairly complex institutional structure that had proved remarkably ready to adopt and extend their social power and political opportunities. The basic and most rigidly maintained distinction between high and low, was the gentry's abstention from manual labour and their belief in the inferiority of manual occupation. Another interesting feature is that unlike other provinces in India there was no dichotomy in Bengal between landholder and the professional middle class : the same "bhadralok" families received rent and supplied men for government service.

14. For an illuminating analysis of the term "social mobilisation", see Karl W. Deutsch, *Social Mobilization and Political Development*, American Political Science Review, Vol. LV, No. 3 (September 1961), pp. 493-502. According to Professor Dectsch, "Social Mobilization is a name given to an overall process of change, which happens to substantial parts of the population in the countries which are moving from traditional to modern ways of life. It denotes a concept which brackets together a number of more specific processes of change, such as changes of residence, of occupation, of social setting, of face-to-face associates, of institutions, roles and ways of acting, of experiences and expectations, and finally of personal memories, habits and needs, including the need for new pattern of group affiliation and images of personal identity. Singly, and even more in their cumulative impact, these changes tend to influence and sometimes to transform political behaviour". He says that it tends to go togeeher in certain historical situations and stages of economic development.

The position of this social elite in Bengal, however, started declining fast during the first quarter of this century. Their ambition was to take part in the development of a system of parliamentary self-government in India, because they knew it fully well that their hopes ultimately rested in the legislative positions. In this sense they were never supposed to be a revolutionary community. The partition of Bengal in 1905 gave them opportunities; during the anti-partition agitation their numbers greatly increased and more and more they were given an active involvement. They also gained experience; moreover, though the agitation achieved its success in 1912 a profound distrust of the political objectives of the Indian government and any strategy based on British co-operation gained ground sharply. There was an outright attack on the old constitutionalist school, their technique, their secular ideals, economic deformation, frustrated ambition and injured pride that made the lower middle class a steady source of recruitment for radical political action. Terrorism was a development of this trend; it was a lower middle class phenomenon to an extent.[15]

After 1905 new opportunities came before the Bengal politicians to participate in representative institutions. The years from 1913 to 1920 gave the Hindu elite the required experience in working within the legislative system. Early in that period high expectations were raised by institutional reforms that would give greater powers to Indians for self-government (e.g., the Morley-Minto Reforms of 1909). The positive significance of the "bhadralok's" experience with the Bengal Legislative Council from 1913 to 1920 was the demonstration of their capacity to work within a parliamentary system and reinforcement of their interest in such a development. The negative significance of that experience was that the "bhadraloks" were discouraged on the one hand from committing themselves fully to the institution because of the lack of power vested in it and on the other from making the effort to establish political control with non-"bhadra-

15. For the growth of extremism in Bengal in the first quarter of this century see, James Campbell Ker, *Political Trouble in India,* 1907-1917, Calcutta: Govt. of India Press, 1917; and *Sedition Committee* 1918: *Report under Mr. Justice Rowlatt As President,* New Age Publishers (P) Ltd., Calcutta, 1973.

lok" by extending the narrow franchise and separate communal electorate.

They were completely unprepared for what happened in 1921 : the enfranchisement of a million new voters of whom the majority were rural illiterates—mostly Muslims. Their appeals for restricted franchise in order to secure competent voters and manageable electorates were disregarded. This synchronised with the transfer to the elected MLCs of first real power through appointment of responsible ministers and promise of more power in the future. Thus the years between 1913 and 1920 was the climacteric period of the Hindu elite's political career. The riot of 1918 also had its effects. It showed that the latest mass discontent could be exploited for personal and communal advantage. This gave new significance to the numerical strength of the Muslim community. Violence now became an effective instrument in the hands of the Muslims. With it a possibility of non-bhadralok influence in the legislative bodies was there. The non-bhadralok people were against the high caste Hindu dominance. It was at this stage that the leadership of the Muslim community launched a series of successful political maneuvres that brought them in virtual control of Bengal politics from the 1920s until 1947. Using their positions in the provincial government and forming coalitions after 1926 with the European and the low-caste Hindu communities, the Muslims gained unprecedented control and authority over Bengal's institutional life in 1930s and 1940s. So the introduction and operation of the parliamentary system through representative institutions became a menace to the Hindu elite instead of being an opportunity to maintain their position in a highly mobilised society. Since they failed to gain legislative majorities in the elections in the 1920s and 1930s, the Hindu gentry lost their hold over the institutional life of the Bengalees and most of them became disillusioned with electoral politics.[16]

The effect of all this was to cut the ground from under the feet of the liberal secularists who readily took to Hindu revivalism to consolidate their position. By 1923, Bengali high-caste

16. For an excellent analysis of this aspect of Bengal politics during the 1920s and 1940s, see Broomfield, J. H., *Elite Conflict in a Plural Society: Twentieth Century Bengal,* Berkeley: University of California Press, 1968, pp. 321 *et seq.*

men had formed defensive communal sabhas based ostensibly on the cult of Sakti, and as the feared legislative attack from below developed over the next decade, the organisations won increasing influence and respectability. The role of the Hindu elite was becoming gradually reactionary, though at the initial stage they wanted to play a secondary role.

But this ambivalence—heritage of liberal ideas and at the same time of their vested interests and lack of capacity to adapt themselves to the changed situation—is demonstrated in their attraction towards extremist movement, itself a lower middle class phenomenon. But this move was also unsuccessful in gaining a mass following, since the various Hindu revivalist movements only tended to create factionalism within the society and since all of them made for greater and greater exclusiveness on the part of the high castes.

While the Hindu revivalist movement and the extremist movement were proving mostly unsuccessful in the 1930s, non-conformism became more and more deep-seated among the Hindu "Bhadralok", who were found readily available for conversion into Marxism. Marxism appealed to the High-caste Bengalis because "it rejected electoral politics, which had led to the loss of bhadralok dominance; because it denigrated orthodox Hindu ideas and behaviour at a time when Bengalis were becoming disenchanted with Hindu revivalism because it promised the overthrow of the hated British and anglicized ruling groups, who were guided by their ideas (and who controlled Calcutta); because it promised a modern society in which the intellectual would have a more prominent position; because it legitimized the terrorist and conspiratorial activities on which the bhadralok had staked their reputations for three decades"[17]

It should be noted that the recruits for the Indian Communist movement were mostly drawn from different segments of the Bengali society. First, as a result of a successful recruitment drive a large number of the former extremists[18] (as many

17. Franda, Marcus F., *Radical Politics in West Bengal,* The M.I.T. Press, 1971, p. 12.

18. For an exhaustive account of the Indian Communists' attitude towards the extremists, see *India and Communism,* a confidential report compiled by H. Williamson, Director, Intelligence Bureau, Government of India, Simla, Government of India Press, 1935, pp.194; 237-238.

as one thousand), who had been active in Bengal politics since 1905, joined the Communist Party during the "Communist Consolidation Movement"[19] in the prisons of Bengal in 1930s.

Apart from a fancy for the Marxism apocalypose another reason that may be adduced is perhaps the extremists' aversion towards the Gandhian philosophy of political struggle. To them Gandhi's "ahmisa" and "satyagraha" were meaningless.[20]

These recruits, however, were not highly educated as they had initially abandoned their education to take part in the organisation of revolutionary movements against the British. On the other hand, the intellectuals in the Indian Communist movement were recruited in Indian and European colleges and universities.

It is rather striking to note that the present Communist movement in India and in West Bengal, in particular, clearly identifies three sharply distinguishable sets of leadership in the CPI and the CPI(M),—first are those who are primarily interested in organisational work, because of their previous experience in the highly institutionalised terrorist (extremist) federations.[21] Almost all of them who had been active in the pre-split CPI's organisational front in this state opted en masse for the CPI(M) because they hoped to make it more militant and less election-oriented. Leaders like Promode Das Gupta, Ganesh Ghose, Hare Krishna Konar fall in this category; in the second group may be included those intellectual leaders of the movement most of whom are highly educated and prominent in theoretical debates in the party.[22] Leaders like Hiren Mukherjee,

19. For an account of the Communist recruitment, see Dutt, Kalpana, *Reminiscences,* Bombay: People's Publishing House, 1945, pp. 87-88.

20. For typical Bengali attitudes towards Gandhi and his politics, see Gordon, L. A., "Bengal's Gandhi: A study in Modern Indian Regionalism, Politics and Thought" in *Bengal Regional Identity,* David Kopf (ed.), East Lansing, Michigan State University Asian Studies Centre, 1969, pp. 87-130.

21. For an interesting analysis of the social basis of the Communist Party split in West Bengal, see Donald S. Zagoria, *The Social Bases of Indian Communism,* Richard Lowenthal (ed.), *Issues in the Future of Asia,* Frederick A. Praeger, New York, 1969, pp. 119-122.

22. The "Class" division in the Party was institutionalised when the Party found it necessary to send representatives to Parliament. Generally it chose well-educated candidates who were fluent in English. This inevitably led to friction between the parliamentary and the orga-

Bhowani Sen, Somnath Lahiri, Renu Chakravarti and Indrajit Gupta who constituted the intellectual core of the undivided Communist Party in West Bengal later joined the Right CPI after the official split in 1964. There is still another group of leaders whose principal interests lie in the legislative politics in the Communist movement; it includes a few prominent leaders like Jyoti Basu and Bhupesh Gupta. And it was during a few years preceding the split in 1964, the CPI leadership in West Bengal became institutionally divided into three fairly distinguishable factions which had informally existed in the party in the 1930s. The intellectual group in the party (who came to be denigrated as Rightists because of their consistent loyalty to the Central Party Organisation and the CPSU) was led by Bhowani Sen and Somnath Lahiri; the Leftists (so known in the party for their most dogged opposition to the Central leadership and the CPSU and militant support for a neo-Maoist strategy of revolution) were led by Promode Das Gupta and Harekrishna Konar and they commanded the support of the bulk of the regular party organisation,[23] and finally there subsequently emerged a third group known as "the centrists" because of their mediation efforts between the Rights and the Leftists. This group was represented by electorialists like Jyoti Basu and Bhupesh Gupta who, however, were virtually dependent on the party's organisational leadership for their successful careers in legislative politics. This group, it may be pointed out, quickly melted with the split because of its leaders' consistent lack of ideological-tactical orientation while Jyoti Basu joined the CPI(M), Bhupesh Gupta became a prominent figure in the CPI's legislative politics. And with the absorption of the centrists in either of the

nizational wings of the Party, since the latter's leaders were generally of more humble origins, less educated, and often anti-intellectual.

23. For more than a decade before the split in 1964 the leadership of the left faction was in virtual control of the state party headquarters. During the period between 1951 and 1954 Jyoti Basu was the party secretary and since he was always involved in legislative politics, he left the organizational machinery to be controlled by the staff of the party headquarter in Calcutta, headed by Promode Das Gupta. And when in 1959 Das Gupta was elected state party secretary by replacing Jyoti Basu, the whole organizational apparatus finally passed into the control of the leftists and this group has still continued to dominate the CPI(M) organization since 1964.

two Communist parties the leadership patterns that have now emerged in the two CPIs in West Bengal may be identified in the following way :

Out of the total 33 members of the West Bengal State Committee of the CPI(M) in 1969-70, as many as 24 belonged to the three highest castes in the province, viz., Brahmins, Kayasthas and Vaidyas and 31 of them had been to college for at least a year; while only 3 members had been engaged in manual labour to earn their livelihood, almost all of the rest were born in the well-off families of landlords, lawyers, doctors and teachers. On the other hand, out of the 9 members of the CPI State Secretariat in 1969-70, 8 were from upper middle class Hindu families and 1 was a wealthy Muslim. All of them are fairly educated and none of them was ever engaged in manual labour.

Compared with the social composition of the leaderships of both the CPI and CPI(M), the central leadership of the CPI(M-L) does not present any different picture. On the contrary the CPI(M-L) leaders are mostly of petty bourgeois origin and with less impressive record of work among the poor peasant and industrial workers.[24] Of the 22 members of the party's first central committee, formed after the First Party Congress in May 1969, as many as 12 were from West Bengal.[25] A screening of social composition of these 12 members shows that most of them belong to the status of petty bourgeoisie.

The following data (p. 177) would be revealing enough for a clear understanding of the twelve CPI(M-L) Central Committee leaders from West Bengal.

The table shows that of the twelve central leaders of the CPI(M-L) as many as ten represent the two high castes of the Hindu community, e.g., the Brahmins and the Kayasthas, while only two—Santosh Rana and Jangal Santhal belong to scheduled caste and tribal community respectively.

24. For biographical data of some of the more important CPI(M-L) leaders see Appendix II. For an interesting analysis of the CPI(M-L) leadership see Satindranath Chakravarti, *"A Party is Born"*, *Now*: A Political and Cultural Weekly, (Calcutta), June 6, 1969, pp. 8-10 and June 13, 1969, pp. 9-11.

25. Eleven of the twelve members are Charu Mazumdar, Kanu Sanyal, Sushital Ray Chowdhury, Jangal Santhal, Asim Chatterjee, Saroj Datta, Suniti Ghose, Sourin Bose, Santosh Rana, Mahadeb Mukherjee and Sadhan Sarkar.

TABLE No. 1

Religion and caste of the 12 CPI (M-L) leaders :

Muslims—Nil	Christians—Nil

Hindus :

(i) Brahmin—4	(iv) Mahisya—Nil
(ii) Kayastha—6	(v) Scheduled caste—1
(iii) Vaidya—Nil	(vi) Tribal—1

Total : 12

TABLE No. II

Class origin of the twelve Bengali leaders of the CPI(M-L)*

Working Class	Nil	Landlord	Nil
Agricultural labour and poor peasant	Nil	Intelligentsia	11
Rich peasant	1	Others	Not available

The foregoing analysis of class origin of the CPI(M-L) leaders from West Bengal clearly reveals that like the two other Communist parties the CPI(M-L) is also essentially an elitist organization. Although attempts were made at a later stage to gain support from the poor, the low castes, and the illiterate, every available piece of evidence would show that the Maoists in West Bengal did not succeed in bringing members of low-status groups into leadership position in the party or in securing the unquestioned backing of such groups. A Communist Party cannot pursue a correct proletarian political line without serious deviations, if its class composition is defective, if the membership from the petty bourgeois and middle class origin is preponderant and if members from the urban and rural proletarian classes do not form the predominant force in the party. In fact, it is the swamping of the Communist parties with members

*Biographical data was obtained by the author through interviews of some CPI(M-L) student leaders and newspaper clippings.

of non-proletarian origin and neglect of the special emphasis on recruitment from the proletarian and semi-proletarian classes that has always atrophied Communist movement in India. And a frank admission to this effect came a few years back from the Central Committee of the CPI(M):

> .... at the states and centre level, a good portion of the members to top and leading committees has inevitably come forth from Communists of bourgeois and petty bourgeois class origin. This is due to the class composition of our society and of our Party.... The intellectuals coming from the propertied classes have the educational and other facilities which enable them to develop the theory of socialism and are in a position to take it to the working class. Due to this, intellectuals belonging to the social status of either the bourgeoisie or the petty bourgeoisie who study and accept Marxist-Leninist theory and practice have come to occupy a dominant position in the leadership of the policy-making committees. We have failed to consciously train and promote cadre of proletarian origin to the leading committees.[26]

A Note on the Agit-prop Machinery of the CPI(M-L)

Unlike the two other Indian Communist parties the CPI(M-L) is by no means a mass organization in the sense that while the two other parties mobilise their full strength through a network of auxilliary mass organisations, the CPI(M-L) has operated strictly as an underground organization as wanted by the party chief Charu Mazumdar. He said:

> Such a revolutionary party will not be a party to fight election campaigns nor will it be based in the cities. A revolutionary party can never be an open party, nor can its main concern be to publish papers etc.; nor can it depend on the revolutionary intellectuals. The revolutionary party must depend on the workers and the poor and land-

26. *Our Tasks on Party Organisation,* a report adopted by the Central Committee of the Communist Party of India (Marxist), at its Calicut Session, October 28 to November 2, 1967 (Calcutta: CPI(M), 1967), pp. 28-29.

less peasants. Peasant struggles and secret organizations must be built up with the villages as their bases. Without this the party will be defenceless in the face of attacks of the counter-revolutionaries.[27]

With this inherent incapacity of the party to function in the open through the normal channels of political operation such as parliamentary or electoral activity, the party has mainly relied on its publications and guerrilla actions for purposes of gearing up its agit-prop programme. It may be very clearly understood that unlike the CPI and the CPI(M) the Maoists in the absence of any mass or front organizations, have never directly approached the masses through public meetings, processions or demonstrations of any kind. Every member of the CPI(M-L), therefore, is not a full-time agitator and propagandist in the technical sense of the terms.[28]

The great paucity of information prevents anything like an exhaustive treatment of the propaganda and agitation machinery of the CPI(M-L). An endeavour is being made in the following paragraphs to throw some light on the most important feature of the CPI(M-L)'s activity in respect of the CPI (M-L) press and other publications.

The CPI(M-L) Press

It should be noted that even long before the final split in the CPI(M) in May 1969 the dissident Maoist leaders in that party had been regularly bringing out a host of pamphlets and news sheets to carry on a pitched ideological struggle with-

27. Charu Mazumdar, "Undertake the Work of Building Revolutionary Party", *Liberation,* October 1968. p. 11.

28. Overstreet and Windmiller have observed that "in Communist usage the term 'propaganda' has a specialized meaning and is differentiated from 'agitation'. This distinction is, in the broadest terms, between the general and the specific. Propaganda is the dissemination of simple ideas, often in the form of......slogans, to a mass audience...... In theory, any Party member is a full-time agitator and propagandist. As an agitator, he must, through the spoken or written word, make daily contact with the masses, stimulating them to action with elementary political slogans related to immediate issues. And as a propagandist he must address a reasoned exposition of the Party's Policy to smaller, more sophisticated groups, with the aim of a fuller conversion". Gene D. Overstreet and Marshall Windmiller, *Communism in India,* pp. 446-447.

in the party.[29] During the Naxalbari peasant struggle beginning in the spring of 1967 the dissidents' attack on the CPI(M) leaders in West Bengal was spearheaded by the Antar Party Sodhanbad Birodhi Sangram Committee (for Inner-Party Anti-Revisionist Struggle) through a series of Journals like *Chinta* (Thought), *Commune, Bidroha* (Rebellion), *Santrash* (Terror), *Chatra Fouz* (Students' Army), *Dakshin Desh* (Southern country) and so on. Later on when the All India Co-ordination Committee of Revolutionaries (AICCR) was organized by the Maoists in West Bengal, a regular publishing apparatus started functioning from a press at Keshab Sen Street in North Calcutta, and subsequently this was taken over by the Central Editorial Board of the CPI(M-L).

The CPI(M-L) had published two types of official organs —an English monthly journal as a central organ and some weekly newspapers published by the provincial units of the Party in various regional languages.

The Central Party organ of the CPI(M-L) first appeared in English in 1968 under the name *Liberation* as a monthly. The journal was edited by Sushital Raychowdhury who formerly had been on the Editorial staff of the *People's Democracy* and the *Desha Hitashi,* the Central and provincial organs of the CPI(M). Subsequently, when in late 1970 a serious ideological rift developed between the Party Chairman Charu Mazumdar and Sushital Ray Chowdhury, Editor-in-Chief of the *Liberation,* the latter was removed from the Editorial Board of the journal and finally expelled from the Party. *Liberation* appeared almost monthly until the end of 1970. As a result of repeated police raids on its office at Keshab Sen Street in North Calcutta the journal's publication became clandestine and very irregular.

The weekly newspapers and journals were being published by the different provincial units of the Party in various languages— the West Bengal unit produced *Deshbrati* (weekly) and *Ghatana Prabaha* (monthly), edited, first by Sushital Raychowdhury and after his expulsion from the Party, by Saroj Datta under the

29. For a list of these inner party publications see, "On Left Deviation or Left Opportunism", Resolution of the Central Committee, Communist Party of India (Marxist), Madurai, August 18-27, 1967.

pen-name "Sasanka";[30] the Bihar Unit brought out *Janayuddha* edited by S. N. Singh and *Jana Sakthi* was published by the Andhra Pradesh Unit and edited by Nagi Reddy until his expulsion from the AICCCR in April 1969. These journals were discontinued as a result of the State Government's repression during 1970 and 1971.

The contents of the official newspapers and journals—both central and provincial, have been theoretical as well as factual. Major theoretical contributions came from Party leaders themselves. In addition, articles by foreign Communist leaders including selected essays from Marx, Lenin and Mao Tse-tung's works were published. Other features included reports on internal party developments and instructions to Party members for political actions.

Since there are no official circulation statistics of the CPI (M-L) newspapers and journals, it is not possible to give any exact figure of circulation of the Party organs—both central and provincial. Before the police raids on the Party press, the CPI (M-L) used to make use of the usual commercial channels for the distribution of its publications—ordinary road-side book stalls and newspaper hawkers in towns and cities, hawkers being given agencies with attractive commissions. Apart from this conventional device the Party used to sell its publications through different book stalls run by either party workers or sympathisers. In fact, the whole of the College Street area, the "Book Market" of Calcutta, was littered with improvised bookstalls selling party literature. In all the 16 districts of West Bengal the party had set up improvised book stalls. It was at the heart of Bolpore in Birbhum district that a bookstall under the name "Nishan" was run by the student cadres of the CPI (M-L) in 1969-70. Later on, it was demolished by police raids.

Furthermore, the CPI (M-L) made every use of its party cadres as salesmen for its literature and for this purpose special sales squads were organised. In fact it had been the

30. When in the middle of 1971 the liberation struggle in Bangla Desh against the ruling military junta of West Pakistan was raging fiercely, the CPI(M-L) took an active interest in it and published a new monthly journal in Bengali entitled "Pub Akash Lal" ("Eastern Sky is Red"). Only a few issues of this journal were brought out in 1971.

general practice within the party to judge the eligibility of the candidate members by appointing them salesmen during the probation to peddle party publications on the city streets, from door to door and at the educational institutions. And it has been found that promotion of the primary members into the regular cadre of the action squads virtually depended on their successful salesmanship.

Apart from these open publications, there is also a technique of highly confidential inner-party communications designed for distribution among provincial and district committees, not the rank and file, and this mainly consists of inner party documents containing reports on party action and ideological differences, letters of instructions written by different leaders to the party units.[31] There are other irregular types of communication media, such as circulars and memoranda. And in addition to

31. Some of the important inner party documents the existence of which has been confirmed by both the press and the police are: the Regulation of Party Organization, adopted at the First Congress of the Party in May, 1970 (Mimeographed); "The Current Party Line and a Summary of Our Experiences": Self-critical report of the Bengal-Bihar-Orissa Border Regional Committee of the CPI(M-L)—it is a critical review of the practical mistakes committed by the Party since 1969 (Mimeographed); "Comrade Charu Mazumdar Replies the Charges of Comrade Purna" (in Bengali), (Mimeographed); "Charges and counter-charges by the Bengal-Bihar-Orissa Border Regional Committee and the *Deshabrati—Liberation* Editorial Board on the liberation struggle in East Pakistan", (inner Party document I) (in Bengali, circulated by the West Bengal State Committee of the CPI(M-L) 1971 (Mimeographed). This document contains a series of charges and counter-charges levelled at each other over the questions of operational strategy and practice of the Party by Charu Mazumdar, the Party Chief, and "Khokan" (pseudonym), organizer of the Bengal-Bihar-Orissa Border Regional Committee: Exchange of Views between Comrade Ashok on behalf of the Nadia District Committee, West Bengal and Comrade Sarat of the West Bengal State Committee on the question of liberation struggle in East Pakistan", inner-party document No. 3 (in Bengali) circulated by the West Bengal State Committee of the CPI(M-L), 1971 (Mimeographed); "Comrade Sourin Basu's letter to Comrade Khokan", 1971 (typescript). This document contains Basu's suggestions on the ideological-practical problems confronting the Party over the questions of the Indian revolution and the liberation struggle in Bangladesh; and Kanu Sanyal, "Beware of those who want to defy the authority of Charu Mazumdar", circulated by the West Bengal State Committee of the CPI(M-L) 1971.

communication downward, there is in theory at least a regular system of report upward. But at the later stages of party's operation this principle of reporting was totally abandoned. Because in order to neutralise the "revisionist" influence of middle class cadre on the action squads, Charu Mazumdar ordered a complete decentralisation of the party organisation. The squads were given full freedom to plan and execute their action without any influence from the party except in cases of gross violation of the broad policy and programme. Mazumdar believed that in the given situation even an adventurist action had its use and no act of defiance should be condemned.

Like the two other older communist parties, the CPI (M-L) has not depended on the Indian postal service for the transmission of private inner-party documents etc. Such communications have been largely exchanged through a network of courier-service between the Central Committee and State units, on the one hand, and between the State and district units, on the other, through a chain of "contact post boxes" (code name for certain selected houses). It was towards the end of 1971 that the whole network was disrupted as a result of intensified police action against the party.

CPI (M-L) Finances

Little information has so far been available regarding the financial position of the CPI (M-L). It has been traditional with all the Indian Communist parties to keep sources of funds the most closely guarded secret even within the Party.[32] Though there have been persistent allegations regarding the regular flow of Peking's financial assistance for the CPI (M-L), there are no concrete evidences in this respect.[33]

32. Before the first split in Indian Communist movement in 1964 Promode Das Gupta and Jyoti Basu were the only leaders who had access to secret sources of the party funds of the West Bengal State Unit and this placed them in a position from which they could control and supervise the overall financial arrangements of the party. After the split the party funds of the CPI and the CPI(M) have been the close preserve of the Secretaries of the State units—Gopal Banerjee and Promode Das Gupta.

33. Though not a direct reference to the question of Chinese financial assistance to the CPI(M-L) was officially made by the Government of

In fact, of the three Indian Communist parties, the CPI enjoys the most sound and stable financial position, because it receives an indirect subsidy in the form of profits on the sales of books, journals and pamphlets supplied free of charges by the Soviet Union and its East European satellites. The CPI(M), on the other hand, does not receive any such subsidies from foreign Communist governments because of its formal break with both the CPSU and the CPC on the ideological level.

The sources of the CPI (M-L) finance are as official as those of the CPI and the CPI(M). These may be divided under three different heads. First, the Party constitution requires that each member pays 10 paise annually.[34] It may be pointed out that this little amount was fixed by the Party as fee just to ensure discipline and loyalty of the party members through the payment of this token membership fee. The CPI(M) constitution, on the other hand, fixes annual party membership at one rupee to be paid by January end of each year to the branch or unit Secretary by the members concerned. If he does not clear it by March end, his name shall be removed from the rolls.[35]

Another source of the CPI (M-L) finance is the levy that can be fixed from time to time upon a party member by the unit to which he belongs after assessing the capacity of the member concerned.[36] The principle and mode of fixing levies on party members, however, have not been clearly laid down in the CPI (M-L) constitution as may be found in the constitution of the CPI (M), which provides that every party member must pay a monthly levy as decided by the Central Committee. Those whose income is of annual or seasonal character have to pay their levy

India, in December 1968 the then Union Minister of State for External Affairs, Mr. B. R. Bhagat, confirmed reports that at least 1000 Naga rebels trained and financed by Chinese for purposes of guerrilla warfare attempting to infiltrate back into India. See *Amrita Bazar Patrika* (Calcutta), December 24, 1968. For reports on Peking's links with the CPI(M-L) and the Naga hostiles, see *Hindusthan Standard* (Calcutta) September 21, 1969.

34. *Constitution of the CPI(M-L)*, (adopted at the First Congress, held in May, 1970), Chapter Two, Article 2(b).

35. See Article IX(i) of the *Constitution of the Communist Party of India* (Marxist), adopted by the Eighth Congress at Cochin, December 23-29, 1968.

36. Constitution of the CPI(M-L), Chapter Two, Article 2(b).

at the beginning of the year or at the beginning of every quarter. If a member's levy dues accumulate for six months, then his name is to be removed from Party rolls.[37] The percentage of monthly income that is to be paid as levy has been fixed by the CPI(M) Central Committee in the following manner.[38]

Monthly Income		*Levy*
Below Rs. 100		$\frac{1}{4}$ per cent
Between Rs.	100-200	$\frac{1}{2}$ per cent
„ „	200-300	1 per cent
„ „	300-500	2 per cent
„ „	500-1000	5 per cent
Over	1000	10 per cent

It should be noted that the collection for the CPI (M-L) funds from the two above-mentioned sources have never been so good as to sustain an underground party like this because the bulk of the party membership has come from students and unemployed youths. Individual contributions from sympathisers, however, have constituted the major source of party funds. It is rumoured that the CPI (M-L) received large contributions from non-sympathisers and even from businessmen. It has been observed by one anonymous writer that in Calcutta itself businessmen, money-lenders and bustee landlords constituted only 12 per cent of the total number of "class enemies" annihilated by the CPI (M-L) in 1970. In contrast, in the rural areas such "class enemies" (businessmen and jotedars) liquidated were 40 per cent of the total killed. He says that this was not because of the fact that there was any shortage of vulnerable "exploiting class enemies" in Calcutta. "But it is characteristic of the basic anti-social urban guerrilla that rather than kill he prefers to collect from them 'subscriptions for party funds' in return for protection . . . What are the sources of finance for the urban guerrilla? Why should a wagon-breaker give up his lucrative

37. Article X of the *Constitution of the Communist Party of India* (Marxist).

38. *Our Tasks on Party Organization,* a resolution adopted by the Central Committee of the Communist Party of India (Marxist) at its Calicut Session, October 28-November 2, 1967, p. 66.

trade to turn a Naxalite? The fact is, protection rackets in the city and the industrial suburbs are safer and more lucrative. Unlike the Tupamaros or Marighella's guerrillas the Calcutta guerrillas do not rob banks or rich houses ; the levy on the residents of particular areas is enough for themselves and for the underground organisational setup (to which some money is indeed siphoned).[39] The author, however, has not given any proof in support of his observation. While it is true that the CPI (M-L) might have an anti-social fringe, it is also possible that to mislead the police some groups or parties resorted to 'Naxalite'-type actions for private gains.

39. "Urban Guerrillas in Calcutta", *Economic and Political Weekly* (Bombay) Vol. VI, No. 28, July 10, 1971.

For an exhaustive analysis of the CPI(M-L)—anti-social link up, see Chapter VI.

CHAPTER VI

THE CPI (M-L) IN OPERATION, 1969-1971

TACTICAL LINE FOR AGRARIAN REVOLUTION

IT HAS already been pointed out that the political resolution of the CPI (M-L), adopted in May 1969, identified the contradiction in contemporary India as "between feudalism and the masses of our peasantry". The stage of revolution was that of people's democratic revolution, "the main content of which is the agrarian revolution, the abolition of feudalism in the countryside".[1] And the countryside, being the weakest link in the chain, naturally came to be the main theatre of operation of the CPI (M-L) cadres in 1970-71.

The broad strategic objective of the Communist revolutionaries in the CPI(M), who had launched the Naxalbari peasant struggle in early 1967, was to liberate the countryside by waging a protracted people's war and then, encircle the cities. Naturally, one of their principal tactical problems related to the mobilisation of the peasantry for armed struggle and creation of liberated areas. It is on record that in his "Report on the Peasant struggle in the Terai" Kanu Sanyal admitted that although initiated by the revolutionaries of the Siliguri Subdivision Peasants' Association, the Naxalbari movement was something of a mass upsurge in which spontaneity and mass initiative far outweighed the planning and discipline required of a revolutionary movement. Without proper politicization, military experience and discipline, the movement suffered reverses in the face of police repression. The very open and public nature of their declaration and preparation for armed struggle had exposed them too much before they could get sufficiently organised. It was for this reason that Sanyal suggested in his "Report" that in the next phase of struggle the revolutionaries would set up party units which would not only be fully armed but also "trained to

1. "Political Resolution of the CPI(M-L)", *Liberation,* May 1969, pp. 5-6.

maintain secrecy". Such units would propagate Mao's thought, intensify class struggle and "as guerrilla units strike and annihilate class enemies".[2]

A conference of the revolutionary peasants of the Siliguri subdivision in September 1968 reaffirmed the tactical line suggested by Sanyal—the building of party units to propagate Mao's thoughts, intensify class struggle and launch guerrilla attacks on class enemies. So far the sole concern of these units, it had been thought, was the launching of armed struggle for the seizure of political power.[3] At this stage, however, Charu Mazumdar came out with some additional suggestions about the tactical line for armed agrarian revolution. He said:

> Isolation from the broad peasant masses constitutes a most harmful political weakness on the part of the revolutionaries. This danger appears at every stage of the struggle. That is why Chairman Mao in explaining the tactics of guerrilla warfare, has said: "Divide your forces to arouse the masses, concentrate your forces to deal with the enemy". This is the first law. This process of arousing the masses is never completed. The second lesson is that guerrilla warfare is, basically, a higher stage of class struggle, and class struggle is the summation of economic and political struggles... While the comrades who are working among the peasants should continue to propagate politics, they should never belittle the necessity of formulating common slogans on economic demands. For, without this, broad sections of the peasantry cannot be drawn into the movement, nor can the backward sections of the peasants be raised to a level where they can grasp our political propaganda nor can their hatred against their class enemy be sustained. "Seize the coming crops"—is a slogan which must be propagated from this moment. Hatred must be roused against the *jotedar* class as it starves the peasants throughout the year". "Peasants should seize the next harvest" is a slogan which will draw broad sections of the peasants into the fold of the

2. For an exhaustive analysis of Sanyal's "Terai Report", see Chapter II.

3. "Resolution adopted at the Convention of Revolutionary Peasants", *Liberation,* November 1968, pp. 54-55.

movement, and our conscious political propaganda will change the nature of this peasant movement.[4]

In another article Mazumdar further elaborated on the problem of mobilising backward sections of the peasantry. While insisting on the necessity of secret political propaganda by the revolutionaries so as not to prematurely expose them to repression, he, however, pointed out that backward peasants would be late in grasping politics under this method. "And for this reason", he wrote, "it is and will be necessary to launch economic struggles against the feudal classes. For this reason it is necessary to lead movements for the seizure of crops, the form of the struggle depending on the political consciousness and organisation of the area". He further pointed out that "without widespread mass struggle of the peasants and without the participation of large sections of the masses in the movement the politics of seizure of power would take time in striking roots in the consciousness of the peasants".[5] However, as the Maoist leadership, which had already consolidated itself in the All-India Coordination Committee of the Communist Revolutionaries in early 1969, there was less and less emphasis on mass organisation and mass participation in political struggles by the party activists. On the other hand, the stress was definitely on secret party organisation and secret politicization. As the party was to operate as an underground organisation, the line of launching mass struggle for economic demands did not quite fit in with the tactics of secret politicization by the party units.

This shift in the CPI(M-L) tactical line for the armed agrarian revolution became rather pronounced in mid-1969 shortly after the formation of the second United Front Government following its overwhelming victory in the mid-term poll held in February 1969.

It may be worth remembering here that the life of the first UF regime in West Bengal was cut short as a result of internal quibblings among its partners arising out of the law and order problems. Trouble was created by the Naxalbari peasant up-

4. Charu Mazumdar, "To My Comrades", *Deshabrati,* August 1, 1968, reprinted in *Liberation,* October 1968, pp. 14-15.

5. Charu Mazumdar, "Develop Peasants' Class Struggle Through Class Analysis, Investigation and Study", *Deshabrati,* October 17, 1968, reprinted in *Liberation,* November 1968, pp. 17-20.

rising and then, a reign of terror was unleashed by the Marxists in the name of labour dispute through *gherao* and coercion. In fact, this view was unequivocally expressed by the then Chief Minister Mr Ajoy Mukherjee in a statement prepared for publication in newspaper in the event of his resignation as Chief Minister on 2 October 1967.[6] He said : "A reign of terror is being created all around through coercion, force, assault and looting in the name of people's committees. A planned attempt is being made (by the left Communists) to make the administration and the police lose confidence and become inactive so that the anti-social activities of these parties may continue as unhindered as possible....Attempts are being made to bring about a much greater catastrophe. The left Communists are pro-China. They want to make a violent revolution with the help of China. Brisk preparations are going on for this....In the left Communist Party an *ultra-left* faction has come up. The Communists are singing full-throated hullelujah to China which attacked India....On the soil of West Bengal Bengali boys and girls are shouting slogans in Chinese language like 'Red Salute to Mao Tse-tung' and 'Red Salute to Red China'. There are six or seven thousand or even more ultras in the left Communist Party alone...."

It was at the height of the tension within the U.F. that the Government was dislodged by the Governor, Mr Dharam Vira on November 21, 1967. At the same time the P.D.F. Ministry under P. C. Ghosh's leadership was sworn in. But amidst a high drama of defection and counter-defection President's rule was imposed on the State exactly a year after the fourth general elections.

The mid-term poll which was held in February 1969 had at least two major surprises in store—one for the State Congress and the other for the CPI(M). While the Congress strength was reduced to a paltry 55 seats from 127 bagged in 1967 elections, the CPI(M) sprang up as the single largest party in West Bengal Assembly with 89 seats as against 43 of the 1967 elections.

With an overwhelming majority of 218 seats out of a total of 280 in the State Assembly the United Front Ministry was installed for the second time in West Bengal.

6. This statement was not published in view of the fact that Mr Mukherjee changed his decision to resign at the last moment.

With the swearing in of the UF Ministry the Maoist revolutionaries set about evolving their new strategy of action which was largely influenced by their attitude towards the CPI(M). It has already been pointed out that contesting only about 100 seats the CPI(M) emerged as the largest party in the Assembly with 83 MLAs, including three independents sponsored by it, and as such it turned out to be the single biggest partner of the UF. And this measure of the CPI(M) electoral success came as a consternation to the Maoist Cadres in West Bengal in particular. Despite the pre-election promise of the UF to release all political prisoners connected with the Naxalbari peasant uprising, the Naxalites had the apprehension that if the CPI(M) could again manage to come to power either directly or through a United Front then the extremists would have to face with even fierce repression than what had earlier been unleashed by the first United Front Government (with the CPI(M) leader, Jyoti Basu as the Home Minister) in order to quell the Naxalbari peasant uprising in 1967.

Anticipating, perhaps, this sort of political development in West Bengal after the 1969 mid-term poll, Charu Mazumdar had raised the slogan of election boycott in December 1968, just three months before the mid-term poll. He wrote that today the Marxist-Leninist revolutionaries could not go in for the parliamentary democratic process. This was true for the colonial and semi-colonial countries as well. In this new era of world revolution the main task of the Marxist-Leninists was to establish rural bases and to build upon a firm foundation the unity of workers, peasants, and all other toiling people through armed struggle. So the slogans like "boycott elections" and "establish rural bases" and "create areas of armed struggle" remained valid for the entire era.[7]

Following Mazumdar's directive the Naxalite activists immediately started operating in the areas known as the strongholds of the CPI(M) in order to campaign more against the CPI(M) election candidates than to incite people to boycott election. They intensified their anti-CPI(M) campaigns especially in Baranagore, the regular constituency of Jyoti Basu, and Kalna in Burdwan district from where Hare Krishna Konar was con-

7. Charu Mazumdar, "Boycott Election--International Significance of the slogan", *Liberation*, December 1968.

testing. But this did not impress the electorate at all as both Basu and Konar won by even bigger margin in the mid-term poll. And when the second United Front Government was sworn in with Jyoti Basu as the Minister-in-Charge of Home (Police) and General Administration, the Naxalites in West Bengal grew violently hostile towards the CPI(M), and this marked the beginning of a series of clashes between the supporters of the two groups. In the face of intense police repression the Naxalites quickly moved into the countryside and started building underground organisations there.

Another factor which lured the CPI(M-L) cadres to go in for underground guerrilla activities in the villages was the situation arising out of the policy of land-grabbing adopted by the CPI(M) Land Revenue Minister, Hare Krishna Konar. It may be noted that as the principal organiser of his party's peasant front, Konar became an excellent link between the department he headed and his party's peasant organisation. And it was under his initiative that the policy of recovery and distribution of benami land and Khas land was adopted by the United Front Government. Whenever land in excess of the permissible ceiling could be detected the owner was served with notice by the land and land revenue department to transfer the land to the Government. But long before the completion of this formality the peasants under the leadership of the CPI(M)'s peasant front forcibly took away the land and distributed among themselves. In this way the CPI(M) Krishak Sabha gained considerably in strength during Konar's two terms as Land and Land Revenue Minister.

Soon, however, the other UF partners became alive to this danger of growing CPI(M) strength in the countryside and they also started vigorously to grab land and settle their own peasant followers on it. As a result, serious clashes among the UF constituents took place over this peasant movement for recovery of land. At this stage, the CPI(M-L) cadres who had been mainly concentrating their attention in and around Calcutta immediately took advantage of this chaotic situation to spread fast into the countryside in order to create bases among the disgruntled and somewhat confused (because of the erratic UF peasant movement) poor peasants and agricultural labourers. And Charu Mazumdar was prompt enough to read into the significance of this strategic shift of his party activists and came out with a detailed theorisation, though somewhat improvised, of underground peasant guerrilla warfare in the countryside.

Defending guerrilla warfare as against mass organisation as the sole form of struggle for the Indian People's Democratic revolution, Charu Mazumdar declared that (a) mass organisation could not make the agrarian revolution, only an underground party could do it; (b) since there were different classes within the peasantry, namely, the poor and landless peasant, the middle peasant and the rich peasant, an organisation of the entire peasantry would be dominated by the rich and middle peasants; (c) such an attempt would strengthen the tendency to carry on open movements through open mass organisations inevitably turning into another set of leaders of revisionist mass organisations; (c) the leadership of the poor and the landless peasants over the peasant movement could be established only through underground party organisations among the peasant masses; and (e) guerrilla warfare was the only tactic for carrying on peasants' revolutionary struggle, and the poor and landless peasants could establish their leadership over the peasant masses only by conducting guerrilla warfare.[8]

Thus abandoning the earlier tactical line of drawing the backward sections of the peasantry into armed struggle by mobilising them first on sundry economic demands, Mazumdar wrote:

> Obviously, the peasantry as a whole does not participate in this guerrilla warfare. What happens is that the advanced class-conscious section of the peasant masses starts the guerrilla war. For this reason, guerrilla war, at its initial stages, may appear as a struggle of only a handful of people.

At the same time, refuting the charge of Parimal Das Gupta, Mazumdar's one time colleague and subsequent detractor, that he had introduced *Cheism* in the party, Majumdar observed.

> . . . . this kind of guerrilla war has nothing in common with what is advocated by Che Guevara—the guerrilla war which is waged by the petty-bourgeois intelligentsia without the peasant masses. The guerrilla war that we speak of, on the other hand, is initiated by the class-conscious elements of the poor and landless peasants and can be led and carried on

8. Charu Mazumdar, "On Some Current Political and Organisational Problems", *Liberation,* July 1969, pp. 14-15

> only with the active cooperation of the poor and landless peasant masses.
>
> This kind of guerrilla war has nothing in common with the kind advocated by Che Guevara for the further reason that this kind of guerrilla war is launched not by relying on arms and weapons—so characteristic of a Che-type war, but is launched without arms and by relying confidently on the cooperation of the masses . . . .

While committing the party fully to guerrilla warfare as the sole form of revolutionary struggle, Charu Mazumdar decried the tendency to organise struggles for economic demands of the peasants as pure economism—"a concrete manifestation of revisionism". He wrote:

> Economism in the peasant movement expresses itself in the form of rejecting the necessity of waging guerrilla warfare, thus concentrating the attention of the peasants on the question of seizing land and crops. Such economic ideas place open struggle above everything else, discourage any thought of building secret organisations or maintaining secrecy, strengthen the tendency towards spontaneity and belittle the role and importance of conscious leadership.[9]

Mazumdar further clarified his stand to explain that mass struggle for economic gains would follow guerrilla action, not precede or accompany it.

In December 1969 Charu Mazumdar made the following observations regarding the tactical line of his party:

> First, the People's Democratic revolution could win victory only through armed struggle, that is, through people's war;
>
> Second, the village was the centre and the peasants were the main force of this people's war;
>
> Third, the people's war could be victorious only under the guidance of Mao Tse-tung's thought as the only weapon both for its theory and practice.[10]

At the same time he put forth some simplistic solutions re-

9. Charu Mazumdar, "Fight Against the Concrete Manifestations of Revisionism", *Liberation,* September 1969, p. 12.

10. Charu Mazumdar, "March Forward By Summing Up the Experience of the Peasant Revolutionary Struggle in India", *Ibid.,* December 1969, p.

garding the basic problem of the operational strategy of guerrilla warfare to be waged by the Indian peasantry.

On the question as to where to start guerrilla warfare Mazumdar wrote:

> The wrong conceptions regarding this question were that guerrilla warfare can be started only in mountainous areas or where there is jungle, and Chairman has taught us that people's war can be waged only relying on the masses; therefore, guerrilla warfare can be started wherever there are peasants. By waging guerrilla warfare in the plains the revolutionary peasants of India have demonstrated that it is possible to wage guerrilla warfare in the plains also, that it is possible to wage it wherever there are peasant masses.[11]

Secondly, as to the question whether it was possible to wage guerrila warfare without mass movement and mass organisation, Mazumdar held that neither of them was indispensable, because they would expose the revolutionary workers before the enemy. So what he suggested was the spreading and propagation of revolutionary politics through secret party organisations.[12]

Then, the third question was: On whom to rely for waging guerrilla warfare? Mazumdar held that the development and expansion of guerrilla warfare was possible only by relying on the poor and landless peasants and no other class, because "their class hatred helps them to remain steadfast in their struggle and they alone can bring about a high tide of revolution by uniting the whole of the peasantry". Wherever the petty-bourgeois intellectuals tried to lead the struggle, guerrilla warfare had failed to develop and it could not be linked up with class struggle.[13]

To the fourth question as to how to start guerrilla warfare, Mazumdar had the following answer:

> . . . . guerrilla warfare can be started only by liquidating the feudal classes in the countryside. And this campaign for the annihilation of the class enemy can be carried out only by inspiring the poor and landless peasants with the politics of establishing the political power of the peasants in the countryside by destroying the domination of the feudal classes. *That is why the annihilation of class enemy is the*

11. *Ibid.,* p. 10.
12. *Ibid.,* pp. 10-11.
13. *Ibid.,* pp. 11-12.

> *higher form of class struggle while the act of annihilating class enemies through guerrilla action is the primary stage of the guerrilla struggle.*[14]

In this analysis the emphasis is clearly on spontaneity and automatism, with a distinct tendency to replace the usual forces of class struggle with "Khatam" or individual assassination. And Mazumdar wanted the 1970's be made the decade of liberation by carrying out the battle of annihilation which was to be the sole form of class struggle.[15] He wrote :

> Select a particular area, a particular unit and a particular squad and then proceed to carry out successfully the battle of annihilation. Then select another unit, another squad, and carry on as before. In this way concentrate your work in one third of your selected area and after our forces are consolidated in that part of the area spread the struggle to the remaining parts. This is the method pointed out by Chairman Mao, and this is the only correct method.

The operational strategy of this annihilation programme of the party was clearly laid down by Mazumdar in "A Few Words About Guerrilla Actions",[16] and may be summarised as follows:

1. *How to Form Guerrilla Units*

Mazumdar prescribed complete secrecy in the formation of a guerrilla unit and a wholly conspiratorial approach to its action. The conspiracy should be between individuals and on a "person-to-person" basis. He said that "the intellectual comrade must take the initiative in this respect as far as possible. He should approach the poor peasant who, in his opinion, has the most revolutionary potentiality, and whisper in his ears; 'Don't you think it a good thing to finish off such and such a jotedar?' This is how the guerrillas have to be recruited singly and in secret, and organised into a unit".

But before the formation of guerrilla action squads, according to Mazumdar, some revolutionary propaganda work for the

14. *Ibid.,* p. 13, emphasis added.

15. Charu Mazumdar, "Make the 1970's the Decade of Liberation", *Liberation,* February 1970, pp. 4-10.

16. *Liberation,* February 1970, pp. 17-23. The "murder manual", like Carlos Marighella's "Minimanual" was published in handy pocket books for the constant use by the cadres of the guerrilla action squads.

seizure of political power should be done among the poor and landless peasant masses. He declared:

> The point that political power has to be seized by armed force must be made very clear, that is, the peasants must be roused, and emphasis must be put on liberating their own villages. The peasants have to seize power locally in their respective areas so that the peasant masses themselves, instead of the feudal exploiters, become the sole authority in settling all their local affairs. This is precisely why we must begin by eliminating the local class enemies. Once an area is liberated from the clutches of class enemies (some are annihilated while some others flee) the repressive state machinery is deprived of its eyes and ears making it impossible for the police to know who is a guerrilla and who is not. . . ."

As regards the organisation of the guerrilla units, Mazumdar held that in order to keep these units well-knit and mobile each unit should not, in general, have more than seven members. And the units must maintain utmost secrecy about (a) the names of the guerrillas; (b) the identity of the particular class enemy to be liquidated; and (c) the date and time of the guerrilla action.

2. *Leader*

A commander should be chosen out of the seven members of each guerrilla action squad.

3. *Investigation*

Mazumdar held that in determining a target that is, a particular class enemy the guerrillas should not be guided by subjective thinking, but by the will of the majority of the people. For this a good deal of investigation work had to be undertaken. Once the target was determined the guerrillas must keep watch over the movements of the class enemy in a thoroughgoing manner so that they could fix the best possible time and place for the attack. This part of the investigation should be done especially by the commander of the unit.

4. *Shelter*

"The most important job before the guerrilla action" according to Charu Mazumdar, "is to make arrangements for safe shelters. This job must be done with utmost care and attention. Every guerrilla must himself arrange for his own shelter in the house of a person he relies upon most. None else should do it for him".

5. *Weapons*

Mazumdar specifically instructed the guerrillas not to use fire-arms during their actions. He insisted that they should wholly rely on choppers, spears, javelins, sickles and such other traditional weapons. The guerrillas should never give unnecessary importance to fire-arms, because, he said, "that might encourage us to put our reliance not on the people, but on weapons, which is dangerous".

6. *Planning*

The petty-bourgeois intellectual should sit together with the guerrilla unit and basing himself on the findings of the investigation, proceed to work out a plan of the attack, including the lines of retreat, and where and when to meet again.

7. *Attack*

Elucidating how a murder plan was to be executed, Mazumdar said:

> The guerrillas should come from different directions pretending, so far as possible, to be innocent persons and gather at a previously appointed place, wait for the enemy and when the opportune moment comes, spring at the enemy and kill him.

He held that since the first attack was of utmost importance, it was better to make several attempts than to make an impatient or hasty attempt and fail. The rich peasant cadre should be removed from the action squad before the first attack and if possible, the middle peasant and petty-bourgeois cadre should also be removed. And at a stage when guerrilla actions would become more frequent, the battlecry would be: *"He who has not dipped his hand in the blood of class enemies can hardly be called a Communist"*.

8. *Dispersal*

After an attack was made the guerrillas should be ordered to disperse and go to their respective shelters. Everything that might serve as a clue must be destroyed.

9. *Political work*

The stage after the annihilation of the class enemy was an important one, because political work had to begin here. The masses should be aroused and their support should be enlisted on the basis of the action that had taken place. The political cadre would work their way forward, pose to be a neutral person and start a whisper campaign among the peasant masses like this: "So, that devil of a man has got killed after all, a good riddance, eh ? Can't find enough words to praise those who have done it. They have done a heroic thing, haven't they? Wish they would carry on with this business until the whole pack of those blood-suckers is finished off. Oh, how fine will be everything then ! Just think, when they are gone, all this area will belong to us, all this land, all the crops, all the riches will be ours ! Because once those scoundrels are gone, how can the police know who is tilling whose land?"

10. *Remobilisation*

At this stage when the morale of the guerrillas was higher than ever, they should be remobilised to carry out further annihilations. Such guerrilla actions would give rise to new guerrilla units and the targets of attack would spread to new areas. The process would repeat itself and the mass participation would also increase steadily. "After some offensive actions take place and the revolutionary political line of annihilating the class enemy is firmly established, the political units, through their practice and work, raise, through a whispering campaign, the broad slogan: 'Seize the crops of the class enemy'. This works like a magic in the villages and even the most backward peasant comes forward and joins the battle. Thus, the fight for the seizure of political power initiated by a few advanced sections is nourished by the tremendous initiative of the masses and mass actions, and the flames of the people's war engulf the whole of the countryside".

Guerrilla Warfare in the Countryside

(A) *Srikakulam*

The annihilation theory put forth by Charu Mazumdar was first tried by the CPI(M-L) in Srikakulam district[17] of Andhra

17. For details. See *Liberation,* July 1969.

Pradesh, which was the largest armed struggle zone of the party after the Naxalbari peasant uprising. The movement among the poor and landless Girijan peasants over an 800-square mile tract in Srikakulam district began in 1959 when the local communists started mobilising them on class demands. By 1968 the movement had acquired a fair degree of organisation and depth under the guidance of the Andhra Pradesh Coordination Committee of the Communist Revolutionaries—the Andhra Pradesh branch of the all-India Maoist organisation, the AICCCR, formed after the Naxalbari peasant struggle. But with the expulsion of the Nagi Reddy group from the AICCCR in February 1969 and subsequently, with the formation of the CPI(M-L) in May the whole movement passed into the hands of the party leaders, who hoped to develop Srikakulam into the Yenan of India. At this stage, however, armed guerrilla action against the feudal landlords remained confined to seizure of their property, crops and guns. And it was not "annihilation" by armed guerrilla action squads.

In September the Communist Party of China showed its sign of endorsement of the Srikakulam peasant struggle, led by the CPI(M-L), by quoting heavily from the latters' English Organ, *Liberation*. It observed :

> A phenomenal expansion of the red area of revolutionary armed struggle is taking place in Srikakulam and various other districts of Andhra, according to a report in the July (1969) issue of the Indian monthly, *Liberation*. Despite vicious enemy suppression campaigns, more than 300 villages have been turned into red areas. Panic-striken landlords have fled for their lives, it adds.
>
> The report says: Here no machinery of the reactionary government operates. Here no forest or revenue official of the reactionary government, no panchayat samiti (village council) man can enter. The guerrillas and members of the village self-defence squads try their best to protect the villages from police marauders. The administration is run, production is looked after and disputes are settled by the ryotanga sangram samithi—the revolutionary mass organisation of the peasants.[18]

Despite the claim of the CPI(M-L) about the emergence of

18. *Peking Review*, September 19, 1969.

"red power" in Srikakulam, the whole movement started frittering away towards the end of 1969. Because from annihilation of the class enemy by the peasants with the help of the guerrilla squads, the operations had by this time degenerated into the more terrorist attacks on individual landlords without any relation to mass movement. In November and December 1969, prominent leaders like Dr Chenganti Bhaskara Rao, Nirmala Krishnamurthy, Subharao Panigrahi, Thamada Ganapathy and Ramesh Chandra Sahu were killed in encounter with the police. In July the intensified counter-insurgency drive of the Andhra Pradesh Government resulted in the death of Vempatapu Satyanarayana and Adibhatla Kailasam, the "brain" of the Srikakulam peasant struggle and the whole movement was brought to a standstill.

With the disintegration of the "red bases" in Andhra Pradesh, the CPI(M-L) leadership started claiming that armed struggles led by the party had been sprouting all over the country. And the Peking media also supported these claims. Noting the major "successes" of the CPI (M-L) in different armed struggles in 1969, *Peking Review* wrote that in West Bengal "the peasant revolutionary armed struggle has spread from Terai region . . . in the northern part of the State to Midnapore and other coastal regions in the South". In Andhra Pradesh, "the peasant guerrillas turned 300 villages (of Srikakulam district) into red areas for launching struggle, and more than 100 guerrillas were active in an area of about 500 squars miles in the Srikakulam mountains. One hundred square miles of mountain area deep in the interior of Parvathipuram Agency came under the control of the peasant forces. The current peasant armed struggle in Andhra Pradesh has spread from the remote mountain area of Srikakulam district to more than 19 rural areas in 10 districts on the spacious plains of Telengana in the northern part of Andhra Pradesh". In Bihar, peasant masses took up arms and organised "small guerrilla squads to conduct operations at Mushahari, in Muzaffarnagar District". Similar armed struggle was also "developing unabatedly in the jungle areas of Gunupur in Koraput District, Orissa State, in areas close to Kalhimpur (Lakhimpur) in Uttar Pradesh, in Bhatinda and some other district of Punjab State and in Kerala State".[19]

19. *Peking Review*, February 13, 1970.

In late 1969 the CPC had already lent its "qualified" support to the "annihilation" line of the CPI(M-L) with an implied "directive" that the Indian Maoists should rely on the masses in annihilating class enemies:

> *Relying on the masses,* the peasant guerrillas in Bihar have been active in unleashing a struggle to wipe out enemy agents and despots, and this had greatly heightened the revolutionary fighting will of the broad masses of the peasantry.[20]

(B) *Debra-Gopiballavpur*

Another major area of the CPI(M-L)'s rural guerrilla warfare was the Debra-Gopiballavpur belt in the Midnapore District of West Bengal. After the Naxalbari peasant uprising in 1967, the movement in Debra-Gopiballavpur was the only significant armed struggle in West Bengal in 1969 and was part of a plan to link up the movements in the Gangetic plains (Bihar and West Bengal) with that of the tribal movement in Orissa and Andhra Pradesh".[21]

Of the two villages selected by the CPI(M-L) activities in Midnapore for waging guerrilla warfare Gopiballavpur has definite strategic advantages. This village is on the border of West Bengal. From Gopiballavpur, Baripada, a sub-divisional town in the Mayurbhanj district of Orissa is 12 miles towards the West, Baharagora in the Singhbhum district of Bihar is only 5 miles to the north. Sprawling over 200 square miles in between West Bengal, Bihar and Orissa, the Santhal-dominated forest area has a direct land connection with Srikakulam in Andhra Pradesh through Orissa. And finally, Gopiballavpur is linked with the rest of Midnapore only by a bridge across the river Subarnarekha. This strategic position would enable the CPI(M-L) cadre to evade the State Police by crossing the borders when pursued, and also to maintain close contact with their fellow activists engaged in similar movements in parts of Bihar and Orissa.

On the other hand, Debra, the other centre of the CPI(M-L) activities in 1969-70 in Midnapore district and far away from

20. "Indian Peasant Armed Struggle Rages like A Prairie Fire", *Peking Review,* September 19, 1969, *emphasis* added.

21. See "Armed Peasant Struggle in Debra, West Bengal—A Report by the Debra Thana Committee, CPI(M-L)", *Liberation,* December, 1969, pp. 62-82.

Gopiballavpur, was chosen as a base of armed struggle perhaps because of the fact that all the CPI(M) leaders of the local unit had come out of the party after the Naxalbari incidents and subsequently joined the CPI(M-L) en bloc. Dangerously open to the forces of law and order, quite close to the railway station and lying parallel to the Calcutta-Bombay National Highway, Debra and about 150 villages under Debra police station were apparently unsuitable for any large-scale guerrilla action. Of course, according to the CPI(M-L) leaders, "integration" of the CPI(M-L) cadre with the poor peasant masses had reached such a stage as the people themselves would ably substitute hills and jungles to protect the guerrilla fighters who could move among the peasants "like fish in water".[22]

Responding to the call of the CPI(M-L) leadership to go to the countryside, integrate themselves with the peasant masses and politicise the poor and landless peasants, many students of Calcutta colleges, some with brilliant academic careers, had given up study to lead the life of political fugitives in remote villages, seeking to indoctrinate the peasants and channel their craving for land into a struggle to grasp political power.

But in Debra-Gopiballavpur, according to the self-critical report of the Bengal-Bihar-Orissa Border Regional Committee of the CPI(M-L) published in *Deshabrati* on April 23, 1970, the party cadre had started with a somewhat nebulous idea of a Naxalbari-type peasant uprising and they had hoped that peasants' guerrilla squads would spontaneously emerge out of armed struggles for the seizure of crops. In practice, however, they could not adopt any specific programme beyond propagation of the politics of seizure of power through armed struggle. On the other hand, by resorting to pure economism and public demonstrations at places they simply exposed the organisation and faced police repression.

"Soon the movement struck as if trapped in quicksand", and a sense of failure and mutual bitterness held sway over the party cadre until the Committee seized on the inspiration provided by the annihilation line, "the great line we had been groping after for one and a half years—the line given us by our beloved leader

22. See Kalyan Chaudhury, "Focus on Midnapore", *Frontier* (Calcutta Weekly), December 6, 1969.

and respected comrade, Charu Mazumdar, of launching guerrilla war by annihilating the class enemy". On August 21, 1969, the Bengal-Bihar-Orissa Border Regional Committee of the CPI(M-L) met at Soormuhi and decided upon launching an annihilation campaign against class enemies. The Debra-Gopiballavpur movement, it was observed by the Committee, would be tactically different from the one which had convulsed Naxalbari in 1967. Trouble had started at Naxalbari with the occupation of land under the leadership of the local Kisan Samiti (Peasants' Association). In Midnapore, however, occupation of land was to be of secondary importance to the party. The main aim of the guerrilla squads was to organise lightning armed raids on the houses of jotedars and money-lenders and they would be killed wherever possible. Their stocks of foodgrains would be distributed among the poor and landless peasants in the area of operation.

This departure from the tactics followed in Naxalbari was deliberate. The movement in Midnapore, to go by *the Report of the Border Regional Committee,*[23] was to represent a higher stage of struggle, that is guerrilla warfare. It further held that along with the movement the work of annihilating the class enemy in the countryside, confiscating his property and establishing peasants' political power would begin.

Once the class enemy had been liquidated, the areas could easily be turned into guerrilla bases. "So no guns", declared the Border Committee Report, "no forests or hills, nor the mechanical slogan of correct investigation; our only task is to inspire the poor and landless peasants with the Chairman's thought".[24]

The shift towards individual terrorism was made in late September and then it was formalised as a strategy within a short time. Significantly, the first murders were committed in an area which was "a clean slate" as far as any record of mass action was concerned. The groups in Debra and Baharagora, with some record of mass work, dragged their feet longer, the Debra unit promising to "spread the prairie fire" if only Gopiballavpur undertook to light the spark ! The Border Report sharply criticised the Debra unit's spirit of legalism and open mass activity and shrinking from the tactics of *Khatam*.

23. "Report of the Bengal-Bihar-Orissa Border Regional Committee", *Deshabrati,* April 23, 1970.

24. *Ibid.*

According to the Border Committee Report, although the first few actions against the class enemies did not succeed, they opened the floodgates of peasant initiative, which would not have been possible through mere "militant economism". In a mood of elation the Report declared:

> As the annihilation campaign proceeds, the peasants' political consciousness steadily rises. We learn to see the programme of annihilating the class enemy as a struggle to develop the new man ....[25]

After two months of guerrilla offensive against "class enemies" in November, thousands of peasants, it was claimed, rose up in arms. Under the leadership of the party armed peasants seized all the crops of oppressive jotedars and those of enemy agents. Many jotedars fled the area; others who stayed on, came to terms with the party. The peasants set up people's courts to try the oppressers. They secured the return of all their property from the money-lenders.

The United Front Government in West Bengal had ignored the CPI(M-L) activities in Midnapore in the beginning. The CPI(M) Home Minister, Jyoti Basu characterised the CPI (M-L) cadre as "half political, half anti-social" people whose strength was being blown up out of all proportions by the bourgeois newspapers.[26] It may be noted that before the election in 1969 the United Front had pledged itself not to use the police force for curbing "democratic movements", nor to apply the Preventive Detention Act against political workers. One of the first decisions of the Cabinet after the election was to release all political prisoners and withdraw all cases started in connection with "democratic movements". In accordance with this decision, all persons arrested in connection with the Naxalbari movement, including those who had been convicted, had been released.

The UF government however, was soon compelled to revise its attitude, as the CPI (M-L) consolidated its position in Debra-Gopiballavpur area, where the writ of the Government had practically ceased to run in a tribal belt of about 200 square miles by late 1969. The police force was considerably strengthened and about 100 people suspected of being CPI (M-L)

25. *Ibid.*

26. See Sankar Ghosh, "The Naxalite Struggle in West Bengal" *South Asian Review* (London), January 1971, p. 101.

activists were arrested. But, as the Border Report declared, "after the taste of liberation they had, any amount of repression would not be able to rob the peasants of their dream of bright days of liberation in future". Faced with the "encirclement and suppression" campaign by the police, the guerrilla squads dispersed over a wider area and carried on their annihilation campaign simultaneously with political propaganda. Finally, however, when the contingents of the Eastern Frontier Rifles and the Central Reserve Police zeroed in and conducted joint mopping up operation in the whole area, the movement quickly petered out. And although the CPI (M-L) cadre tried to create afresh "red bases" in the southern parts of the 24-Parganas district, in West Dinajpur, Purulia and subsequently in Birbhum, all the flames of the Maoist peasant insurrections by and large flickered out in the face of severe police and military action. The collapse of the Debra-Gopiballavpur movement marked the climacteric point in the CPI (M-L)'s armed agrarian revolution. In August, Charu Mazumdar himself made an oblique admission of the retreat of guerrilla warfare in the countryside : "The inexorable laws of history cover temporary setbacks, which will make it seem as if the tide of struggle is running out".[27] This retreat was mainly because of mistakes committed by both the leadership and the inexperienced cadres, who carried some unreal picture of the revolution in their minds and did not know how to discard the wrong notions. The reckless application of the "annihilation" line for liquidating the class enemies did not lead to the creation of "liberated areas" because killing of landlords and other "bad" elements in the villages was not actually destroying a system. On the other hand, the new line invited reprisals and "white terror" which the organisation was not strong enough to withstand, and it was admitted in the Border Committee Report .

> The police encirclement was responsible for our guerrilla squads' absolute loss of initiative. Our aggressive tactics of launching offensives steadily degenerated into an escapist mood of passive defence.[28]

27. *Deshabrati*, August 15, 1970.

28. After Debra-Gopiballavpur the CPI(M-L) tried to develop a "Red Zone" in Birbhum in April-July 1971 under the leadership of Asim Chatterjee, who hailed from that district. The Naxalite activities were

Meanwhile, Charu Mazumdar had indicated the only possible way out of the morass of frustration: intensification of terrorism to stiffen the morale and greater mobility—"leaving a place quickly" as the Border Committee Report puts it—to escape the consequences. In fact, the revolutionaries made a habit of "leaving a place quickly" as soon as a murder was committed. Full of admiration for their own "mobility", the "heroes" were rather casual about the "white terror" the local people had to face. The real limitations of the movement were reflected in the stories of disillusioned villagers handing the CPI (M-L) guerrillas over to the police. Thus the mass line of the CPI (M-L) became literally a line of retreat from the masses. It was a retreat to the sound of phrases that glorified isolated acts of terrorism, and enhanced the moral value of murder for the bewildered young men who had to practice it, as it was declared by the party that annihilation or *Khatam* was a means to solve all social problems and fulfil all political tasks. The Political organisational Report of the CPI (M-L)'s Foundation Congress held in May 1970, published under the appropriate title "We Will Solve All Our Problems Through Class Struggle, That Is Annihilation" made the point that "annihilation was the key to the social revolution". It said:

> The battle of annihilation .... removes from the minds of the people poisonous weeds of self-interest, clan interest, localism, casteism, religious superstitions, etc..... Thus the battle of annihilation can bring the East Wind of the splendour and glory of Man .... The battle of annihilation had linked together our two sacred tasks—the task

simultaneously initiated at Bolpur, Dubrajpur, Rampurhat and Suri with the annihilation of "class enemies" and gun-snatching at a large scale. As many as 159 arms were taken away from policemen and private citizens upto the middle of 1971. The CPI(M-L) movement in Birbhum, however petered out in the face of intensive combing operations of military and the Central Reserve Police. It was admitted by the CPI(M-L) itself that the movement had to beat up a retreat because the activists paid too much of attention to the adventurist acts of gun-snatching and not to the organisation of base areas. As a result, they could not withstand the 'encirclement and suppression' by the military. See "A Review of Armed Struggle in Birbhum". Report of the West Bengal-Bihar Border Regional Committee of the CPI(M-L).

Liberation, July 1971—January 1972.

of liberating our country and the people, and the internationalist task of ending imperialism and imperialist war.[29]

The annihilation programme, however, did not finally solve the problem of the CPI (M-L)'s action strategy. In fact, it created a series of problems, ultimately leading to the total disintegration of the party itself.

The CPI (M-L)'s Urban Guerrilla Movement

As it has been already pointed out, the Communist Party of India (Marxist-Leninist) claimed itself to be the only "genuine" Communist Party in India, based on Mao Tse-tung's thought. And it was, therefore, natural that in the scale of strategic priorities liberation of countryside would come first. But the major emphasis of the CPI (M-L) on organising the landless and poor peasants as a "rural-based party" and on using the liberated countryside to encircle and finally capture the cities led the party to the point of neglecting the work in the cities—among the working class, petty-bourgeoisie and students and youths.

It may be remembered that during the Naxalbari peasant uprising and immediately after it in early 1967 the Maoist revolutionaries in the CPI(M) had no definite tactical line as to how best the Indian revolution could be organised. This nebulous political thinking was duly reflected in the declaration of the

29. *Liberation*, May-July 1970, p. 24.

It may be noted that urban guerrillas all over the world share an unflinching faith in violence (including annihilation) not only as a means of bringing about quick social change, but also as a "cathartic" force as it can create true revolutionaries by liberating the personality from all sorts of inhibitions. For example, Frantz Fanon describes violence as "the cleansing force". (Frantz Fanon, *The Wretched of the Earth*, Penguin Edition, 1970, p. 74). Again, John Gerassi is a bit too overzealous when he speaks on violence. "The exhilaration", according to Gerassi, that comes with street-fighting is not as Establishment (i.e. adaptation-oriented) psychiatrists insist, escapism, parental rejection, narodnism, sadism etc. On the contrary, it is achieving selfhood independence, the feeling that one is a man, taking pride in oneself and one's comrades. It is just as Fanon said, "an act of growing up, not of adolescent nihilism". (John Gerassi (ed.), *Towards Revolution*, London, 1971, Vol. 2, pp. 465-466). Carlos Marighella appeared to be too sadistic as he said: "The urban guerrilla's reason for existence, the basic condition in which he acts and survives is to shoot". (Carlos Marighella, *Minimanual of the Urban Guerrilla*, Grassroots Publication, London 1970).

Maoists in November 1967, when they stated that their immediate task would be "to develop militant, revolutionary struggles of the working class and other toiling people to combat economism and to orient these struggles towards agrarian revolution".[30]

In keeping with this line the Maoist revolutionaries in the CPI(M) tried to organise students and a section of workers, (specially at the different units of the West Bengal State Electricity Board (WBSEB) under the leadership of Parimal Das Gupta, a prominent Maoist leader in West Bengal) for demonstrations in support of the Naxalbari peasant struggle. The success of the Maoists was so instant that the Calcutta University and Presidency College buildings on College Street were almost covered with posters bearing slogans like "Naxalbari Peasants Lal Salam". (Red Salute to the Naxalbari Peasants), "Naxalbarir Lal Agun Dike Dike Chhariye Dao" (Spread the Flames of Naxalbari to All Directions). And it has already been mentioned that a Maoist organisation, "Naxalbari Krishak Andolan Sahayak Samanvaya Samiti" (Co-ordination Committee for the Assistance of the Naxalbari Peasant Movement) had been functioning under the chairmanship of Promode Sen Gupta, another Maoist leader in West Bengal. The Committee organised street-corner meetings and demonstrations throughout 1967, demanding the unconditional release of those peasants who had been arrested for alleged complicity with the troubles at Naxalbari, and also for raising funds for the assistance of the Naxalbari peasants.

At this stage Charu Mazumdar set forth in greater detail the tasks of the Maoist revolutionaries in the cities. Highlighting the pivotal role of the students and youth in this respect, he observed that their lack of self-interest and spirit of dedication and courage "make them an asset for the revolution". First of all, he wanted them to integrate themselves with the peasants and propagate revolutionary politics. But "those who are unable to go to the villages at present", he instructed, "should also engage in doing propaganda work among the workers in the

30. See *Liberation,* December 1967, quoted in Abhijnan Sen, "Naxalite Tactics in Cities", *Frontier,* October 3, 1970.

cities. Their aim should be to organise democratic struggles in the cities in support of the peasant struggles in the villages".[31]

Apart from these stray instructions, however, there was as yet no clear programme of the Maoists for the cities. At the Democratic Convention of the Communist Revolutionaries in Calcutta on March 22, 1968, the operational strategy of the democratic struggles in the cities was spelt out in greater detail. Apart from waging struggles in support of the peasants, the industrial workers were instructed to build militant organisations for the defence of their own class interests. It was decided that struggles would be launched against the Preventive Detention Act, automation, retrenchment, lay-offs, lock-outs and police repression. Charu Mazumdar, however, put forth a new line by which he laid the greater stress on the agit-prop work by the students and youth in the cities. He said:

> ....the political task of the student and youth workers is to study this new and developed Marxism—the thought of Chairman Mao—and to put it into practice. He who shuns this task can never acquire any knowledge about the principles of Marxism...As Chairman Mao has said, there can be only one criterion by which we should judge whether a youth and student is a revolutionary. This criterion is whether or not he is willing to integrate himself with the broad masses of workers and peasants, does so in practice and carries on mass work".[32]

Thus understood, "the political organisation of the youth and students must necessarily be a Red Guard Organisation",[33] and dissemination of Mao Tse-tung's thoughts and propagation of armed struggle were to be their main tasks.

Despite the latest instruction from their chief theoretician, the students and youth supplemened their agit-prop work with movements for partial demands of their own and on behalf of the people in general, throughout 1968. Processions and demonstrations were organised against the tramfare rise and rise in food prices. Rationalizing this line of action in the cities, espe-

31. *Deshabrati,* November 23, 1969, p. 87.

32. Charu Mazumdar, "To the Youth and the Students", *Liberation,* April 1969.

33. *Ibid.* p. 9.

cially in Calcutta where the influence of the Maoists had been largely confined in 1967-68, the Draft Political Programme for the Revolutionary Students and Youth Movement first published in *Deshabrati* on February 20, declared:

> Revolution cannot succeed with the help of a handful of advanced elements of students and youth. But it is difficult to draw in numerous backward elements by simple political propaganda. To unite and lead this section of students and youth into joining a revolutionary movement it is necessary to wage struggle for food, employment, education and culture and direct all the discontent and anger of the youth to the path of long-term revolutionary struggle. At every stage of such struggle they would follow such tactics and carry on propaganda in such a way that there is a mass participation by students and youth and they become more active and politically conscious".[34]

It may be pointed out that before the formation of the CPI(M-L) in April 1969, the AICCCR, which had been working as a loose confederation of a spectrum of Maoist factions, did not have much control over these factions. Therefore, there was hardly any co-ordination of the activities of these groups. But as the AICCCR was moving in the direction of forming a party in 1969, a clear picture of its action pattern started emerging, and the first move towards a definite change could be noticed in the Draft Organisational Report of the CPI(M-L), circulated in April 1969, immediately after the formation of the party. The main line of argument of their Report was that if the party was to be a secret underground organisation, launching of mass or democratic struggle was ruled out. It held that "though the party should learn to utilise all possible legal opportunities for developing its revolutionary activities, it should under no circumstances function in the open". Whether front organisations should be created for this purpose was not made quite clear. It was briefly noted that the party would give priority to the kind of work by which the working class could be prepared "to assume the role of leadership of our revolution,

34. For an English rendering of this Draft Political Programme, see *Liberation,* April 1969, pp. 57-67.

rather than carry on economic and cultural activities in the cities".[35]

This quick shift from the tactic of mass organisation and mass participation to that of underground party organisation and secret politicization created sharp differences in the CPI(M-L) as a section in the party's West Bengal State unit under the leadership of Parimal Das Gupta contended that "work in the cities is being neglected".[36]

Reacting strongly to the charge, Charu Mazumdar said :

> . . . . if everyone concerns himself with building mass organisation, who is to build up the underground party organisation? Do we expect the mass organisations to organise the agrarian revolution? Certainly no one is thinking like this, and it is correct not to think like this".[37]

Further clarifying the tactical line of the party among the industrial workers, Mazumdar said :

> We must understand that the members of a trade union do not necessarily turn into Communists simply because its leader happens to be a Communist. The Party units have to shoulder a great responsibility. They must independently propagate the revolutionary politics, that is, the politics of agrarian revolution, among the working class . . . They must do so, because the proletariat will never be able to grasp the necessity of carrying out agrarian revolution by waging its struggle for economic demands. The politics of agrarian revolution must be brought to the proletariat from *without, from outside the trade union struggle.* For this, we require revolutionary cadres, equipped politically, that is, equipped with the thought of Chairman Mao. And such cadre can be brought up only through underground Party organisations".[38]

Trade unions, he observed, could serve as training schools for political education for the industrial proletariat, when there was no revolutionary situation and the bourgeoisie appeared to

35. *The Draft Organisational Report of the CPI(M-L)*, April 1969, Mimeographed.

36. For details of the charge, age Charu Mazumdar, "On Some Current Political & Organisational Problems," *Liberation*, June 1969, p. 14.

37. *Ibid.*

38. *Ibid.*, p. 17-18, italics added.

be quite strong and the proletariat considered itself very weak. "In such a situation," he said, "trade union struggle creates self-confidence among the workers and increased their confidence in struggle and they learn the tactics of fighting in the course of their struggle against the bourgeoisie. In this way, trade union struggle becomes a training school for the proletariat."

He strongly argued that in a country where the situation was revolutionary and where every struggle was fast turning into a violent clash with the State power ,trade unions were not enough to tackle such a situation. At this stage the party was the class organisation of the workers. Turning to the Indian situation, Mazumdar observed:

> . . . particularly in a country like India, where the main centre of revolution lies in the rural areas, the party is called upon to shoulder much heavier responsibility and the task of building party organisations among the proletariat becomes urgent.

This is so because the proletariat would play its leading role without the Party organisation. "So when we say", he held, 'that a revolutionary situation now prevails in India, it necessarily follows that in India, *our task to-day is to build underground revolutionary Party organisations and not mass organisations.* It is this underground Party organisation that will lead the mass struggle. We must remember what Chairman Mao has taught us: 'Never forget class struggle'. Only through such struggles can the broad masses of workers feel the necessity and inevitability of smashing the existing state apparatus and realise that an agrarian revolution is necessary in order to seize State power. Only thus can the proletarian leadership be established over the agrarian revolution".

While the CPI(M-L) was moving away from work in the urban areas under the express instruction of its General Secretary, Charu Mazumdar, a fresh directive came from him at this stage, which asked the student cadre of the party to shun union activities at the educational institutions and propagate revolutionary politics only among workers and peasants. In a signed article entitled "Party's Call to the Youth and Students" in *Deshabrati* on August 21, 1969, Mazumdar paid a glowing tribute to the revolutionary tradition of the youth of the country. He said:

"At every stage of India's struggle for national free-

> dom, the youth and students of India made enormous sacrifices, carried the call of freedom to the villages, resisted police repression, and discontinued their studies and voluntarily destroyed the prospects of building careers for themselves in order to become wholetime political workers.[39]

At the moment, he said, the task of the revolutionary students and youth was to shoulder the important responsibility of propagating revolutionary politics. But one big obstacle in the path of the students taking up wholeheartedly the cause of revolution was their fascination for union activities at educational institutions. Deprecating this tendency, he said :

> These college unions cannot solve any problem of education that confronts the students. On the other hand, the college unions fail to provide leadership to the youth and the students in their revolt against the existing education system. By encouraging a sort of economism, the student unions blunt their revolutionary edge. As a result, the union leadership, in most cases, is found to sink deep into the mire of opportunism, and careerism begins to develop among them while the temptation of staying on in leadership drags them into all kinds of opportunist alliances, and thus destroys their revolutionary morality.

Finally, Mazumdar made this clarion call to the students and youth :

> Today, the Party has only one appeal to make to our students and youth : Integrate yourself with the workers and the poor and landless peasants. Integrate ! Integrate !

In March 1970, Mazumdar called upon the students to realise the "hollowness" of the present bourgeois education system and to leave their respective institutions to work for the revolution which was "round the corner".

> Leave your schools and colleges and plunge into the revolutionary struggle.....It will give me the greatest pleasure if you plunge yourselves into the revolutionary struggle here and now instead of wasting your energy in passing examinations.[40]

39. For an English translation of the full text of Mazumdar's article, see *Liberation,* September 1969, pp. 5-7.

40. Charu Mazumdar, "A Few Words to the Revolutionary Students

The students were further instructed to go to the villages to integrate themselves with the poor peasants. Only after they had passed this admission test as revolutionaries, "could they return to the cities to integrate themselves with the workers." He declared somewhat eloquently :

> The students and youth of Bengal have a glorious tradition. So if you carry out this task of yours conscientiously, I can assure you that the PLA (People's Liberation Army) will march in the sprawling plains of Bengal by the beginning of 1971, if not in 1970.[41]

A very queer thing happened at this stage,revealing confused political thinking of the party's chief theoretician, Charu Majumdar himself. While in response to his directive, scores of students in and around Calcutta had left their schools and colleges and moved into villages to organise armed peasant guerrilla bases, he retracted his previous stand on the question of trade union work in a comprehensive document entitled "the Party's Tasks Among the Workers" published in *Deshabrati* on March 12, 1970.

Explaining the reason for the long spell of silence of the Central leadership on the tactical line regarding trade union work, Mazumdar said that unless politics had been finally grasped by the workers, the new tactics of working class could well degenerate into militant economic struggles. Since the party cadre had gathered some experience through political work the time was considered opportune for laying down the new line. This new line marked a departure from the earlier position of total rejection of trade union work. Though Mazumdar reiterated his stand that "it is not our task either to organise trade unions, or to bring them under our control, or to bother ourselves about the trade union election",[42] in the same breath he said:

> But trade unions are there and will be, mainly under revisionist leadership. Struggles would also be waged

and Youth", *Deshabrati,* March 5, 1970, reprinted in *Liberation,* March, 1970, pp. 11-12.

41. *Ibid.,* p. 91.

42. For the full English text of Mazumdar's article see *Liberation,* March 1970, pp. 5-10. Also see Charu Mazumdar, "To the Working Class" *Ibid.,* pp. 1-4.

> through trade unions, and since struggle is in the nature of the workers, he will also join in this. We can never oppose any struggle of the workers against their class enemy. Such opposition is an expression of idealist petty-bourgeois thinking. We shall not make the workers dependent on us for their struggles for economic demands or against any attack of the capitalists; we should inspire them with revolutionary politics so that they take initiative independently. We should never make the workers mere followers of our Party cadres nor jump in to lead them.

The party cadre, he said, should concentrate on building secret party units through the propagation of revolutionary politics. If such work succeeded in developing self-confidence and initiative among workers, some of them would go forward to give able leadership to the trade union struggle and also fight the revisionists there. But it should be ensured that the workers themselves did not develop revisionist tendencies.

Laying down in detail the tactical line for the working class movement Mazumdar observed:

> While we should encourage the workers in any struggle they wage, we must nonetheless, constantly explain to them that, today, the weapons like hartals and strikes have become largely blunted in dealing with the attacks of the organised capitalist class (such as lockout, lay-off, closure etc.). To-day, the struggles can no longer develop peacefully or without bloodshed. To develop, the struggles must take the forms of gherao, clash with the police and the capitalists, barricade, annihilating the class enemies and their agents etc. according to the given situation . . . The working class, through such actions, will then invent newer ways of waging struggles. The party will not invent these for workers, but will give the workers revolutionary politics, and it is they who, with the help of this politics, will themselves invent them.

The party would pay special attention to the organisation of agitations and other kinds of struggles in support of the workers if they were attacked. Mazumdar further instructed the workers not to clash with fellow workers if they raised revisionist slogans at this stage. It would help to cement the solidarity among the workers. He further instructed his party cadre to develop self-respect among the workers. If, through political propaganda, a sense of prestige could be rekindled in him, he would grow into a daring firebrand revolutionary. He would transcend the fear of losing his job and even his life. If retrenched, he would become a good party organiser in the city or would join the peasant struggle in the countryside.

It becomes clear from the foregoing analysis that by March 1970 the CPI(M-L) Central leadership had deveolped two parallel and complementary tactical lines—one for the organisation of armed peasant guerrilla bases in the countryside, and the other for organising the industrial proletariat through militant trade unionism and other violent struggles in order to join the peasant masses in the party's final bid for the encirclement and capture of cities from the liberated countryside.

Despite this strategic planning of the CPI(M-L) leadership in early 1970 for the forthcoming revolution which it had in view, Calcutta and other towns of West Bengal started witnessing scenes for which Charu Mazumdar and his other senior colleagues were not at all prepared. Between March-April 1970 and June-July 1971, Calcutta and its suburbs were in the grip of urban violence of an unprecedented proportion. At this stage, many students and youth who had moved into villages to "integrate" themselves with the poor and landless peasant masses, swarmed back into the urban centres, especially Calcutta. Despite their simmering spirit of adventurism, they could not be left long in the rural environment. Their illusion of "integration" with the peasantry popped off with a whimper when they found themselves easily spotted by the police in the countryside, or worse, when disillusioned villagers handed them over to the police. Moreover, the gory orgies of the ruthless annihilation programme sickened a large number of young student activists who had dreamt to take part in a mission of liberation and not assassination.[43]

43. Again, the practical difficulties attending such a course of action were enormous. Very revealing is the serio-comic experience of the Presidency College "Red Guards" who went to a village and talked to a group of people about seizure of power, only to find them still "somewhat influenced by revisionist politics of parliamentarism" (*Liberation*, April 1970, p. 30). Then they asked a perfect stranger to kill a jotedar whom he appeared to hate, but "owing to his insufficient clarity about

Since the party had no programme of urban guerrilla action except agit-prop work in the cities, the students improvised their own programme, which started with destruction and desecretion of the statues and portraits of Gandhi, Rabindranath, Subhas Chandra, Vivekananda, Vidyasagar and a host of other national figures, and also bonfire of the Gandhian, American and Soviet literatures. The first significant action of the CPI(M-L) student activists in Calcutta took place on March 24, 1970, when about 50 students of Jadavpur University stormed into the Vice-Chancellor's office to protest against the arrest of a student. This was followed on April 10 by a raid on the Gandhi Study Centre and the Adult Education Centre on the Jadavpur University Campus. On all occasions, the general pattern of these raids was that a few young man would enter the institutions, throw bombs to scare away the possible resisters, ransack the office rooms, break statues and portraits of national leaders and depart after hoisting the red flag of the party.

The CPI(M-L) leadership's first reaction to the city actions of the student cadre was indifference, though it sought to justify the attack on Gandhism with a total denigration of the Mahatma as the "prime agent" of the imperialists and the comprador bourgeoisie, who betrayed the movement for national liberation by his insistence on non-violence. Justifying these actions of the students, a party theoretician wrote:

> It is no wonder that Rajani Palme Dutt, P. C. Joshi, Hiren Mukherjee, Namboodiripad and other revisionist agents of imperialism have tried hard to cover up the treachery of Gandhi and the Congress leadership and depicted them as representatives of the progressive bourgeoisie leading India's struggle for freedom till 1947. For, their purpose was the same as that of Gandhi and men of his to betray the Indian revolution. That is why, far from trying to fight and eliminate the influence of the comprador bourgeois leaders on the revolutionary masses, they strengthened it. Today, after the armed peasant struggle for the overthrow of imperialism and feudalism and for the liberation

class analysis" the man simply brought along some "rich peasants and bad elements" to harass the revolutionaries who promptly "left for the nearest railway station". *Ibid.,* p. 39.

of the country has broken out, the revolutionary youth are exposing all that fraud, not in so many words but through deeds—by trampling under foot the images of the men who were lackeys all.[44]

It should be noted that although the student activists of the CPI(M-L) did not wait for any specific directive for their rampages in Calcutta, in particular, they had drawn their inspiration from the Programme of the party itself, which denigrates the Gandhian leadership in the strongest of words in paragraph 4:

> The Indian bourgeoisie, comprador in nature, intervened to divert the Indian Liberation Struggle from the path of revolution to the path of compromise and surrender. Beginning from the Champaran peasant struggle, the Gandhian leadership representing the upper stratum of the bourgeoisie and the feudal class, with its ideology of ahimsa, satyagraha, passive resistance and Charka, sought to tailor the national movement to serve the interests of the British imperialist rule and its feudal lackeys.[45]

As the iconoclastic trend became a regular feature with the party, the student cadre bringing education to a standstill in West Bengal, Charu Mazumdar not only overlooked this apparent deviation from the accepted party line, but hailed it and rationalised it with ideological arguments. The ground for this had already been laid by him some time ago in a directive to the party's student cadres, in which he had asked them "to extend the party's area of operation beyond those registered through peasant revolution" in Debra and Gopiballavpur of the Midnapore District of West Bengal and in other States.[46] But the sudden topsy-turvey in Mazumdar's ideological orientation was glaringly revealed when he came out with a queer theorization of the "vandalism" let loose by the students in Calcutta. In a special edition of *Deshabrati,* August 15, 1970, he wrote

44. Partha Chowdhury, "Deshbandhu and an Important Phase of Indian History", *Liberation,* pp. 68-69.

45. This was also the point of view of Soviet, British and Indian Communist theoreticians roughly up to the death of Stalin. The communist reassessment of Gandhi came in the late fifties in the wake of the Sino-Soviet conflict and improved Indo-Soviet relations. The CPI(M-L) programme, therefore, did not say any thing new or original. See Appendix No. I.

46. See *Deshabrati,* April 23, 1970.

that the attacks on Gandhi and other bourgeois leaders and the hoisting of red flags in educational institutions and factories were a spontaneous movement born of the revolutionary intuition of students and youth, which the leadership had failed to point out.

The students, he said, were making "a festival of breaking statues", and in factories the workers were making a "festival of hoisting the red flag, enjoying the sense of fear among employers and helplessness among the police and military". The students and youth, according to Mazumdar, were doing the "correct thing". A revolutionary education and culture could not be created without destroying the colonial education system and the statues erected by the comprador bourgeoisie. But he took care to remind the students that the movement was neither novel nor self-sufficient. It was not a movement like the great Proletarian Cultural Revolution launched some time back by Mao Tse-tung in China. He further said that a cultural revolution need not wait till victory in the civil war had been achieved; in India the two should go together. He rationalised the city actions of the student activists as being born out of the revolutionary tide that had been created in the countryside by the annihilation programme. He said:

> The students and youth have become restless for the sake of the agrarian revolution and they are striking blows at the statues of those who had always tried to pacify the armed struggle of the peasant masses. So this struggle of the students and youth is a part of the agrarian revolution.

The peasant armed struggle in the countryside, he said, was smashing the base and in the process encouraging attacks on the bourgeois superstructure which in turn was accelerating the process of destruction of the base. In other words, Mazumdar said that the current movement was an off-shoot of the peasant struggle, though not a permanent feature of the People's Democratic revolution in India.

It should be noted that while Mazumdar whole-heartedly approved the city actions of the student cadre, he at the same time cautioned them against neglecting the primary task of integrating with the workers and peasants. He observed that "it is easy to do one or two revolutionary things but very difficult to remain a revolutionary for ever".

The urban guerrilla activity in Calcutta which had been initiated with hit-and-run raids by students on educational institutions soon took a zig-zag course, first swerving into violent inter-party clashes and finally escalating into murderous attacks on the class enemies—mainly the police and military personnel.

A major clash between the CPI(M-L) and the CPI(M) cadre early in May 1970 marked the second phase of the CPI(M-L) guerrilla activity in Calcutta. It may be pointed out that even since the foundation of the CPI(M-L) in 1969 the only party which had been actively opposed to the Maoists in West Bengal was their parent party—the CPI(M). With the proliferation of CPI(M-L)-led peasant armed struggle in different parts of the State, the CPI(M) started toying with the idea of a partial partisan struggle in its area of influence since it feared that in the emerging pattern of political alliances in the country, it might not be able to share power in any State, far less at the centre. Its young cadre were fast getting disillusioned with the parliamentary process; they were restive and only a slender line separated the extremist fringe of the party from the CPI (M-L) activists. It was in order to prevent an erosion of party ranks before the partial partisan struggle could be launched that the CPI(M) waged an undeclared war against the CPI(M-L) cadre whose response was rather ferocious.

With encounters and clashes between the two parties taking place frequently, Charu Mazumdar instructed his party cadre that they should always "be alert and retaliate against any party that dared attack the CPI (M-L)". This amounted to official clearance to hit back at the CPI(M). As to the method of attack he said that in order to break the morale of "fascist gangs" they should go in a group of 5 or 6 and "launch swift, guerrilla-style attacks from a very close quarter".[47]

In April 1970 violence erupted in a wide area under the Jadavpur police station, first involving people connected with Jadavpur University.[48] A teacher, Mr Soumen Pal, reported to be a CPI(M) supporter, was assaulted in his north Calcutta

47. Charu Mazumdar, "A Few Words to the Revolutionary Students and Youth", *Deshabrati,* March 5, 1970.

48. The facts presented here mostly represent an eye-witness account

residence. On April 29, Rajat Ghatak, a CPI(M-L) student activist was murdered near Jadavpur University. On the same night a CPI (M-L) student sympathiser was assaulted in the university campus. The next day, the University was closed sine die, violence being anticipated. The same night, however, a group of CPI(M) supporters raided the dining hall of the University S. P. T. Hostel and stabbed Manik Mahapatra, a boarder of the hostel, to death. The boy was reportedly a CPI(M-L) sympathiser, but had no direct party affiliations. After this incident an orgy of violence was let loose by the CPI (M-L) student cadres in and around Jadavpur University. It may be pointed out that Professor G. C. Sen, Vice-Chancellor of Jadavpur University, was murdered in December, 1970 at the height of the inter-party rivalry between the CPI(M) and the CPI(M-L).

Finally, the third and the most gruesome phase of the CPI (M-L) urban guerrilla activity in Calcutta was started with the extension of the annihilation line of the party to the city. This began in July 1970. Following the killing of some leading CPI(M-L) figures like Vempatapn Satyanarayana, Adibhatla Kailasam, M.F. Ramanamurthy and others in Andhra Pradesh the party had called upon the peasants to hit back by killing landlords. Finally it was at a meeting of the Calcutta District Committee of the CPI(M-L) in July that the party decided "to take revenge of the murder of the heroic comrades in Andhra and West Bengal by annihilating the police, CRP, blackmarketeers and capitalists"[49] In August, Charu Mazumdar put forward the theoretical justification for this new party line. He held that with the intensification of guerrilla war in the countryside the jotedars had started flocking into the cities and turning them into strong-holds of "white bourgeois terror" with the help of the army and police. Against this white terror, Mazumdar said the revolutionaries should let loose "Red terror" by annihilating police and military personnel, businessmen, bureaucrats and so on. And the instant result of this directive was a spate of individual killings in and around

of the happenings by the author who is employed at Jadavpur University and resides in the Jadavpur area.

49. *Deshabrati*, July 9-16, 1970.

Calcutta.[50] Murderous attacks on policemen became almost a daily occurrence; more than 400 policemen were injured and nearly a score were killed in the first six months of the President's rule in West Bengal after the fall of the second U.F. regime in March, 1970.

In Calcutta, initially, the common targets among the police force were the unarmed traffic constables. Although these constables were later armed with pistols and posted in groups, number of Naxalite attacks on policemen went on increasing fast. As a result resentment started mounting in the state police force and some violent demonstrations were organised by the policemen in Calcutta, Krishnagar and Berhampur. In all these cases the rebellious policemen had to be disarmed and confined to barracks.

It should be noted that the action of the CPI(M-L) cadres in the cities was projected more as one of supporting action for struggle in the countryside and resistance to police repression in the cities than one designed to achieve a particular strategic objective. And the fact that intelligence agents and Special Branch Police were special targets of the CPI(M-L) attack indicated perhaps an attempt to shut off the "eyes and ears" of the State power. In the final consideration it may be pointed out that the murderous attacks in the cities were not a chance extension of the Naxalites' annihilation programme, for in his "Terai Report" on the Naxalbari movement of 1967 Kanu Sanyal had clearly stated that one of the lessons of the movement was that liquidation of the police and other enemy agents was necessary for creating base areas in the countryside. These actions had been on the agenda for quite some time; perhaps they had to be delayed to prepare the party organizationally to withstand the counter-insurgency measures of the authority that it would invite on itself once attacks on police and military personnel had started.

THE CPI (M-L)—ANTI-SOCIAL LINK-UP

The annihilation programme which was the result of Mazumdar's sadistic and subjective thinking sent his party into serious convulsion. By his directive to the urban cadres who had fled

50. Pages of reports giving details of *Khatam* in various places of West Bengal appeared in *Deshabrati*, February 15, 1971. Among the victims mentioned by names were Dr Gopal Chandra Sen, Vice-Chancellor of Jadavpur University and a Congress leader from Suri, Birbhum.

the countryside after their failure in the villages, to participate in the so-called "cultural revolution" and annihilation programme, Mazumdar left them in a serious predicament, because when the CPI(M-L) student and youth activists had moved into villages, the vacuum in the cities was instantly filled in by the anti-socials and bad characters, and on their return they lost their identity and got mixed up with the local ruffians, who pretended to be Maoist to suit their own designs. In the villages the clumsy way of committing murders, the use of traditional weapons like choppers, spears, iron rods etc. and the common farming implements—all this points to the fact that the killers were not professionals. In the cities, however, many of the murders showed a finesse quite unattainable without experience and practice.

Professor Myron Weiner has very ably sketched a fine profile of the underworld elements operating in the cities of South Asian countries. He writes:

> They (the "rowdies") are unorganized or loosely organized criminal elements found in many major South Asian cities. They are the pimps, procurers and pickpockets of the city. Probably because the police are under Central and State rather than municipal control, rowdy elements have not been able to establish high-level ties with the police. The well-organized, fabulously wealthy underworld of American cities does not exist. The rowdies, or *goondas* as they are sometimes called, are loosely organised into small groups throughout the city. Available evidence from Calcutta indicates that they are not new-comers, but long-established urban residents. Often, but not always, they are unemployed except for their criminal activities. The rowdies are the major catalyst of any mass violence; they take advantage of the disturbances and excitement which always accompany any kind of mass activity to attack and loot shops. Given the level of discontent, the lack of adequate organisation and machinery to deal with such discontent, and the rootlessness of the population, a large part of which comes from rural areas, the street-dwellers of Calcutta often need only a catalyst to arouse them to violence.[51]

51. Myron Weiner, *Political Change in South Asia,* Calcutta, Firma K. L. Mukhopadhyay, 1963, pp. 73-74. For a very recent analysis of

The anti-socials in Calcutta consist of middle and lower middle class *mastans* (local ruffians) and the under-class lumpen-proletariat representing the goondas, smugglers, wagon breakers, pimps etc. The nature of their social composition will be best understood if a quick look is taken at the social symbiosis of the Calcutta metropolis. Northern and central Calcutta is less a city than an agglomeration of slums, knit together by modern roads and a transport and communication network. In the eastern suburbs of the city the population settlements are around the railways, the canal trade and the fisheries. These lower middle class and under-class habitations almost gradually merge into the bustees—the slums of which Calcutta and Howrah have as many as 3000. These slums are not like "ghettos"—there is no ring of racial tension around them. On the other hand, there is a great deal of social mobility resulting from the socio-psychological affinity between the bustee and the indigent localities. Consequently the middle class and lower middle class "mastans" cannot always be separated from the lumpen-proletariat of the slums.[52]

The agony of slum life was further intensified in recent decades by congestion. In the last forty years in the city alone the population per square mile increased from 54,528 to 79,023. This was not due mainly to the population explosion, but also to the influx of refugees after 1951. According to a review of the Government of West Bengal a total of 42,00,880 displaced persons came over to West Bengal from East Pakistan up to August 1967. Of them 12,21,474 (29.08%) alone rehabilitated themselves in the Calcutta metropolis which accommodates about 25% of West Bengal's total population with around 2% of the State area.[53] With the present housing conditions[54] in the city it could

the anti-social elements in Calcutta see "The Tentacles of the Underworld", in *West Bengal: An Analytical Study,* Bengal Chambers of Commerce and Industry, Calcutta, 1971, pp. 129-140.

52. The sociological difference between the "mastans" and the lumpen-proletariat is that while the former, though violent and lawless persons, are not social cast-aways, the latter are a wholly excommunicated lot. Again while the anti-socials are professional criminals, the "mastans" are the byproducts of socio-economic frustrations and anomie.

53. See *Economic Review*: 1967-68: Government of West Bengal, West Bengal Government Press, Alipore, Calcutta, 1968, p. 14.

54. For an analysis of housing conditions in Calcutta, see "A City in Agony" in *West Bengal: An Analytical Study, op. cit.,* pp. 70-72.

be seen that only the bustee accommodation was somewhat elastic and could stretch under pressure; in the middle class and lower middle class areas it was not possible to expand housing quickly enough. The bustees and the refugee colonies, therefore, had to bear the burnt of this explosion, thereby aggravating the city's law and order problem beyond measure.

The ravages of the anti-social elements, the ingenuity with which they operate, the infighting between different rowdy and "mastan" groups have reached such alarming proportions in recent years that law and order in the city has become a casualty. The most serious and menacing aspect of the whole situation is the unholy link-up of the anti-socials with political forces in the State. It may be pointed out that few political parties in West Bengal can honestly claim that they do not have an anti-social fringe. But what others have been doing from expediency the CPI(M-L) did as a matter of policy.

In fact Charu Mazumdar welcomed the infiltration of the anti-social elements into his party in spite of bitter opposition of some of his senior colleagues. He argued that the anti-social elements had turned against society because they were its victims, and they would be good revolutionary staff if their animus could be directed into a correct political channel.[55]

The real consideration for Mazumdar's action, it may be pointed out, was tactical. The indoctrinated hard-core of his party undoubtedly came from the middle class. The students did certainly take part in the urban guerrilla insurgency in the city and suburb. The party had also cadres from among teachers, engineers, lawyers, research scholars etc. Their activities were mainly confined to attacks on schools and colleges, destruction of libraries and laboratories, disfigurement of statues, bomb attacks on cinema houses etc. However, the fact remains that they had not been of much help in the annihilation programme. Because in spite of their ideological commitments the students could not get over their class inhibitions and join the anti-socials whole-

55. The exchange of views between Charu Mazumdar and Khokan (pseudonym) on the recruitment of the lumpen-proletariat into the party and other problems is contained in an inner-party document entitled "On Some Questions Concerning National Liberation Struggle in India", (Document No. 2), circulated in Bengali by the West Bengal State Committee of the CPI(M-L) in April 1971.

heartedly in killing people in cold blood. On the other hand, Mazumdar was fanatical about annihilation. He believed that on it depended the success of his revolution. He, therefore, wanted to replace the faint-hearted middle class cadres by people who would have no qualms about killing the "enemy".

Thus the fact is that the anti-social fringe in the CPI (M-L) framework in the megalopolis was very formidable in 1970-71. But the question is how much they were politicised. Originally some efforts had been made by party ideologues without any significant effect. This was chiefly because of the fact that they had joined the CPI(M-L) not so much to further the party cause, as to further their private designs. And as a result of the *carte blanche* for reckless terrorism granted by Mazumdar the lumpen-proletariat elements got the upper hand over the student activists of the party. Finally, intense "putschism"[56] struck roots in the party, thereby hastening the pace of liquidation of the party organisations in the cities. At the initial stages of the urban insurrectionary activities launched by the CPI(M-L), the police seemed baffled. There was a wide intelligence gap. However, the police realised that conventional methods would not pay and gradually switched to counter-insurgency methods. Small units of policemen in plain clothes (seven or eight men in each group) armed with pistols and revolvers instead of the conventional police rifles, moved into the CPI(M-L) hideouts, tracked down the guerrilla insurgents, drew them into open encounters and killed or rounded up many of them. At least 4000 people suspected to be CPI(M-L) activists were arrested by the police. Finally, with the promulgation of the PVA (Prevention of Violent Activities Act) the urban guerrillas started dispersing to the country-

56. Mao Tse-tung has identified the following points as the syndromes of putschism.

"(1) blind action regardless of subjective and objective conditions; (2) inadequate and irresolute application of the party policies in the cities, (3) slack military discipline, especially in moments of defeat; (4) acts of house-burning by some units; and (5) the practices of shooting deserters and of inflicting corporal punishment, both of which smack of putschism. In its origins, putschism is a combination of *lumpen*-proletariat and petty-bourgeois ideology". Mao Tse-tung, "On the Remnants of Putschism" in *Selected Writings*, National Book Agency (Private) Ltd., Calcutta, 1967, pp. 575-76.

side of the neighbouring states like Orissa, Bihar, Assam and Tripura.[57]

Disintegration of the CPI(M-L)

In 1971 the last flickers of the CPI(M-L)'s revolutionary action could be seen in two bids to strike terror in West Bengal. The first was the snatching of rifles from the enemy to arm the guerrillas. It had been reported that the CPI(M-L) was maturing its plan for a "long march" in some of the western districts of West Bengal to prove that it had already raised a "liberation" army. Mazumdar thought that the foundation of a liberation army could be laid with only 100 rifles and 250 country-made guns. And in order to reach the target he called upon his party cadres to snatch arms from the police and military personnel. He said :

> To-day the government are trying to murder the people. So on behalf of the people we should take upon ourselves the task of avenging this murder through murder. This is called 'tit-for-tat' struggle. Chairman has said time and again that tactics of our struggle should be tit for tat. That is why it is the task of every revolutionary today not only to wipe out the police force but to seize rifles and to arm the squads of the present guerrilla with those rifles.[58]

Immediately after Mazumdar's call, party workers started snatching arms from policemen. The party journal reported 300 such acts of arms-snatching carried out at Magurjan, Rupaskundi, Behala and at different places of the Birbhum district of West

57. Statistically, the decline of the urban guerrilla activities had been clear by June 1971. The movement started operating in educational institutions around March/April in 1970; within a year's time 331 schools and colleges were left in shambles. Around November and December more than 50 schools and colleges had to be closed down. The Presidency College closed down for months. But by April 1971, all the 57 colleges in the city were functioning again; of the 471 schools, 454 were open. By the middle of June most of the major examinations were held. For further details, see *Economic and Political Weekly* (Bombay), July 10, 1971.

58. Charu Mazumdar, "Seize the Rifles and Arm the Peasant Guerrilla Squads", *Liberation,* January-March, 1971, p. 4.

Bengal.[59] The cadres who had seized rifles were depicted as "fulfilling the thousand-year-old dream of thousand of peasants". Applauding the act of rifle snatching by the guerrillas at Magurjan, Majumdar wrote:

> The peasant and worker guerrillas of Naxalbari captured six rifles and many bullets by attacking a police post at Magurjan. This has raised the peasants' armed struggle to a higher state. Despite their best efforts the West Bengal and Bihar Police have failed to recover either the rifles or the bullets. This incident is of much significance, for the successful attack was carried out even after all the intellectual and old leaders of that area had been arrested. This incident has given the peasants' armed struggle the character of a liberation war. So we declare that it is already time to build up the People's Liberation Army. If we do not take up the task of building the People's army, the peasants' armed struggle will enter a blind alley. The ruling classes also have realized that the day is not far off when Bengal will become another Viet Nam . . ..[60]

Finally, in February came the news of the formation of the People's Liberation Army. Giving this information *Liberation* wrote:

> In Asia, Africa and Latin America, especially in Cambodia, Laos and Vietnam the People's Liberation Armies are winning everyday resounding, thrilling victories. U.S. imperialism's blatant aggression against Cambodia, resumption of its savage air raids on the People's Republic of Vietnam and its frenzied invasion of Laos, which is a direct threat to Socialist China and constitutes one more step in its drive towards another world war, are meeting with staggering defeats at the hands of the People's Liberation Armies of the three countries. Indeed, U.S. imperialism, Soviet social-imperialism and their stooges are today in the throes of their

59. In Birbhum alone more than 100 licensed guns were taken by the CPI(M-L) activists. Gun snatching had reached such an alarming stage by June 1971 that the police authorities ordered the licensed gun-holders to surrender their arms immediately at the local police stations. See *Hindusthan Standard* (Calcutta), June 30, 1971.

60. Charu Mazumdar, "Build up the People's Liberation Army March Onward", *Ibid.* ,*p.* 1.

> death-bed struggle. In this excellent revolutionary situation the Indian People's Liberation Army has been founded. It is out of the many guerrilla squads of landless and poor peasants who have been waging revolutionary armed struggle in various parts of West Bengal under the leadership of Charu Mazumdar and the Communist Party of India (Marxist-Leninist) that the People's Liberation Army has emerged ....The capture of rifles and bullets from an armed police camp at Magurjan in the Naxalbari area by peasant guerrillas and the formation of the People's Liberation Army, which welds together all the scattered squads of poor and landless peasants, mark a decisive turning point in the history of the Indian revolution. Led by the Party, the P.L.A., now a small force, will grow from strength to strength as it will fight and annihilate the enemy and his armed forces, *conduct propaganda among the masses, organise them, arm them and help them to establish revolutionary political power. The sole purpose of this army will be to stand firmly with the Indian people and to serve them whole heartedly.*[61]

The Second new feature of the CPI(M-L) action was the jail-break and jail-front idea, which took a terrible toll in dead and wounded Maoist prisoners in several jails in West Bengal like the Presidency Jail and Dum Dum Central Jail at Calcutta, the Central Jail in the Murshidabad District and in the prisons of Darjeeling, Maldah and Birbhum districts. To go by a recent report of the Calcutta *Statesman* dated 7 May, 1975 as many as 84 Naxalite prisoners had been killed in the last four years. Exactly what happened, and the full political implications could only be revealed after an impartial inquiry, but there is no doubt that the insatiable leadership of the CPI (M-L) was calling for more blood and greater sacrifices. Commending such acts of jail-breaking, Charu Mazumdar wrote :

> The revolutionaries who are today in the prison of West Bengal have created a new history of struggle that none ever came across in the annals of prison-life. These comrades realize and feel from the core of their hearts that revolutionaries remain revolutionaries even while in prison: they are quick to rise up and fight every humiliation. They have

61. "Hail the Formation of the Indian People's Liberation Army", *Liberation,* January-March, 1971, pp. 6-9, italics in original.

made jail-breaking a common place affair. Two hundred year-old imperialist rule built up the prison as the strongest base within the administrative system; today that two hundred year-old structure is crumbling. This is proof of the fact that imperialism built up its structure on very shaky foundations. Today the prison is a centre of revolt; to-day the comrades in prison are repeatedly making a mockery of it by escaping from it. Though the reactionary government murders prisoners and pursues a policy of savage repression, it fails to and will ever fail to stop jail-breaking and to put down the revolt within prisons. That is why I offer red salute to the comrades in prison.[62]

Finally, it would be wrong to consider these new CPI(M-L) moves as an indication of increased strength. Both rifle-snatching and jail-breaking attempts were extremely daring acts presupposing a certain degree of organisation, but viewed as a part of the general situation, they must be seen as a last gamble on the part of those whom the logic of left-sectarian politics had driven up the blind alley of reckless terrorism. No such movement can be without its myth, and the CPI(M-L) leadership visualized the pounding march of rifle-holding guerrillas towards a "peasant raj" round the next corner, while the monstrous waste of lives under its care continued. And the conclusion seemed to present itself at this stage that the urban guerrilla warfare along with sporadic rifle-snatching and jail-breaking activities had lost all link with the struggles in the countryside, and as such it was unlikely to be replaced by any new turn towards the villages. Whatever the truth about the projected "long march"[63] of the People's Liberation Army from Midnapore to Purulia in West Bengal, the CPI(M-L) was not certainly to "make the seventies the decade of liberation"[64] as declared by Charu Mazumdar a year back.

62. Charu Mazumdar, "Red Salute to the Comrades Behind Prison Bars", *Ibid.*, p. 5. Jail-breaking was such a great feat of revolutionism to Mazumdar that at one stage he frowned on Kanu Sanyal's hunger-strike in jail to secure the status of a political prisoner in 1971.

63. For details of the "long march", see *Statesman* (Calcutta), January 5, 1971.

64. Charu Mazumdar, "Make 1970's the Decade of Liberation", *Liberation*, February 1970, pp. 4-10.

A couple of observations may be reduced from the study of the ideas and operational techniques of the CPI(M-L) in West Bengal in particular. First is the failure at each successive stage to achieve the ends of the movement with the means to which it was supposedly committed. From Naxalbari to Calcutta through Debra-Gopiballavpur-Birbhum was a "a long march" (!) which was all along marked with retreats (not "strategic retreats" in the Mao style) and the focus of the action consistently shifted to less and less meaningful forms and targets. Second, the extreme ideological confusion of a leadership which "parrotted" Mao had already reached the point where ideological orientation was replaced almost entirely by personal obsessions and ideosyncrasies.

CHAPTER VII

THE CPI (M-L) AT THE DEAD END: DEEPENING IDEOLOGICAL CRISIS AND FINALE

THE EXTREMIST opposition within the CPI(M), growing into a powerful breakaway group by 1967, subsequently leading to the foundation of the CPI(M-L) in 1969, did not remain united long enough as a strong centralised organisation or a credible theoretical platform. Within a year of its formation, the CPI(M-L) started suffering from chronic splittism because of acute ideological and personality differences and because of "its extremely sectarian and bureaucratic attitude from the very beginning", as was alleged by one of the subgroups into which it broke up.[1] In West Bengal, in particular, almost a dozen factions sprouted in 1969-70, all swearing by the "Thought" of Mao Tse-tung. Apart from the CPI (M-L) with its English and Bengali organs, *Liberation* and *Deshabrati,* the other Maoist groups in West Bengal were the Maoist Communist Centre (MCC) or the Dakshindesh group, the *Lal Jhanda* group led by Swadesh Mitra, the *Proletarian Path* group of Parimal Das Gupta, the *Forward* group of Promode Sengupta, the *Communist* group of Amulya Ganguli, the Communist Unity Committee (CUC) or the *Marxist Review* group of Ajit Roy and so on.[2] It is interesting to note that all these factions came to be known by the respective journals they published.[3]

CHARU MAZUMDAR VS. ASIT SEN

In 1970 a severe setback was experienced by the CPI(M-L) central leadership when a very powerful section of the party's membership branched off from the CPI(M-L) and organised a

1. *Forward,* No. 2, February 1970, p. 1.

2. The fragmented Indian Maoist movement had many nuances. In the absence of a term that can describe them adequately "Naxalites" (after the 1967 Naxalbari peasant revolt) has become a generic term denoting the whole spectrum of Maoist formations in West Bengal including the CPI(M-L).

3. Among other Maoist journals in West Bengal the more prominent were *Bhitti, Puber Hawa, Muktiyuddha, Gana Mukti* and *Istahar.*

separate group styled as the Preparatory Committee of the Revolutionary People's Struggle, and started criticizing Charu Mazumdar's political line in its own journal *Liberation War*. The main object[4] of this group, it was reported, was to propagate what its convenor, Asit Sen called the correct teachings of Mao Tse-tung and to highlight the "gross deviations" of the CPI(M-L) line from Maoism. It was contended by this group that the activities of the CPI(M-L) cadres directed against educational institutions were nothing but the romanticisation of petty-bourgeois revolutionism. These terrorist activities would not help the people much towards revolution. On the other hand, such a programme would isolate the revolutionaries from the general mass of the people. Asit Sen said:

> The cadres participating in these activities are undoubtedly militant, sincere and courageous, but I cannot help feeling that they have been led into the wrong path. Burning of books on or by Gandhi would not erase Gandhism from the minds of the people. Gandhism would be defeated only by educating the masses about its bourgeois class character.

No revolution, he pointed out, was possible without a qualitative change in the class structure of the society which invariably determined the nature of the state and before embarking on action, one had to determine which class one wanted to overthrow and which class one wanted to bring to power. He further observed:

> These students who are doing all this do not constitute a class and their actions such as attacks on schools and colleges do not serve the interests of any revolutionary class. No action can lead to revolution unless it serves the interest of the class whom you want to bring to power. These students do not even seem to have any such class programme.

Characterising Charu Mazumdar's article "A Few Words About Guerrilla Action" as "an admixture of Narodism and Guevara's petty-bourgeois romantic theory of revolution", Sen observed:

> A revolution is a violent war involving killing and no revolutionary opposes killing in principle. I am opposed to

4. For the details of this groups programme see "Present Political Situation and Our Task", *Liberation War,* June 1971, pp. 9-22.

this programme (of annihilation of class enemies) because abortive revolutions in history have proved futile and, as Lenin pointed out, killing cannot be the method to revolution and should be totally rejected. These actions in killing individual jotedars here and there amount to individual terrorism and cannot mobilise and organise the masses for revolutionary violence. Only when millions of workers are mobilised, then, and then only can killing have real meaning.[5]

Later on, in an article Sen held that his vital ideological-ctical differences with the CPI(M-L) further widened by the ct that the cult of Charu Mazumdar had been institutionalised the party. He said:

> A sectarian effort was made to project Charu Mazumdar as the "authority" of Indian revolution. Moreover, in following Marxism-Leninism and Mao's thought in the Indian context the revolutionaries were boastfully asked to follow everything in the light of Charu Mazumdar's view. He was regarded to have added a new chapter to Marxism-Leninism after Mao Tse-tung and hence this science acquired a new epithet, Marxism-Leninism-Mao Tse-tung's Thought and Charu Mazumdar's teachings.[6]

5. For further details of Asit Sen's views, see author's "Ideologial Bases of the CPI(M-L)", *Journal of Constitutional and Parliamentary tudies,* Special Number on Indian Political Parties, October-December 971, pp. 474-476. Also see, Asit Sen, *Another Dangerous Line,* a Benali booklet. No Date.

6. Asit Sen, "A Few Words About CPI(M-L)", *Liberation War,* une 1971, p. 58.

In fact, contrary to all the norms of democratic centralism, Mazumar's authority was definitely sought to be established in the party. In n article entitled "To Win Victory in the Revolution We must Establish he Revolutionary Authority" the observer wrote:

We must conscientiously and seriously wage a struggle to establish he revolutionary authority of Comrade Charu Mazumdar. Our slogan : Internationally, we must follow Chairman Mao, Vice-Chairman Lin iao and the great glorious and correct Communist Party of China as he world-lessons of the Great Proletarian Cultural Revolution; nationlly, we must be loyal to Chaiman Mao, Vice-Chairman Lin Piao and he Communist Party of China and must fully accept the revolutionary uthority of the leadership of Comrade Charu Mazumdar.

For details, see *Liberation,* February 1970, pp. 39-50.

MAZUMDAR VS. SUSHITAL RAY CHAUDHURY

With the exit of the Asit Sen group from the CPI(M-L intense splittism caught on the party leadership. At this sta the major challenge to Charu Mazumdar's authority came fro Sushital Ray Chaudhury, Satyanarayan Singh, and Sheo Kum Misra, the three secretaries of the party's state units in West Be gal, Bihar and Uttar Pradesh. Charging Mazumdar with "spl ting activities and reckless adventures" all these leaders argu that in applying Maoism in India Mazumdar had introduced ma innovations which were fundamentally in conflict with the Mao thought.

The differences between Mazumdar and Ray Chaudhu which were contained in a secret inner-party document releas by the West Bengal State unit of the CPI(M-L),[7] centred rou a few tactical issues like the attacks on educational institution desecretion of statues of national leaders and the annihilation pr gramme of the party. While differing from Mazumdar's thes on "base and superstructure" put forth in the August 15, 197 issues of *Deshabrati* regarding the attacks on educational instit tions and statues, Ray Choudhury, writing under the pen-nam "Purna" argued that by its indiscriminate attacks on education institutions and the statues of national leaders the party had was ed the energy of the students and youth and alienated itself fro the masses; and he had great doubt if it would even be possib to force the party cadres to return to the countryside from th cities. Drawing the lesson from the Chinese experience, Ra Chaudhury said that although in China the revolutionary stude and youth movement of May 4, 1919 had ushered in the Ne Democratic revolution, it never degenerated into reckless attack on educational institutions and desecretion of statues. Mazumdar' instructions, therefore, were fundamentally in conflict with th lessons of the Chinese revolution and the thought of Mao Tse tung as well.

In his reply Charu Mazumdar said that those leaders who "Purna" considered as the "intellectual leaders" of the India

7. "Comrade Charu Mazumdar's Answers to the Charges c Comrade 'Purna' ", inner-party document in Bengali circulated by th West Bengal State Committee of the CPI(M-L), no date, 16 pp. For report on this document, see *Statesman* (Calcutta), December 9, 1970.

rgeois democratic revolution against the British imperialists ever took an active role in driving out the British but through ir activities sought to perpetuate British rule in India. On the er hand, leaders like Rammohan, Vidyasagar, Vivekananda , who took part in reformist movements for the national re- eration of the Indian people, sought to do so in order to ert the attention of the revolutionary people from the path of uggle for independence." There was, therefore, no scope of crimination between the Gandhian and Congress leaders and social reformers in destroying their statues. Mazumdar fur- r pointed out that since the action programme had been ap- oved in the party's foundation Congress held in May 1970, it s to be strictly followed. He also accused Ray Choudhury of i-party activities bv challenging the party's decisions in this pect. The inevitable result of the clash between Ray Chau- ury and Mazumdar on the ideological front was that the former s immediately removed from all the key posts of the party in- ding his membership of the Politbureau of the Central Com- ttee of the CPI (M-L), Secretaryship of the party's West Ben- State unit and also from the post of Editor-in-Chief of *Libera- n* and *Deshabrati*. And although he was not formally thrown t of the party,[8] the whole matter came to an end with his death e to heart attack on March 13, 1971.

CHARU MAZUMDAR VS. ASIM CHATTERJEE

The Mazumdar-Ray Chaudhury polemics had already dis- pted the CPI(M-L) organisation in West Bengal. And the ad end came in early 1971 with the sharp division within the rty between Charu Mazumdar and his right hand man, Asim atterjee, known in the party circle as "Comrade Kaka". There s evidence that for sometimes past factions led by the two lead- s had been publishing rival inner-party documents each claim- g to be more genuine in its adherence to Maoism than the other. atters came to a head when Chatttrjee mounted a severe fron- attack on Charu Mazumdar in an inner-party document en-

8. The indication that Sushital Ray Chaudhury was not formally pelled from the CPI(M-L) came when the news of his death was re- rted along with other "martyrs" of the CPI(M-L) in a column entitled omage to Martyrs" in *Liberation*, January-March, 1971, see 95-96.

titled "On Questions Concerning the Indian National Liberatic Struggle" under the assumed name "Comrade Khokan." In th document he charged Mazumdar with betraying China an liquidating the party".[9]

Chatterjee's main charges against Mazumdar were that th latter had ignored mass organisations and mass movement an heavily relied on the lumpen-proletariat with the sole emphas on annihilations. All this forced the party to deviate from th Maoist political line of armed guerrilla warfare in the countr side and instead, to indulge in urban guerrilla action. Chatterje alleged that he had insisted on an immediate meeting of the Cen tral Committee for thorough ideological discussions. He also de manded a personal meeting with Mazumdar. But he regrette in his document that he had been greeted with repeated rebuf from Mazumdar.

At the height of this bitterness Asim Chatterjee severed a connections with Charu Mazumdar and started strengthening h own organisation "the Border Regional Committee of th CPI(M-L) for West Bengal, Bihar and Orissa." Immediatel after the clash between Mazumdar and Chatterjee it was reporte that Mazumdar lost support of many important leaders of th party in West Bengal and his influence was confined to Calcutt and suburbs and a few fringe districts only.

The ideological differences between the two rival leade which had so long proved irreconcilable were climaxed by th developments in Bangla Desh, following the military crackdow there in March 1971.[10] At the initial stages of the nation liberation struggle in Bangla Desh the official CPI(M-L) line co demned it as a part of a world-wide anti-China conspiracy by th US "imperialists", Soviet "revisionists" and Indian "reaction aries." And as such it could not be regarded as a liberatio struggle. According to the party literature,[11] actual liberatic struggle in East Bengal had been launched by the East Pakista

9. For a report on this document see *Statesman* (Calcutta November 11, 1971.

10. For an account of the series of events leading to the politic convulsions in Bangla Desh in March 1971, see A. K. Roy, "Nationali and Communist Forces at Cross-roads in Bangla Desh," *United As* (Bombay), May-June, 1971, pp. 164-171.

11. *Liberation*, January-March 1971, pp. 72-75

Communist Party (Marxist-Leninist) under the leadership of Mohammad Toyah and it should be the endeavour of the revolutionaries to transform the upsurge in East Bengal into a class struggle under the leadership of the EPCP(M-L).

In an editorial of the January-March 1971 issue of *Liberation* it was observed:

> The revolutionary armed peasant struggle that has developed in several districts of East Bengal under the leadership of the Communist Party of East Pakistan (Marxist-Leninist) struck fear into the hearts of the imperialists and the Pakistani landlords and comprador bourgeoisie. If the armed agrarian revolution spread, this age-old paradise for plunderers would be lost to them : Their dream of turning East Bengal into one more link in the ring of imperialism's bases encircling Socialist China and launching a new world war would be reduced to . . . The Indian reactionaries too were afraid, for in no distant time the peasants' armed struggle in East Bengal would forge close links with the peasants' armed struggle raging in West Bengal and the two would become one vast, irresistible tide that would sweep imperialism, social-imperialism and the reactionaries of the two countries into their graves.[12]

Giving an account of how the world-wide anti-China conspiracy has been hatched up in East Bengal, the editorial declared:

> . . . when, on November 12 (1970), a terrible calamity befell the people of East Bengal, when cyclone and a huge tidal wave lashed its islands and coastal areas and took a toll of about one million lives, the U.S. and British imperialists swooped like vultures on this unfortunate land. In the name of providing relief to the distressed people they rushed large armed forces to East Bengal. The accidental crash of a Soviet plane at Panagarh near Asansol in W. Bengal carrying Soviet military personnel bound for East Bengal, gave the secret out that the Soviet social-imperialists were working hand in glove with the U.S. imperialists in reducing East Bengal into a neo-colony and military base of theirs.

12. 'People of East Bengal Will Smash the Counter-Revolutionary Plot", *Liberation*, January-March, 1971. pp. 72-73.

Mounting a severe attack on Sheikh Mujibur Rahman and his Awami League the editorial said:

> This running dog of U.S. imperialists, the Soviet social-imperialists, the Indian reactionaries and East Bengal's feudal oppressors and comprador bourgeoisie has raised the slogan of *"Jai Bangla"* (Victory to Bengal), slogan of the Bengali people's national liberation. Thus he seeks to exploit the people's fervent nationalism which has today grown very intense because of the brutal exploitation and oppression they have been suffering from at the hands of the Pakistani ruling classes. The landing of foreign troops in East Bengal, the elections, the slogan of *"Jai Bangla"*—all these form one pattern and have one aim: to confuse the people, to divert them from path of armed struggle, to disrupt and suppress it and to drag Pakistan into global strategy of U.S. imperialism and Soviet social-imperialism....Today, as the running dogs of U.S. imperialism and as lackeys of East Bengal's landlords and comprador bourgeoisie, Mujib and his men have raised the demand for sham national liberation—a manoeuvre to strengthen the imperialist and feudal fetters and to fulfil the aspirations of East Bengal's comprador bourgeoisie....Far from wanting to smash the present state machinery, he seeks to retain it . . .[13]

The difference between Charu Mazumdar and Asim Chatterjee which had been lying somewhat below the surface ever since the declaration of independence by the Awami League Chief, Sheikh Mujibur Rahman in East Pakistan in March 1971, exploded following the repeated Chinese statements at the U.N. Security Council and General Assembly in support of Yahya Khan's military dictatorship in its actions.[14] Chatterjee criticised the official CPI(M-L) line as "vile and hated centrism" amounting to a total deviation from the political line of the "great, glorious and infallible" Chinese Communist Party. He further contended that by following this centrist line the CPI(M-L) leadership was simply helping indirectly the world-wide conspiracy of

13. *Ibid.*, pp. 73-74, italics in original.

14. For an analysis of the Chinese attitude towards the political crisis in Pakistan in 1971, see Ashok Rudra, "China in the Bullshop", *Frontier* (Calcutta Weekly), December 25, 1971.

the American imperialism and the Soviet social-imperialism to attack China. Quoting exhaustively from an article entitled "What the Indian Expansionists Are After" in *Peking Review*, April 11, 1971, Chatterjee held that since the Chinese Communist Party had firmly stood by the Yahya regime in Pakistan for its "just war" to protect its own sovereignty, independence and territorial integrity against foreign intervention and aggression, the CPI(M-L) must extend its full support to Yahya Khan. Chatterjee even went to the length of putting Yahya Khan and Prince Narodam Sihanouk of Cambodia (now deposed) in the same group of anti-imperialist forces.[15]

In his reply to the charges of Asim Chatterjee, dated June 29, 1971 Mazumdar, however, took a sobre view on the Bangla Desh issue, more in line with the popular anti-colonial mood of the people of Bangla Desh in general. Mazumdar held that Asim Chatterjee in echoing the Chinese view had called Pakistan's war with India a "just war", because India had not attacked Pakistan as yet, but had been "intervening in the internal affairs of Pakistan through subversion" in East Pakistan could be called "just" enough. Though the fear of being branded anti-Chinese prevented Charu Mazumdar from supporting the liberation movement in Bangla Desh, he pin-pointed the reactionary nature of the Yahya regime and referred to his banning Communist movement in Pakistan and to his dependence on the bureaucratic comprador-bourgeoisie and the big feudal landlord class. He, therefore, concluded that the Maoists on either side of the international border should tackle a two-pronged attack of the enemy—on the one hand, the aggression launched by the imperialists of all hues and the Indian "expansionists on the people of Pakistan, and the encirclement and suppression campaign of the Yahya regime against the Maoists in Pakistan. For this the Maoists should wage a protracted people's war on their own independent initiative by mobilising the peasant masses through clsas struggle."[16]

15. Inner-party Document published by the Border Regional Committee for Bengal, Bihar and Orissa in "On Pakistan and the Deshabrati—Liberation Line", Inner-party document No. 2, July 1971. For press report on this document, see *Hindusthan Standard* (Cal.) July 7, 1971.

16. "Comrade Charu Mazumdar's Statement", June 29, 1971, *Ibid.*

PEKING'S REACTION

The deepening ideological crisis in the CPI(M-L) resulting from its steady disintegration drew in formal attention of the Chinese Communist Party which had been lending out its unqualified support to the CPI (M-L). It is interesting to note that in reproducing the CPI(M-L) formulations and reporting the exploits of the armed peasant struggle in different parts of India, the CPC had been persistently trying since the formation of the Indian Maoist party to keep before it the essential features of Maoism, without which it would be impossible to mobilise the peasantry for a revolutionary agrarian programme.[17]

But when in 1970-1971 Charu Mazumdar widely deviated from the Chinese directives through his "revolutionist" impatience, his insistence that the CPI(M-L) must function as a secret party, and the guerrilla should operate in small, self-sufficient squads, his neglect of building up broad peasant support, the absence of any clear-cut agrarian programme of the party, and finally his drift towards urban terrorism, CPC showed its tacit disapproval of the CPI(M-L)'s action pattern by suspending the publication of reports of the exploits of the Indian Maoists in its media. A review of revolutionary situation in Asia in October 1970 extolled the "peasant armed struggle" waged by "revolutionary people of India" under the leadership of the CPI(M-L) and predicted its ultimate success against the "reactionary" India government, but did not mention the urban guerrilla activity of the CPI(M-L) in Calcutta during this time.[18] But the first sign of open Chinese displeasure with the CPI(M-L)'s tactical line came in May 1971, when a review affirmed China's full support for the insurgent movements in South-East Asia and predicted the "eventual downfall" of the "reactionary governments" of Burma, Thailand, Malaya, the Philippines, Indonesia and North

17. For a study of the consistent pattern of reporting on the armed peasant struggles led by the CPI(M-L) in the Chinese press, see the *Peking Review,* July 11, August, 6, September 19, and October 31, 1969; January 2, January 30, and February 13, 1970. Also see Shao Yung-hang, "Hail Rising Revolutionary Storm of the Indian Peasants", *Peking Review,* September 9, 1969. Shao's article was clearly designed to tell the Indian Maoist revolutionaries how to organise peasant armed struggles on Maoist lines.

18. See *Peking Review,* October 13, 1970.

Kalimantan but dropped the usual reference to India.[19] This amounted to censure of the CPI(M-L)'s tactical line in the cities as well as in the countryside.

The CPC's displeasure with Charu Mazumdar was further discernible through Radio Peking broadcasts during the whole of the first week of October 1971. These broadcasts mentioned "a spurt of CPI (M-L) activities" in parts of West Bengal and the formation of peasants squads, equipped with guns looted from the police and the "class enemies." In this connection, the Peking broadcasts specifically mentioned Asim Chatterjee's Border Regional Committee for Bengal, Bihar and Orissa. This was indicative of Peking's possible recognition of Chatterjee's faction and the rejection of Mazumdar as CPI(M-L)'s supreme leader at that stage. The broadcasts also mentioned that the Chinese Communist party had come across CPI (M-L)'s inner-party documents carrying in full the ideological clash between Charu Mazumdar and Asim Chatterjee.[20]

Meanwhile the intervention of the CPC in the affairs of the CPI(M-L) became more pronounced as the documents seized by the Calcutta Police from different Maoist hide-outs in Calcutta showed that the CPC had made "bitter criticisms" of the CPI (M-L)'s style of work and the writings of Charu Mazumdar, published in the party's periodicals *Deshabrati* and *Liberation*.[21]

There were four main points in the CPC's criticisms. First the revolutionary struggle in India led by the CPI(M-L) had not been organised on correct ideological lines marked out in Marxism-Leninism and Mao Tse-tung's thought. A considerable revolutionary fervour had been wasted in the urban areas, particularly in and around Calcutta, at the cost of struggles in the rural areas.

19. See *New China News Agency* report, May 20, 1971.

20. See *Statesman* (Calcutta), October 11, 1971.

21. *Ibid.* Of these the most important document was a 135-page paper prepared by Sourin Basu (now an under-trial prisoner) who had reportedly slipped into Peking through Nepal in late 1970 and met top CPC leaders including Mao Tse-tung. Interesting excerpts of this document written in Bengali was published in *Darpan* (a Calcutta Bengali weekly) in its April-May 1971 issues. The document, which bears the date of 29 October 1970, contains two main reports of what Premier Chou En-lai and Kang Sheng, a member of the standing committee of the politbureau of the Communist Party of China had said about the basic formulations of the CPI(M-L) General Secretary, Charu Mazumdar.

In this connection, detailed references were made to "similar deviations" in China during the years prior to 1927. Secondly, the achievements in some rural areas (viz. Srikakulam in Andhra Pradesh, Lakhimpur in U.P., Mushahari in Bihar, Debra-Gopiballabhpur in West Bengal etc.) were not consolidated by the formation of mass peasant bases and peasants' armed force, the CPC observed. Thirdly, the CPI (M-L) had failed to involve the whole peasantry in a revolutionary struggle through a broad-based agrarian policy.

Finally, in the Chinese criticisms there were references to Mazumdar's "sweeping" formulations at different times. On the basis of an article written by Charu Mazumdar in the September 1969 issue of *Liberation,*[22] the CPC observed that he had discarded the entire Communist movement in India prior to the formation of the CPI (M-L). This according to the CPC, was a wrong view, because the people's struggles had continued; they had been only led by "wrong" leaders. While further criticising Mazumdar's politics the CPC made these following observations:[23]

1. The Chinese party grew and developed by fighting alien trends—both left adventurism and Right deviation.
2. The Chinese Revolution became successful with three magic weapons : (a) the Party, (b) the People's Army and (c) the United front.
3. To call a Chairman of one Party as the Chairman of another party is wrong and even it will wound the national sentiment of the working class of this country.
4. The idea....that United Front will come into being only after the formation of some base areas .... is a mechanical understanding .... The United Front comes into being at every stage of struggle, and again it breaks down. This is not a permanent organisation. There is no doubt that the worker-peasant unity is its main basis.

22. The article in question is "Fight Against the Concrete Manifestations of Revisionism."

23. For these observations, see "Open Letter to Party Comrades" addressed by Kanu Sanyal, Chowdhury, Tejeswara Rao, Sourin Bose, Nagabhusanam Patnaik, Kolla Venkaiah and Bhuvan Mohan Patnaik, see *Mainstream,* October 21, 1972.

But .... the characterisation of the bourgeoisie as a whole as comprador is wrong.

5. Regarding the formulation that the open trade union, open mass organisations and mass movements as out of date, and taking to secret assassination as the only way : This idea needs rethinking. Formerly we misunderstood your (Mazumdar's) word 'Annihilation.' We used to think that the idea is taken from our Chairman's war of annihilation. But in July 1970 issue of *Liberation* we come to understand that this annihilation means secret assassination.
6. You have applied Lin Piao's People's War Theory in a mechanical way. Lin's guerrilla war theory is a military affair. During the anti-Japanese resistance war when we had an army of 10 lakhs, at that time some comrades in the army raised a slogan that positional warfare and mobile warfare are the way to mobilise the people. In reply to their wrong theory, Comrade Lin said that guerrilla was the only way to mobilise the people. This military theory has no relation with political and organisation question.
7. Regarding the formulation that if a revolutionary does not make his hand red with the blood of class enemies, then he is not a Communist. If this be the yardstick of a Communist then that Communist Party cannot remain a Communist Party.
8. No stress has been given on agrarian revolution and the slogan for the seizure of the State power is counterposed to the land problem....
9. Without mass struggle and mass organisation, the peasants' armed struggle cannot be sustained. The Communist Party of China supported Naxalbari struggle, not merely as a struggle, not merely of State power. The article 'Spring Thunder'.....will clarify it.
10. The authority and prestige of a leader cannot be created but grows and develops.
11. The general orientation of the CPI (M-L) is correct but its policy is wrong.

It may be noted that the views of the Chinese Communist Party regarding the policies of the CPI (M-L) had reached the party's head-quarters in West Bengal in early 1971. Mazumdar and his associates who had been in control of the party head-quarters were charged by Asim Chatterjee and his compatriots in the Border Regional Committee with having suppressed the Chinese documents.

Finally, the inner-party crisis in the CPI (M-L) took a new turn with the expulsion of Charu Mazumdar and some of his old colleagues from the party and the election in his place of Satya Narain Singh (who had been the General Secretary of the Bihar unit of the CPI (M-L) as General Secretary by the Central Committee which met at Deoghar in Bihar in the first week of November 1971 on the occasion of the 54th anniversary of the October Revolution. It was reported that Mazumdar had been persistently refusing to convene a meeting of the party's Central Committee for the last one-and-a-half-years. Therefore, the Central Committee meeting had been converted at the instance of the State units of West Bengal, Bihar, Orissa, U.P., and Punjab. Curtain rang down over the final act of the CPI (M-L) drama with the arrests of Asim Chatterjee on November 3, 1971 at Deoghar in Bihar, and of Charu Mazumdar on July 16, 1972 at a place in Central Calcutta and with his death at the police lock-up on July 28[24]

The Last Flickers

In an interview at the Jamshedpur prison the British Naxalite, Mary Tyler (Sen), who had been arrested by the Bihar police along with 51 others on May 28, 1970 from the Jaduguda forests thirty miles from Jamshedpur, told a *Statesman* correspondent quite emphatically that "revolution is the only path for change......The Naxalite movement has not fizzled out, the revolution comes in waves, you take it from me our comrades are meeting again and a new wave is rising......"[25]

The waves of class struggles transforming themselves into a revolutionary deluge, however, did not come true. With most of their acknowledged leaders dead or in prison, the Naxalites were yet to compose the ideological and political differences which went on plaguing the CPI (M-L) even after Charu Mazum-

24. For detailed information on Mazumdar's arrest and his subsequent death see *Statesman* (Calcutta), July 27 and 29, 1972.

25. *Statesman* (Calcutta), 30 September, 1973.

dar's death. The crisis of leadership in the party deepened further in early 1973 as the attempts by at least four major factions to forge unity among various splinter-groups received a setback. The newly reconstituted Central Committee of the CPI (M-L) led by Satyanarain Singh met in Calcutta in April 1973. It was reported in the meeting that Satyanarain Singh and a few other members of party's Central Committee met some representatives of the Andhra Pradesh Revolutionary Communist Party led by Chandrapulla Reddy in order to discuss the problems of unity. A joint appeal for unity was issued after the Andhra meeting. It was signed by Satyanarain Singh, P. Vasudev Rao, Secretary, CPI (M-L) Srikakulam Regional Committee and also member of the Central Committee, R. Ram Narsiah, Secretary, Andhra Pradesh Revolutionary Communist Party, and Venu Gopal, a State Committee member of the APRCP.

This appeal, however, lost much of its weight as Nagi Reddy and his group rejected the unity proposal, maintaining that in the current stage of Indian revolution it would be unwise to boycott parliamentary elections which could be used as one of the many forms of struggle.

Further, a few other documents believed to be of Naxalite origin, which were in circulation in 1973-74 betray the anxiety of the CPI (M-L) leaders to bring the various factions together. For example, two contradictory statements, one issued from Delhi in the name of the General Secretary and the other circulated from Calcutta by Satyanarain Singh, elected General Secretary of the CPI (M-L) in November 1971, created total confusion in the party ranks. The Delhi statement declared that the CPI (M-L) would henceforth confine itself to "democratic movements" which by implication meants that it would cease to be an underground organisation. On the other hand, contradicting this statement of the "other" General Secretary, Satyanarain Singh's circular claimed that the Delhi statement had been issued by the faction led by Suniti Ghosh, a former member of the CPI (M-L) Central Committee, who had been subsequently "displaced along with Charu Mazumdar"[26]

Finally, the debunking of the former Defence Minister, Lin Piao at the Tenth Congress of the Communist Party of China held

26. See *Hindusthan Standard* (Calcutta), 6 February, 1974.

in August 1973 brought about a further division in the already divided ranks of the Naxalites.

It may be noted that the reticense so long observed by the Chinese leaders regarding the Naxalite movement in India since May 1971 could also be marked in the political report presented to the Tenth Congress of the CPI by Chou En-Lai. The political report to the Ninth Congress, prepared by Mao Tse-tung himself and presented by Marshal Lin Piao had noted that the armed struggles of the peoples of several countries, including India had been steadily growing in strength. The CPC had also expressed its "firm support" for the revolutionary struggles of the people of Laos, Thailand, Burma, Malaya, Indonesia, India, Palestine and other countries and regions in Asia, Africa and Latin America". Obviously, the reference was to the Naxalite movement in India. Chou's political report to Tenth Congress, however, did not refer to the armed struggle in India and this was obviously understood as the continuation of Chinese disapproval of the Naxalite tactics in India. On the contrary, the total denigration of Marshal Lin Piao came as a great blow to the CPI (M-L) which was accustomed to regard everybody not owing complete allegiance to Chairman Mao and Vice-Chairman Lin as revisionist. Initially, the reports of conflict between these two Chinese leaders and of the Marshal's death in a planecrash had been dismissed by the Naxalites as canard. But after the Tenth Congress as they came face to face with the stark reality, they were thrown into a serious dilemma. If they endorsed the line of the Tenth Congress, they would have to revise their tactical line thoroughly, for the Naxalite theory that the entire masses could be mobilised through guerrilla war alone was an adaptation from Lin Piao. Had there been any reference to the armed struggle in India in Chou Enlai's political report, the CPI (M-L) could have taken that as a signal to persist in its old line.

In fact, until the first half of 1973 the CPI (M-L) factions kept their differences rather confined within matters relating to the tactics and strategy of the on coming revolution in India. But the opening of the Lin Piao issue in the Tenth Congress of the CPC proved to be the point of no return for them. And a careful screening of the documents published by the Naxalites following the Tenth Congress shows that the CPI (M-L) had broadly divided itself into three major factions by the end of

1973; (1) those under Bihar's Satyanarain Singh, totally opposed to Charu Mazumdar's line and constituting the smallest faction, (2) those who follow Charu Mazumdar to the letter and believe that the Chinese criticism of Mazumdar was because of internal dissensions in the Chinese Communist Party at the time in which the revisionists were out to overthrow Lin Piao; hence their continued reverence for Lin; and (3) a powerful faction which owes allegiance to Charu but accepts the Chinese criticism and admits that Charu Mazumdar made many mistakes in his execution of "armed revolution".

The dispute over the Lin Piao issue, it may be pointed out, was of such tactical significance for all those factions, especially the last two that after a careful review of the proceedings of the Tenth Congress they were reported to have held their respective party congresses to review their revolutionary strategies.

The second group held the second Congress of the party under the leadership of Mahadeb Mukherjee in December 1973 in a rural region of India within "the iron bastion of poor and landless peasants aroused by the thought of our respected leader comrade Charu Mazumdar and under the careful and vigilant protection of the people's liberation army built personally by him."

The Congress, according to a communique issued by the "Control Committee" of the CPI (M-L), adopted a resolution reaffirming the party programme of 1970, "which is the only correct programme for the entire period of India's People's Democratic Revolution and which most aptly and boldly upholds the correct line of Comrade Lin Piao. Guerrilla warfare is the only way to mobilise and apply the whole strength of the people against the enemy". The communique ended with Red Salute among others, to Lin Piao[27].

On behalf of the third faction, the "Central Organising Committee[28] of the CPI (M-L) issued a statement on the basis of its own second congress held in March 1973, congratulating the Chinese Communist Party on the successful conclusion of its

27. Communique of the Control Committee of the CPI(M-L), *Liberation,* 3 December, 1973.

28. This Committee included some members of the CPI(M-L) Central Committee, elected at the First Party Congress held in 1970. Among them was Suniti Ghosh.

Tenth Congress which had "consolidated the victory of the proletariat over the anti-party clique led by Lin Piao, the bourgeois-carrerist, double-dealer, spy and traitor."

This document did not reaffim the group's faith in the 1970 programme of the CPI(M-L). While acknowledging Mazumdar's death as a great loss to the party, the organising Committee recorded that the struggles had received "a set back because the party committed certain errors and all the people whom it is necessary to mobilise or/and organise for the triumph of revolution could not be mobilized and organised".

In the central organising committee's view the country was objectively ripe for revolution and it was for the party and the revolutionary people to make the much-needed subjective preparations. To this end, the committee laid down four immediate tasks—(a) propagation of Marxism-Leninism-Mao Tsetung thought among the people, (b) unity with all genuine Marxist-Leninists, (c) participation in and leading mass struggles on all fronts, and (d) intensification of class struggles of the working class and other working people.[29]

Despite the factional rivalries among different groups within the CPI(M-L) the pro-Lin Piao faction under the leadership of Mahadeb Mukherjee became quite active in as many as seven districts of West Bengal—24 Parganas, Howrah, Hooghly, Nadia, Burdwan, West Dinajpur and Midnapur. Although the police had been able to flush out the CPI (M-L) activists from the tribal-populated Kanksa[39] (Garh Jangal) area near Durgapur in the Burdwan district, the pro-Lin group reestablished their bases in the area towards the middle of 1973 by taking advantage of the serious economic backwardness of the area. During that time also they built up CPI(M-L) strongholds at Kalinagar and Petuabhanga in Nadia, at Sheoraphuli and Chandanagore in Hooghly, at Kamalpur in Burdwan, at Banshihari, Tapan and Kaliagunge thana areas in West Dinajpur and in the Haldia, Tamluk, Balichak and Kharagpur towns of Midnapur district.

29. Resolution adopted at the second Congress of the CPI(M-L), February, 1974.

30. In 1973 the entire Kanksa thana area was described by the administration as a "disturbed area" and as many as six police camps had to be opened encircling the area in order to contain the Naxalites operating there.

This group resumed quite vigorously the party's old programme of annihilation and encounters with the police. The police adopted the "fish-in-water" strategy to enlist mass support in order to contain the CPI(M-L) activities in different areas. By July 1974, altogether 19 members of the police, Railway Protection Force and National Volunteer Force were killed and 30 firearms snatched. The police in reply killed 12 activists, recovered 29 firearms and arrested 1,270 activists of the party.[31]

It was reported that towards the end of 1974 ideological dissensions had started following the failure of the latest phase of violence unleashed by the CPI(M-L) faction under the leadership of Mahadeb Mukherjee and the whole organisation faced severe disintegration as a result of a revolt against its "strongman" Mukherjee himself. A large section of the cadre, had become sore about Mukherjee's "autocratic authority" and the Central Committee held a secret meeting on October 30 to discuss the situation but the problems could not be resolved. At the emergency meeting held on 3 November, which turned into a 'virtual underground court' Mukherjee was charged on several counts and severely indicted. He resigned then and there. After this the police followed Mukherjee close on his heels and finally arrested him at Shillong in December 1974.

While all the CPI(M-L) factions have been lying low for some time in West Bengal, many areas in Bihar are now bustling with extremist activity especially after the fluid political situation created in that State by the call for "total revolution" of Jaiprakash Narayan.[32] While the anti-Lin Piao faction of the CPI(M-L) is operating in the Shahabad, Barh and Lenada areas, the pro-Lin Piao extremists have been fast regrouping in Dhanbad, Giridih, Berneo, Patna and Arrah (Bhojpur) regions and the Maoist

31. See *Statesman* (Calcutta) 12 November 1974. Of then the most significant police action took place at Kamalpur village on the Hooghly Burdwan border, reported to be a very important stronghold of the pro-Lin group which had held its second congress there in November 1973. For details see *Statesman* (Calcutta) 19 September 1974.

32. For a fairly exhaustive account of Jaiprakash Narayan's political views see Ajit Bhattacharyya, *Jaiprakash Narayan,* Vikas Publications, New Delhi, 1971. Recently Mr. Narayan appealed to the CPI(M-L) leaders in Bihar to devote their revolutionary zeal to the cause of "the total revolution". See *Amrita Bazar Patrika* (Calcutta) 24 May, '75.

Communist Centre is also busy trying to bring into their fold the poverty-stricken tribals in the Hazaribagh-Giridih belt.

In every case the story is quite the same—land being the dividing factor. A recent survey on the socio-economic conditions in the Madhuban-Dumalchak areas in Arrah district shows that severe economic exploitation of the poor landless Harijans by the upper-caste people is at the root of the present troubles in the area. But violence is not new to these villages. For long there has been terror in the land. But till recently the perpetrators have been the wealthier farmers and their men, all belonging to the higher castes, who became the ruling elite with the abolition of the Zamindari system in 1975. Although the Bihar Government had decided to distribute land to the landless, the decision was never seriously implemented and the upper-caste people started grabbing the land of the Harijans. This is exactly what happened in Madhuban which was once a dense forest before the Government decided to rehabilitate the poor landless Harijans in 1968, where they started ploughing the lands after cleaning the Madhuban woods. The wealthy people from the nearby villages came and forced them to sell the lands at throw-away prices. Gradually exploitation and fortune of the Harijans by the rich higher caste people started mounting. And the Naxalites who had been operating in these areas since 1970 became successful in turning the caste war into class war, because the caste and class lines are the same with almost all the land belonging to the upper castes. About 80% of the people are daily-wage labourers with wages varying between 25 and 50 Paise.[33]

With the area well irrigated and fertile, the farmer using improved technology under the new wave of "Green Revolution", have been growing even richer. Tractors and harvestors have made it possible to cultivate large areas, with fewer people and the poor landless people have been finding it difficult to get jobs or even to subsist.

It is, therefore, no wonder that the Naxalites would consider this sort of socio-economic situation in the district a good ground for unleashing class war. Even a rather conservative estimate shows that there are more than 1,000 hard-core Naxalites in the district and their sympathisers must run into tens of thousands.

33. See *Amrita Bazar Patrika* (Calcutta), 22 May 1975.

The Bihar administration has conceded that the trouble in Arrah-Bhojpur area is "fundamentally agrarian" and cannot be contained by sheer force. Force was tried in 1971. But this has left the Naxalites much more well-organised than before, which has been proved by the ever growing incidence of murders committed by armed extremists in different areas of Bihar.

Recently it has been reported that extremist leaders from over a wide area encompassing India, Bangladesh and Nepal have formed a Joint Committee of Action and intensified extremist propaganda. The Indian Naxalites who under Kanu Sanyal's guidance had built up a sanctuary in the eastern-most Terai district of Jhapa in Nepal along the Naxalbari border, are working in close collaboration with the Nepalese Maoists under the leadership of Mohan Chandra Adhikari, a Politbureau member of the pro-Peking faction of the outlawed Communist Party of Nepal. In the wake of the liberation of Bangladesh they were reported to have collected modern arms and dumped them at different places in eastern Nepal.[34] With the easy flow of arms from Bangladesh and eastern Nepal's potential as a sanctuary and operational base, there would be little surprise if the resurgence of large scale Naxalite activities take place in that area where the "spring thunder" had set off the first sparks in 1967.

The Union Government under the able leadership of the Prime Minister, Mrs Indira Gandhi was prompt enough to realise the gravity of the situation and on 4 July 1975 the Government of India banned the Rashtriya Swayamsevak Sangh, the Anand Marg, the Jamait-é-Islami and a host of Maoist and ultra-leftist factions including the CPI(M-L) on the ground that they had been indulging in violent activities prejudicial to internal security, public safety and maintenance of public order. This action of the Government came on the ninth day of the proclamation of national emergency arising out of internal disturbances. The Union Government issued four separate orders under Rule 33(1) of the Defence and Internal Security of India Rules, 1971, to impose the ban. The Government orders laid down that "any person who manages or assists in managing any of these organisations, promotes or assists in promoting a meeting of any members of these organisations, attends any such meetings, publishes

34. See *Hindusthan Standard*, 13 August 1 74.

any article or advertisements relating to any such meetings, invites persons to support these organisations is liable for action under the law."

In a radio broadcast to the nation Mrs. Gandhi said:

The CPI(M-L) and its various factions have been responsible for a large number of murders and violent incidents. None of these organisations have anything common among themselves nor can their activities be at all called political in a legitimate sense. There has been an overwhelming opinion in favour of banning the activities of these organisations.[35]

35. See *Amrita Bazar Patrika,* 3 July 1975.

Chapter VIII

SUMMARY AND CONCLUSION

From the fore-going analysis it has been found that the history of the Indian Communist movement during the decade under review (1962-1971) is one of fragmentation and disorientation. The Indian communists have divided themselves during this period into three parties—the CPI, the CPI(M) and the CPI (M-L)—and a host of *ultra-leftist* and centrist groups. Also a large number of communists have kept themselves outside all organised groups and parties. It is also true that while before 1964 the Indian Communists, despite their sharp ideological and political differences, were at least formally committed to a single political line worked out by the united CPI, to-day each communist party, each communist group (and also each atomised communist individual) has its own approach to national and international issues which often conflicts with that of other communists.

The split of 1964 in the Indian Communist movement, it has already been observed, was not merely the reflection of the Moscow-Peking ideological schism. It had deep roots in the history, tradition and the social composition of the CPI. And it is these factors that prepared the internal, indigenous setting for the response to Peking's call for a split. Thus the Chinese pressure only accentuated the process and the so-called "Dange letters" provided a convenient device to force the split. But the real reason was that the two trends could no longer co-exist in a single party and had to test their ideas on the touch-stone of mass action.

But the real character of a political party seldom tallies with its own consciousness. The more the CPI and the CPI(M), freed from the restraints of functioning inside a single party, put their respective ideas into practice, the more identical became their practice. These main issues, it may be pointed out, had been advanced as the political grounds for the split in 1969; (1) attitude to the Congress; (2) attitude to the Parliamentary system; and (3) the attitude to China. The leaders of the CPI(M) believed that the CPI was too anti-China, pro-Congress and had a reformist's faith in the parliamentary system. They wanted to build a genuine revolutionary party which would not fall victim to any nationalist prejudices but try to learn from the teachings of all great Marxist-Leninists, especially Mao Tse-tung. The CPI, on the other hand, considered the CPI(M) adventurist, incapable of persuing a national mass policy and having a "blind" faith in Mao's dogmas.

However, as the two parties went into action, they exchanged their concepts as it were. As the 4th General Elections approached, the CPI became as anti-Congress as the CPI(M). If the CPI(M) in Kerala entered into an alliance with the Muslim League, the CPI did the same with the Jan-Sangh in U.P., Bihar, Punjab and Madhya Pradesh. The CPI(M) on its part, entered the parliamentary game as enthusiastically as the CPI. Not only did both the parties participate with equal zest in coalition-making, there was hardly any difference in the way their respective ministers, M.Ps. and M.L.As functioned. While the CPI, in other words, embraced the tactical orientation of the CPI(M), the latter accepted its strategical concepts. In the face of this identity of practice between the two parties, their theoretical differences over such questions as National Democracy and People's Democracy lost all significance.[1]

While there is no controverting the fact that without the Chinese Communist leadership calling for an open schism the organisational split in the CPI in 1964 would not have taken place, it is at the same time correct to hold that this split did not clearly represent a Sino-Soviet polarisation as[2] it transpired later.

1. The split of 1962-64, however disastrous it might have been for the two Communist Parties politically and organisationally, served to establish the patriotic bonafides of Indian Communism, especially after the 4th General Elections of 1967, when the communist movement got itself rehabilitated and legitimized within the Indian political process. The CPI could no longer be condemned by its opponents as a foreign agency or the expression of a foreign movement. The second stage in the process of rehabilitation of communism as an Indian movement came almost at the same time when the CPI(M) started disentangling itself from Peking's "pseudo-revolutionism".

2. Under the impact of the Sino-Soviet ideological rift while most of the communist parties clearly took either a 'pro-Soviet" or a "pro-Chinese" stand, some parties called for "open split" meaning that there

The CPI, which had already committed itself to the Soviet position in the ideological debate, was accorded recognition by the CPSU as the only legitimate Communist party in India. The left Communists, on the other hand, formed a party of their own on the basis of a programme minus an unequivocal ideological stand. And this "opportunist procrastination" of the CPI(M) leadership left all such issues absolutely open to various interpretations by party members.

It is in this perspective that the Naxalbari Peasant Uprising assumes significance. This extremist trend in the Indian Communist movement, which can be termed the Indian Variant of the New Left[3], was born as a reaction to the calculated ambivalence of the CPI(M) central leadership towards ideological issues, and also to the negative aspects of the parliamentary politics as followed by the CPI, CPI(M) and other left parties. The chief achievement of the Naxalbari Communists is the total abjuration of parliamentary politics and thereby providing the missing extreme of the ideological spectrum. Quite understandably, therefore, the split in the Indian communist movement took final and defined shape only with the definite emergence of the Naxalbari communists.

It would, however, be wrong to consider the rise of the Maoist wing in the Indian communist movement as a purely Chinese-inspired phenomenon. The Chinese ideological inspiration was definitely there as it would be evident from the fact that India has always had a central place in the Maoist strategy of people's war commended to the Third World by Lin Piao in his thesis entitled "Long Live The Victory of People's War" in September 1965. The Indian Communist Movement has been the battleground of the Sino-Soviet ideological dispute on issues

were two parties, one pro-Soviet and one pro-Chinese. There were still others which sought to take an "independent" position as these were critical of both Moscow and Peking rather than neutral in the sense of avoiding trouble with either of them. For details of alignment of the Communist parties the world over in the Sino-Soviet dispute see *World Strength of the Communist Party Organizations.* Bureau of Intelligence and Research, Department of State, U.S.A., 1968.

3. For an excellent analysis of the New Left, the revolutionary tide of which swept the world in the 1960's, see Cranston, Maurice, (ed.),*The New Left,* The Bodley Head, London. First Indian Edition by National Academy, Delhi, 1973.

like peaceful transition to socialism and the concept of national democracy which are patently Soviet innovations, considered "revisionist" by the Chinese leadership. In fact, the publication of the Lin Piao thesis should be viewed as the beginning of the series of attempts made by the Chinese ideologues throughout 1966 and 1967 to project a Maoist revolutionary line to India when they saw "excellent" revolutionary situation. And with the CPI(M) finally settling for "respectable parliamentarism" by bringing its tactical line in focus with that of the "revisionist" CPI and other left parties, the CPC called for a Maoist revolution in India in mid-1967 by asking the "revolutionaries" within the CPI(M) ranks to fight against "neo-revisionism" and "demarcate themselves from it politically, ideologically and organisationally".

The Maoist movement in India made its debut[4] in the spring of 1967 with a militant mass upsurge of the peasants in the sleepy non-descript Naxalbari Police Station of Darjeeling District, West Bengal, led by the local section of the CPI(M). Though the movement was initially launched as a struggle for land by the poor landless peasants, it subsequently went beyond the limited aim of land redistribution by giving the call for the seizure of state power.

It is rather pertinent to point out that the lack of influence over the peasantry on a whole has been a traditional weakness of the Indian Communist movement. Only on the eve of independence did the country witness some organised peasant movement led by the communists—for example, the Tebhaga movement in Bengal, land struggles in U.P. and Bihar and the great peasant upsurge against the oppressive rule of the Nizam and the Deshmukhs in Telengana. But no such movement or mass upsurge in the countryside could be witnessed since independence. And in that "revolutionary" environment of the immediate post-independence years, the Indian countryside had remained on the whole quiescent even as the towns were seething with mass unrest occasionally. And there was no sustained pressure for

4. Indian Maoism, in fact, predates the final victory of the Chinese Revolution in 1949. In its first appearance at Telengana, it was a short-lived phenomenon of the late 1940's and was suppressed by international communist intervention. After nearly two decades, it returned in a somewhat changed situation.

any structural agrarian reforms, the Congress Government never felt the compulsion to introduce anything more than modest reforms. The slow pace of urbanization, the persistence of traditional agriculture, and the tenural reform made it possible for the rural rich to continue to exploit the rural poor without political upheaval in the countryside. On the other hand, the pre-split Congress grew to rely on the big and middle landowners "for crucial support" in trying to preserve its dominance in the rural areas.[5]

This unstable rural equilibrium based on such pronounced social stratification began to be disturbed in the early 1960s and agrarian unrest started mounting. Three major developments were responsible for this. "One was an acute food shortage.... in the mid-1960's. This resulted from two successive years of severe drought in vast expanses of the country. The second was the split of the old CPI in 1964. Since the rump body remained strong among India's relatively sparce industrial workers, the breakaway CPI(M) felt compelled to turn to the peasantry as an alternate base of support. The third was the so-called "green revolution" and the birth of "capitalist farming".[6]

This "green revolution", it may be noted, has stemmed from a combination of things—scientific development of high-yield varieties of grain, greater use of fertilisers, efforts to increase the amount of ground water, the availability of better seeds, and

5. It should be noted that while the peacemeal agrarian reforms, implemented by the Congress Government in India, bolstered up the political, social and economic positions of the upper rural strata and thereby helped tension accumulate considerably, the partition of India in 1947 brought about a spontaneous "quiet revolution" in the socio-economic milieu in East Bengal, and as a result of this, a qualitative change swept away the highly stratified social system of East Bengal. While the Hindu landlords and jotedars were at the higher rung of the social and political leadership, the poor landless Muslim peasants were mostly down-trodden. But along with the mass exodus of the Hindus from East Bengal into India after partition, the whole feudal social structure of that part of Bengal automatically crumbled down and the poor Muslim peasantry became owners of land almost overnight. For further details on the "Quiet Revolution", see the present author's "National and Communist forces at the Crossroads in Bangladesh" *United Asia,* Special Number on Bangla Desh, May-June 1971, pp. 165-166.

6. See Bhabani Sengupta, "Indian Communism and the Peasantry", *Problems of Communism,* January-February, 1972, p. 5.

the expanding employment of tractors. Thus it holds forth the promise of a major breakthrough in agricultural production. Yet parodoxically, it has also created condition which have worsened the lot of the poor. It has been found thus far that the demand for labour per hectare has not been significantly curtailed by the "green revolution". This is because of the fact that increased use of farm machinery has also led to multicropping and more intensive agriculture. However, the nature of labour demand has changed. For instance, more talented labourers are sought after for year-round employment. Also, at peak periods, such as harvesting, labour demand has become more critical because of the need to quickly clear the land and prepare it for the next crop. This has resulted in high wages at harvest times, and, in fact, throughout the year. The farmers consequently are seeking harvesting combines and other machines to replace slow and increasingly expensive manual labour. It seems fairly clear that demand for labour will diminish as agriculture becomes more mechanised. Further, larger landowning farmers are becoming prosperous with the help of government agencies, banks, and cooperative societies. They are investing in capital intensive equipment in order to enhance their direct control over agriculture and also their income. The small cultivators and the landless labourers, on the other hand, are losing out in several ways. For instance, the demand for their traditional services has diminished, availability of land on crop-sharing basis is reduced, inflation has kept their real wages almost constant, and alternate employment opportunities have lagged behind need. Consequently, the two classes are becoming polarised and increasingly antagonistic to each other. In so far as West Bengal is concerned, the worsening economic position of the poor peasants and agricultural labourers during the decade following 1961 may be better understood from the following table.[7]

What emerges from an analysis of the data given above is the fact that almost throughout the state the agricultural workers have multiplied amazingly, thereby further intensifying pressure on land. And in a highly competitive job market they have to accept wages far below the subsistence level. According to a

7. *Census of India,* 1971, Provisional Population Totals, West Bengal. Paper I of 1971; published by the Director of Census Operations, West Bengal, pp. 66-67.

Percentage of agricultural and other workers to total workers in West Bengal and the districts in 1961 and 1971.

	Cultivators		Agricultural		Other Workers	
	1961	1971	1961	1971	1961	1971
West Bengal	38.5	31.75	15.3	28.75	46.2	42.50
Darjeeling	37.5	29.28	2.9	10.42	59.6	60.30
Jalpaiguri	43.5	39.98	3.0	8.75	53.5	51.23
Cooch Behar	74.1	67.57	7.1	15.02	18.8	17.41
West Dinajpur	61.8	57.88	21.1	28.01	17.1	14.11
Malda	49.8	45.32	14.4	33.32	35.8	20.86
Murshidabad	44.2	38.84	19.7	35.31	36.1	25.85
Nadia	42.9	37.42	16.7	27.17	40.4	35.36
24-Parganas	31.4	24.14	17.6	26.79	51.0	49.07
Howrah	14.3	11.39	9.5	18.90	76.2	69.71
Hooghly	30.3	24.31	19.7	30.12	50.0	45.57
Burdwan	28.4	24.05	17.7	29.69	53.9	46.26
Birbhum	43.7	36.90	30.6	41.80	25.7	21.30
Bankura	52.4	40.45	24.6	33.71	27.1	20.66
Midnapore	55.6	45.63	20.3	33.71	27.1	20.66
Purulia	69.9	45.02	13.7	33.37	16.4	21.61

report published by the Indian Institute of Public Opinion in 1968, the income of about one-third of the Indian Population fell below the poverty line; and those of a little more than one-fifth, below the destitute line.[8]

In spite of the appalling poverty of the landless peasants and the agricultural labourers, little has been done by the communist and other left parties to organise them, compared with their trade union activities in the industrial field. The Kisan Sabhas have always remained dominated by the middle peasantry and until 1967 the organisation of the poor agricultural labourers was almost non-existent. And it should be noted that it is the Naxalbari Communists who, for the first time in West Bengal at least, came to recognise the growing importance of the socio-economic

8. For details, see Indian Institute of Public Opinion, *The Anatomy of Indian Poverty*, New Delhi 1968, and V. M. Dandekar, "Poverty in India", *Economic and Political Weekly*, January 2, 1971.

conditions in the countryside, and launched a peasant struggle by pitting the landless peasants against the big land-owners and rich peasants, and subsequently, by converting a partial struggle for land into the final struggle for power.

The Naxalbari peasant movement was quelled fairly easily, and had not the Chinese media hastened to hail the uprising as the "spring thunder" of the oncoming Indian revolution, it would have been quickly buried in oblivion. But the Chinese plaudit for the Naxalbari Communists as the true Communist revolutionaries in India changed the whole situation qualitatively and encouraged the radical elements in the CPI(M) in several other states—notably Andhra Pradesh, Bihar and Kerala—to organise local peasant uprisings. By August 1967, the rebellion of the Girijan tribals in the Srikakulam region of Andhra Pradesh had assumed the colour of armed guerrilla resistance, and "dozens of Naxalbaris" had sprouted in West Bengal, Orissa, Bihar, U.P., Kerala and Punjab.

Apart from the Chinese endorsement of the Naxalbari insurrection, what attached special significance to this miniscular peasant uprising in North Bengal was the fact that it had flared up in a State with a United Front Government in power and with the CPI(M) as its leading partner, and further, that it was this party's dissident members in the Darjeeling district who actually engineered the movement. And this last feature, it is striking to note, was common in most of the states where similar armed actions broke out. All or almost all of the leaders of the new movement were the members of the CPI(M). This naturally created the general impression at the initial stage that :

A. The CPI(M) was opening a new, militant front in the countryside, parallel to gheraos that had been developing in the cities; and

B. All those insurrections in different parts of the country were the result of a centrally planned and coordinated strategy of the CPI(M) to go in for armed, guerrilla struggle behind the parliamentary façade.

It may be recalled how the Congress, Swatantra, Jana Sangh, SSP, PSP, and other parties of the Right and the left, including the CPI, mounted a severe propaganda offensive against the CPI(M) for encouraging, even clandestinely engineering, the Naxalbari movement, citing as their evidence, first, the fact that the leaders of the movement were CPI(M) members and the failure until then, of the CPI(M) leadership to denounce them. It was further alleged that the CPI(M) had been building up the Naxalbari movement especially in the sensitive border areas with a view to capturing power with the help of the Chinese Red Army.

This forced the CPI(M) leadership, anxious as it was to regain constitutional respectability (in the fond hope that while occupying the ministerial positions, they could offer substantial relief to the people) to come out in open denunciation of the Naxalbari movement. Indeed, the CPI(M) leadership was in complete disagreement with the Naxalbari peasants' armed resistance to the jotedars' attempts to seize the bargadars' harvest and to evict them. The leadership advised its members at Siliguri to be patient and to allow the U.F. Government to settle the disputes.

But once it was constrained to make its disagreement with the Naxalbari Communists public, the CPI(M) could not avoid agreeing to police repression, since the clashes were becoming more violent and widespread. This was followed by the expulsion of the CPI(M) members, actively associated with the movement or supporting it. Thereupon the Chinese Communist Party called upon the 'revolutionaries' within the Indian Communist movement to form a Maoist Communist party in India.

Shortly after this, the Communist "revolutionaries" in West Bengal who had been expelled from the CPI(M) established a coordination committee to mobilise the radical elements within and outside the party; similar bodies sprung up in Andhra Pradesh, Bihar, U.P. and other States. However, faced with police repression, and yet to be organised into a party with a clear programme and properly formulated strategy and tactics, the Naxalbari Communists began to follow hit-and-run tactics rather desperately. Indeed, if the columns of *Deshabrati* were any index, one could find almost each contributor expressing a shade of views, not unoften the same person contradicting himself in two different issues of the same journal. This was perhaps inevitable, since, firstly, they had all been fighting under a difficult situation, and secondly, the pooling of the variegated experiences and understanding of the individuals and groups and the working out of a meaningful act of strategies and tactics were not yet feasible. As a result, serious tactical differences began to crop up among the different Maoist leaders. The differences became sharper after the formation of the All-India Coordination Committee of Communist Revolutionaries (AICCCR) in 1968 and especially after the founding of the Communist Party of India (Marxist-Leninist) on April 22, 1969.

In its Foundation Congress held in May 1970 the CPI(M-L) adopted a constitution and a programme of people's democratic revolution in India, in which the party identified the "contradiction" between feudalism and the peasant masses as the "principal contradiction" in the Indian society; and it defined "the main content" of the "peoples' democratic revolution", the party's strategic goal, as "the agrarian revolution, the abolition of feudalism in the countryside". To accomplish "a people's democratic revolution", it went on, the working class must forge an alliance with not only the poor and landless peasants but also the middle peasants, under proletarian leadership; the alliance under the working-class guidance would have to employ armed revolution as its fundamental tactics. The party, therefore, would firmly reject parliamentarism and pursue armed peasant guerrilla warfare in the countryside in order to encircle and finally capture the cities. The party would, for that matter, function as a secret organisation, keeping its main cadre underground. Thus from 1970 onwards, all open mass activities of the party ceased, and work was carried entirely on a secret and conspiratorial manner. Scores of youth, especially students, had abandoned their academic career and gone to the countryside to organise guerrilla bands and start guerilla warfare. The Maoist movement continued to spread. In 1969, peasant guerrilla warfare was going on not only in Srikakulam but also on a limited scale along the Bengal-Orissa-Bihar border (Debra-Gopiballavpur), in parts of southern Bihar, and along U.P.'s border with Bengal in the terai region. There had also been similar isolated incidents in Punjab, Assam, Madras and Kerala.

From what had started as peasant uprisings in the countryside, the CPI (M-L) movement quickly slide down to reckless individual terrorism against jotedars in the villages and ritualistic and irrelevant violence in the urban areas, and finally ended up with desperate attempts at gun-snatching and jail-breaking in several areas of West Bengal. Confusion deepened further in the party's rank and file because of the tactical blunders resulting from the "petty-bourgeois revolutionism" of the city-bred leadership, which did not have a very high level of ideological articulation and training in guerrilla warfare. The rot, however, had already set in with the induction of large-scale lumpen-proletariat elements into the party. As a result intense "putschism" gripped the party.

Above all, the CPI (M-L) leadership's total disregard for the concrete socio-economic reality of the country and formularistic repetitions of catechisms from Mao's thoughts, even if these could earn ready plaudits from Radio Peking, did not really conform to Mao Tse-tung's theory of revolution, the main lesson of which is the need for the synthesis of the universal truth of Marxism-Leninism and the concrete reality in each country.

It has been already seen that the phenomenon of *ultra-leftism* or what may be called "Naxalism" in West Bengal in the late 1960's had a deeper political-ideological background, deeper in the sense that the extremist left-wing in the CPI(M) was gifted with a "logical consistency" insofar as it sharpened and then gave a definite shape to the inherent ideological inconsistencies in the Indian Communist movement, and all this has already been carefully analysed.

But although tht Naxalbari movement was launched with a sharp ideological-tactical breakthrough, it soon developed neo-anarchist propensities as it came to be swallowed up by the routine of Bengali middle class political life. The leadership and the majority of the supporters of the Naxalite movement came from the urban petty bourgeoisie[9]. And, therefore, the movement truely 'reflects' the mood of this class in the urban areas—desperation, rage and craze for violent action. With this one can possibly explain the vitality and attraction of Naxalism and its powerful impact on the students and youth of West Bengal in particular.

There is thus hardly any doubt that in the present social context Naxalism does represent to a large extent the adolescent revolt in the Indian middle class homes against all established

9. Though this class is itself in a transitional stage, it is inexorably being proletarianised. And almost a century ago or more Marx and Engels had discovered the class-roots of anarchism in the objective fact of the ruin of the petty bourgeoisie.

values and norms, and it would be more understandable even if a cursory glance is taken at the socio-psychological milieu of the Bengali middle-class life in its historical setting.

Since in every political system the process of modernisation or the dynamics of change is inextricably bound up with the phenomenon of social mobilisation,[10] two vital stages of the process have to be reckoned with : (1) the stage of uprooting or breaking away from old settings, habits and commitments; and (2) the induction of the mobilised persons into some relatively stable new patterns of group membership, organisation and commitment. The growth in the number of these people produces mounting pressures for the transformation of political practices and institutions, with a great potential for political tensions and violence.

Bengal, it may be recalled, experienced fundamental changes in the character of her land tenure system, local and provincial administration, commercial and industrial economy and educational network, which modified the social structure of Bengal. In the realm of politics, changes in the position of various political classes were no less dramatic. The political leadership and influence exercised by zamindars in the mid-19th century declined as Indians were admitted into the newly created colleges and universities and as opportunities for appointments into government administration and commercial houses increased. The rapid increase in the number of intermediaries in the land system in the latter part of the 19th and early 20th centuries, combined with an expansion in higher education without a commensurate expansion in employment opportunities, was accompanied by the emergence of more impatient, more extremist political movement. Similarly, Naxalism, which developed certain classic features of terrorist movement, had also its social roots. It has been aptly pointed out that "there is a stream in the national movement which finds its natural continuation in the Naxalbari party. This is the trend of anarchism, popularly designated as terrorism. It will be recalled that in the jails and the underground days of colonial rule many of the best terrorist or

10. For a more detailed analysis of social mobilisation, see Chapter V.

anarchist leaders came over to the Communist party. Now, from the communist movement some have trekked back".[11]

What is thus quite clear to any political observer is the monstrous fact of economic, social and psychological pressures building up the Naxalite explosion. Frustration and anger deepened over the critical employment situation, high cost of living, overcrowded and insanitary homes[12] and the crisis of the academic system. This sense of decay in Calcutta's life further intensified the mood of alienation. Analysing the mind of an average middle class Bengali, Professor Myron Weiner writes :

"A sense of mobility seems to have disappeared among the middle class or, more accurately, aspiration levels remain high while expectation levels have dropped ... In a society in which individuals feel a sense of downward mobility (as in West Bengal), where individuals do not envision a wide range of choices, a more rigid ideological view of politics can be afforded without any personal risks. Middle class Bengalis share a pessimistic view of the political process, as they share a pessimistic view of their own life chances. Individuals have confidence in no institutions—the universities, the press, civic bodies, even the government (except in the abstract). For this, institutions are viewed as being impotent and are thought to be dominated by men concerned with their own well-being, not the public weal".[13]

To the prevailing social and political tensions already injecting a mood of alienation and militancy, was added the steady influx of refugees from East Pakistan ever since the partition of 1947.[14] This large mass of humanity, a considerable part of which was yet to rehabilitate itself properly, had imposed as unbearable burden on the already overstrained resources of this

11. Mohit Sen, "What Is The New Left?", *Seminar,* December 1968.

12. For exhaustive data on these problems see *West Bengal : An Analytical Study,* published by the Bengal Chambers of Commerce and Industry, 1971. For outstanding analysis of how deprivation breeds alienation, see Huntington, Samuel, P., *Political Order in Changing Societies,* New Haven, 1968. and Gurr, Ted Robert, *Why Men Rebel,* Princeton University Press, 1970.

13. Myron Weiner, *Political Change in South Asia,* Firma K. L. Mukhopadhyay, Calcutta, 1963, pp. 240-241.

14. For figures regarding the influx of refugees from East Pakistan between 1947 and 1971, see *West Bengal : An Analytical Study, op. cit.* pp. 22-23.

truncated State. Since about a third of the total influx that remained within West Bengal preferred to hang on to the area now referred to as the Calcutta Metropolitan District, it added to the tremendous pressure already existing in this region. It has been revealed in an inquiry undertaken by the Calcutta Metropolitan Planning Organisation (CMPO) that "the suburbs, closest to Calcutta—North and South—Dum Dum, Kamarhati, Panihati, Garden Reach and the South Subarban areas—have almost overnight become substantial communities. And within the city itself the fastest growth has occurred in the low-lying, unsewered, poorly drained areas in Tangra, Tapsia and Kasba, along the eastern fringes of the city bordering its pestilent marshes of the Salt lakes and the wards of Tollygunge.[15] And what this means in terms of human misery is beyond description.

The influx of the large number of displaced persons into the highly congested metropolitan area has a number of significant sociological implications, the most serious of which arises from the relatively high incidence of literacy among the refugees.[16] This better educated and, therefore, more articulate mass forced by circumstances into utterly depressed and suffocating conditions of living have added to the already high accumulation of the already combustible material in this extremely over-crowded city and its environs. Much of the present unsettling conditions in the Calcutta Metropolitan District owes its origin to this legacy of the partition of Bengal"[17] A personal investigation made by the present author in the three selected areas of Calcutta megalopolis, viz., Jadavpur, Behala and Dum Dum, reveals that these areas overwhelmingly populated by the displaced persons (more than 95%) have sent recruits, mostly in their teens, into the CPI (M-L) ranks. And it has also been found that as high as 80% of the CPI (M-L) cadres are drawn from among families belonging to the category of displaced migrants, with, of course, a heavy anti-social fringe.

It has been pointed out by a political sociologist that the "pre-industrial" or the "partially industrialised" political sys-

15. CMPO, *Basic Development Plan,* 1966-1968.

16. For statistical data on literacy among the displaced migrants, the ordinary migrants and the original residents, see S. N. Sen, *The City of Calcutta,* Bookland Private Ltd., Calcutta, 1959, p. 224.

17. See *West Bengal : An Analytical Study,* op. cit., p. 26.

tems (e.g. India and other countries in South and South-East Asia) have a large potential for violence because of the tension of modernisation and of the "cultural-moral lag" arising out of it. And it is, therefore, found that the role-structure in such a political system (especially in those areas of such a system with definite regional, ethno-conceptual and psychological moorings) has a tendency to institutionalise violence[18].

Thus understood, the forms of violent actions practised by the CPI (M-L) cadre like the destruction and desecration of statues of political and other leaders, ransacking of laboratories and libraries, disruption of examinations and stray murders are nothing novel but simply a hangover from the continuum of organised-anomic violence in Bengal's socio-political environment. This time, however, violence put on a convenient idelogical garb insofar as this urban guerrilla tactical-ideological setting was an interpolation on the classical Maoism of the Naxalites.

In the final analysis it may be pointed out that an average middle-class Bengali has always had a sneaking admiration for violence and adventurism emanating, perhaps from his own socio-psychological predicament[19]. And terrorism in the first quarter of this century grew partly out of this psychological make-up of

18. Although the general notion is that political violence is a phenomenon confined to West Bengal exclusively, a survey of the incidence of crimes committed in different States of India revealed that West Bengal ranked much below in 1968-70. It was found that in 1969 the number juvenile crimes was the highest in Tamil Nadu (17,261) and lowest in West Bengal 1,780. In terms of the volumes of crime per 100,000 population in 1969 while Madras ranked first (571.6), Calcutta was at the bottom of the list (448.9). Even if the number of violent incidents resulting in the death of policemen in different States in 1969-70 is taken into account, West Bengal occupied the third rank (415) next to Maharastra (645) and Andhra Pradesh (460). In Bombay the number of policemen killed in 1969-70 was 342 whereas in Calcutta, even at the height of the Naxalite activities, the number was only 170. For details, See *Amrita Bazar Patrika* (Calcutta), 30 May, 1972.

19. For an analysis of this aspect of the Bengali character, see Chapter V.

It may, however, be pointed out that appeal of violence is not a phenomenon exclusively confined to the Bengali middle class people. What is rather interesting is the fact that in recent times all the violent political movements the world over have been engineered by the urban petty bourgeois leaders, posing themselves as the revolu-

the Bengalis, and with it an heroic tradition in politics. They were thrilled not only by the sensational acts of terrorism but also by the acts of martyrdom and self-destruction committed by the extremists. Naxalism, it should be noted, also thrived on this psychological background of Bengali antagonism to authority and the urge towards adventurism. And it had to dissipate itself quickly as it failed, like an anomic movement, to offer a set of values beyond self-destructive nihilism. It is feared that with the roots of alienation having struck much deeper, such violent anomic-political upheavals may burst forth from time to time, thereby frustrating the country's search for identity and prosperity.

tionary elites. For example, almost all the terrorist organisations including the National Liberation Action in Brazil, the Tupamaros in Uruguay, the Weathermen in America, the Quebec Liberation Front in Canada and the JVP in Sri Lanka have all drawn their cadre especially from the disgruntled middle-class youth. For a fascinating study on why the youth are easily drawn to violence in the Latin American countries, see Alstair Hennessy, "University Students in National Politics" in Claudio Veliz (ed.), *The Politics of Conformity in Latin America*, London, 1967, pp. 119-157.

APPENDIX—I

CONSTITUTION OF THE CPI (M-L) ADOPTED AT THE FIRST PARTY CONGRESS, HELD IN MAY 1970

CHAPTER—1
GENERAL PROGRAMME

1. The Communist Party of India (Marxist-Leninist) is the Political Party of the proletariat of India.

2. The Communist Party of India takes Marxism-Leninism-Mao Tse-tung Thought as the theoretical basis guiding its thinking. Mao Tse-tung Thought is the Marxism-Leninism of our era in which Imperialism is heading for total collapse and Socialism is advancing to world wide victory.

3. The basic programme of the CPI (M-L) is the complete overthrow of the rule of the Bureaucratic Bourgeoisie and the Big Feudal Landlord classes, the agents and lackeys of U.S. Imperialism and Soviet Social Imperialism, the establishment of the People's Democratic Dictatorship led by the proletariat in place of the Dictatorship of the Bureaucratic Comprador Bourgeoisie and the Feudal Landlord classes. The ultimate aim of the Party is the realisation of Socialism and Communism.

4. To overthrow the rule of the above enemies of the people, CPI(M-L) places the path of armed struggle before the Indian people. It rejects the parliamentary path for the whole of the strategic period. The people's war in semi-feudal and semi-colonial India is the peasant's war under the leadership of the working class. As pointed out by Comrade Lin Piao, our strategy of People's War is "to rely on the peasants, build base area, resort to persistent armed struggle and to use countryside to encircle and finally capture the cities".

5. In order to defeat the enemies of our people and to win victory in the revolution the three tasks before the CPI(M-L) are : (i) the building and strengthening of our Party with the method of criticism and self-criticism and link with the masses of the people; (ii) A People's Army under the leadership of our

Party; and (iii) United Front of all revolutionary classes and all revolutionary groups engaged in armed struggle under the leadership of our Party.

6. The CPI (M-L) regards the Communist Party of China as the leader of the international communist movement and recognises China as the centre and base of the World Revolution.

7. The CPI (M-L) upholds Proletarian Internationalism; it firmly unites with Marxist-Leninist parties and groups the world over, unites with the proletariat and the oppressed peoples and nations of the whole world and fights together with them to overthrow Imperialism headed by the U.S. Imperialism, Modern Revisionism with the Soviet Revisionist renegade clique as its centre, and the reactionaries of all countries and to abolish the system of exploitation of man by man on globe so that all mankind will be emancipated.

8. The CPI(M-L) is composed of the advanced elements of the proletariat. It is the vanguard of the proletariat and the revolutionary masses in the fight against the class enemy.

9. Members of the CPI(M-L) dedicate their lives to the struggle for Communism. They must cherish love of the people and adopt the attitude of serving and learning from the people. They must be over vigilant about imperialist conspiracies and modern revisionist manouvers. They must be resolute, fear no sacrifice and surmount every difficulty to win victory.

Chapter II

NAME AND MEMBERSHIP

1. The name of the Party is the Communist Party of India (Marxist-Leninist).

2. Flag : the flam of the Party is Red flag with white hammer and sickle.

3. Membership : (a) Any member of the working class, the toiling people, the peasantry, revolutionary middle class or any other revolutionary element who resides in India and has reached the age of eighteen years is eligible for membership of the Party, provided he accepts Marxism-Leninism-Mao Tse-tung's Thought as the guide to action, accepts Programme and Constitution of the Party unit and pays regularly Party membership

dues and levy as fixed by his unit according to his capacity and is ready to go to rural area for rousing peasant masses for agrarian revolution any moment when directed by the unit to do so.

(b) Membership fees will be 10 paise annually. Levy can be fixed by the unit to which a member belongs after assessing the capacity of the member concerned.

(c) Admission of the member will be on individual basis and generally through the basic unit of the Party.

(d) An applicant must be recommended by two Party members who know him well and provide the Party with all necessary information about him.

(e) At least six months' record of the work among the people for the applicants from the working class and poor peasantry, one year's record of work for applicants from middle class and middle peasant origin and two years record of work for others should be checked up before admitting one in the party.

(f) Members from the exploiting classes will not be allowed into the Party unless they relinquish their property at the disposal of the Party and have thoroughly integrated themselves with the masses.

(g) Careerists, double-dealers, bad characters and enemy agents will not be admitted.

4. Members of the CPI(M-L) should:

(a) Consantly study and apply Marxism-Leninism-Mao Tse-tung Thought in a living way and try to become the best disciples of Chairman Mao.

(b) Subordinate their personal interests to the interests of the people and the Party.

(c) Develop initiative.

(d) Be bold in making criticism and self-criticism.

(e) Be deft at uniting with the great majority including those who have wrongly opposed them but are sincerely correcting their mistakes.

Chapter III

ORGANISATIONAL PRINCIPLE OF THE PARTY

1. The organisational principle of the Party is Democratic Centralism. The democratic centralism means centralised lead-

ership based on inner-party democracy and inner-party democracy under the guidance of centralised leadership.

(a) All higher organs shall be elected except in exceptional circumstances;

(b) Individual is subordinate to the Party unit;

(c) Lower unit is subordinate to the higher unit;

(d) All units and members are subordinate to the Central Committee;

(e) Leading committees are to give regular reports to their subordinate units and promptly convey their decisions;

(f) Leading committees shall take decisions only after full considerations and on the basis of thorough knowledge of the conditions of the people and lower units;

(g) Free and frank discussions within Party units on all questions regarding Party policy and work;

(h) Every unit is free to take full initiative in working out the methods of implementing the general line given by the leading organs;

(i) Every party member must belong to a party unit;

(j) Every member of a leading committee must be assigned a particular area of struggle to which he gives particular guidance and from which he gains direct experience. Exception to this rule may be made only in case where it becomes necessary in the interest of some specific party work;

(k) Factionalism is incompatible with the principle of Democratic Centralism;

(l) Every party member is free to send his opinions, criticisms and appeal upto the Central Committee;

(m) When a party member violates discipline, the party organisation at the level concerned shall take disciplinary measures—warnings, serious warnings, removal from the posts of the party, placing on probation within the party.

CHAPTER IV

STRUCTURE

1. The highest organ of the party is the All India Party Congress.

2. The Party Congress shall be convened every five years.

Under special circumstances it may be convened before its due date or it may be postponed by the Central Committee.

3. The Party Congress will review the political situation and work of the Party, check out general line for the whole country and, if necessary, change or amend the Party Constitution; and even the Programme. The Congress will also elect the Central Committee.

4. The Central Committee will elect a Polit-bureau and set up other necessary standing committees.

5. The Central Committee is fully empowered to change the area under the jurisdiction of any State Unit.

6. The highest organ for the State is the State Conference which will elect a State Committee. In between the period of two State Conferences the State Committee is the highest organ in the State.

7. Below the State Committee there will be Regional Committee, elected by the Regional Conferences.

8. Below Regional Committees there will be Area Committees elected by area conferences.

9. Cells will be the basic units of the Party.

10. The Central Committee and the State Committee will convene their extended meetings from time to time to review the work and policy matters.

APPENDIX—II

BIOGRAPHICAL SKETCHES ON SOME OF THE LEADERS CONNECTED WITH THE NAXALBARI PEASANT UPRISING AND THE COMMUNIST PARTY OF INDIA (MARXIST-LENINIST)

It is always imperative to collect exhaustive biographical information on the leading figures connected with a political movement of any kind in order to understand the social background of such a movement. Since the Naxalbari Peasant Uprising of 1967 and the subsequent Maoist movement in West Bengal, which was a byproduct of that uprising, created a great stir throughout the country during the last five years, it is all the more important to have accurate information on the social background of those who led the movements. Unfortunately however, because of the secrecy that has all the time pervaded the CPI (M-L) affairs since its formation, it has been rather difficult for the author to obtain adequate data on the social composition of the party's leadership. Nevertheless, great caution has been taken while collating information from diverse sources like the daily newspapers, journals and interviews with party activists. Some names, however, have been reluctantly left out only because no data were available.

Banerjee, Kamakshya

Born in 1930, received education up to the Matriculation standard. Originally a member of the Siliguri Local Committee of the Praja Socialist Party. Expelled from the party in 1961 on various charges including some dubious ones. Joined the Samyukt Socialist Party but was again expelled for similar reasons. Finally became a member of the Siliguri Local Committee of the Communist Party of India (Marxist). Active leader in the Siliguri Peasant Convention organised by the extremists in the CPI(M) in 1967. Expelled from the CPI(M) for leading the peasant revolt at Phansidewa. Now absconding.

Bose, Sourin

Born in 1925, at Alipurduar in the Jalpaiguri District; a graduate. Joined the CPI at a young age. Arrested during the Sino-Indian border war in 1962 for alleged anti-state activities; after release joined the CPI(M) in 1964. A member of the Darjeeling District Committee of the Party. Expelled from the party along with Charu Mazumdar in 1967 for organising the Naxalbari Peasant uprising. A founder-member of the Communist Party of India (Marxist-Leninist). Included in the Party's Central Committee at its Foundation Congress held in 1970. Reported to have slipped into China through Nepal in 1970 and had discussion with some senior Chinese leaders at Peking over the tactics to be followed by the CPI(M-L). On his return, developed ideological differences with Charu Mazumdar and joined Asim Chatterjee's faction. Now an under-trial prisoner.

Chatterjee, Asim

Born in 1944, son of a rich and influential congressman of Birbhum, West Bengal. Known in the party circle as "Kaka" and "Khokan". Graduated from Presidency College, Calcutta. A leading figure in the Presidency College students' union controlled by the BPSF(L), the students' wing of the CPI(M). Expelled from the BPSF(L) for organising students' movements at the Presidency College and Calcutta University in support of the Naxalbari peasants. Formed a Marxist students' organisation—the Presidency College Students' Consolidation. In 1969 on Charu Mazumdar's call to work among the peasants in the countryside, Chatterjee along with his close associates, left for Debra-Gopiballavpur in Midnapur to organise agrarian movements. After the failure of the peasant movement in that area he developed differences over ideological-tactical questions especially over the Bangla Desh issue with his mentor, Charu Mazumdar and built up his own organisation, the Bengal-Bihar-Orissa Border Regional Committee. Formed an alliance with Satyanarain Sinha, Secretary, Bihar State Unit of the CPI(M-L). Elected member of the party's Central Committee in 1970. Tried to organise "Red bases" in the countryside of Birbhum but failed. A "Proclaimed Offender" with an award of Rs. 5000 on his head, Chatterjee was arrested at Deoghar in November

1971. At present detained at the Hazaribagh Central Jail, Bihar as an under trial prisoner.

Datta, Saroj

Born in 1913 at Jessore, East Bengal (now Bangla Desh); received education upto the Post-Graduate standard. Took up the career of a journalist. Joined the *Amrita Bazar Patrika* as a sub-editor and rose to the position of Editor-in-chief at the night shift of the daily's office. Lost his job in 1949 for participating in violent and subversive activities which the CPI had launched during the "left sectarian" period under the leadership of B. T. Ranadive. Known in the party circle for his extremist views; was one of the editors of the *Swadhinata*. Arrested in 1962 for anti-state activities; joined the CPI(M) after the split in the CPI in 1964; elected a member of the Calcutta District Committee of the party and appointed one of the members of the Editorial Board of the *Deshahitaishi,* weekly Bengali organ of the CPI(M) West Bengal state unit. Expelled from the party in 1967 for supporting the Naxalbari Peasant Uprising. Was one of the founder members of the Communist Party of India (Marxist-Leninist) and elected to the Central Committee of the Party. Appointed Editor-in-Chief of the *Deshabrati,* the weekly Bengali organ of the CPI(M-L)'s West Bengal State Unit after the dismissal of Sushital Roy Chaudhury (who had developed serious ideological differences with the Party Chief, Charu Mazumdar) from that post. Had a very powerful and facile pen and used to write under the pen-name "Sasanka" His whereabouts are not known at present.

Ghosh, Suniti

A former lecturer in English in the Vidyasagar College (Evening section), Calcutta, Ghosh was known to have always taken extreme positions in his political views. Became politically active after the Naxalbari Peasant Uprising of 1967 and joined the CPI (M-L) in 1969. Was a close associate of Charu Mazumdar and elected to the Central Committee of the party. Took over charge of the CPI (M-L) English organ, *Liberation* in 1971 as its Editor-in-Chief after the expulsion of Sushital Roy Chaudhury from the party. Wrote under the pen-name "Soumya". Now reported to be absconding.

Mazumdar, Charu

Son of Bireswar Mazumdar; born in a zamindar family of Siliguri, Darjeeling in 1918. Matriculated from the Siliguri Boys' School in 1936. Joined the Edward College at Pabna (now in Bangladesh). In 1938 joined the then outlawed CPI and started working in the party's peasant front in the Jalpaiguri District. Organised the Tebhaga movement in the 1940's mainly in the three police stations of the Jalpaiguri District: Boda, Pachagarh, and Debiganj. After the failure of the movement, devoted himself to organising the workers of the then Bengal Dooars Railway at Domohani. Censured by the Jalpaiguri District Committee of the CPI for plunging the peasants of Boradighi Jote in the Dooars in a premature and militant movement which resulted in the first police firing in the region leading to the death of 12 men and women. During the period of Zhdanovist adventurism followed by the CPI under the Ranadive leadership in the late 1940's, Mazumdar organised the tea-garden workers of the Darjeeling District. Arrested in 1949. After release in 1952, resumed trade union activities. In early 1960's raised the banner of Maoist revolt against the "revisionist" leadership of the CPI. Arrested in 1962 for anti-state activities during the India-China border war. Released in 1963, contested a bye-election as the CPI candidate to the West Bengal Assembly from Siliguri and was defeated. After the split in the CPI in 1964 joined the CPI(M). In 1965 issued a circular in the name of the CPI(M); condemned and suspended temporarily by the party. In 1967 on the decision of the CPI(M) to join the United Front Government, wrote a series of eight letters to party members urging them to launch an immediate armed struggle on the Maoist line. Soon after installation of the UF Government he masterminded a peasant uprising in the Naxalbari area of Darjeeling district in the spring of 1967. Expelled from the CPI(M) for this towards the end of 1967. Formed the All-India Coordination Committee of the Communist Revolutionaries (AICCCR) in 1968. On May 1, 1969 the CPI(M-L) was formed with Mazumdar as its first General Secretary. The party started disintegrating from the middle of 1971 when different leaders challenged Mazumdar's leadership and his tactical lines on "annihilation of class enemies" and urban guerrilla action. A "Proclaimed Offender" in 1971 with an award of Rs. 10,000/- on his head, Mazumdar was arrested in Calcutta on July 16, 1972. Died of a heart attack on July 28, 1972 in the police custody at Lal Bazar, Calcutta.

Mallik, Kadam

Born in 1935 at Siliguri; received education upto the High School standard. Joined the Indian Communist movement in the late fifties; detained in 1962 for pro-Chinese views and anti-government activities. Shifted his allegiance to the CPI(M) in 1964. Elected a member of the Siliguri Local Committee of the party. Active among the tea garden workers and landless peasants. Elected Secretary of the Siliguri Sub-divisional Kisan Samity. Organised the peasant revolt at Kharibari and Phansidewa in 1967. Arrested in 1969.

Mazumdar, Khokan

(Allias Abdul Hamid)

Born in 1932, at Barisal in East Bengal (now in Bangladesh) in a poor Muslim peasant family. His father migrated to Siliguri prior to independence. Worked as a work-boy at the Lake Medical Hospital in Darjeeling, but was dismissed in 1948 because of his leftist political affiliations. Worked as a compounder in several medical establishments in the district until 1952, when he joined Kanu Sanyal in organising the peasants of Darjeeling district under the banner of the BPKS, the peasant wing of the CPI. Actively participated in the peasant uprisings at Naxalbari, Kharibari and Phansidewa in the spring of 1967. Now absconding.

Rahaman, Mujibur

Joined the CPI in 1946, but was expelled from the party in 1957 for violating party discipline. In the 1962 election he worked for the Congress candidate for the Phansidewa Assembly Constituency, but after the Indo-Pak conflict in 1965 he established relations with the Left Communists. In the 1967 general election he worked for Jangal Santhal who was a CPI(M) candidate from the Phansidewa constituency. He actively participated in the peasant uprising in the Naxalbari-Phansidewa-Kharibari belt and later joined the CPI(M-L). Now detained as an undertrial prisoner at the Darjeeling Jail.

Rana, Santosh

Born in a Scheduled Caste family in 1944 at Gopiballavpur in Midnapur, West Bengal; an M.Sc. from the University of Calcutta. Inducted into the Maoist movement in West Bengal immediately after the Naxalbari Peasant Uprising 1967. Active in the PSCC, a Maoist students' organisation throughout 1968-1969. Organised peasant guerrilla warfare at Debra-Gopiballavpur, Midnapur District in 1967-1970. Elected to the CPI(M-L) Central Committee in 1970. Developed tactical and ideological differences with Charu Mazumdar and joined Asim Chatterjee's Bengal-Bihar-Orissa Border Regional Committee. Married Jayashri Rana, who had actively led the tribal peasants at Debra-Gopiballavpur. Arrested in early 1972.

Raychaudhury, Sushital

Born in 1917 at Hooghly in West Bengal; graduated from Calcutta University. Joined the Indian Communist movement at a very early age. Elected Secretary of the Hooghly District Committee of the CPI in 1943. Wrote extensively in the party weekly *Swadhinata* and other papers like *Matamat* (Views), *Sambad* (News) on the *Tebhaga* movement in Bengal in the early 1940's. Transferred to the Calcutta District Committee of the party after independence and joined the Editorial Board of the *Swadhinata.* Gravitated to the Left Communist faction during the inner-party squabbles following the India-China border war of 1962. Joined the CPI(M) in 1964 and was elected to the Editorial Board of *Deshahitaishi,* the Bengali weekly organ of the CPI(M) West Bengal State Unit. Known for his extremist views. In 1965 wrote a series of articles in *Chinta* (Thought), challenging the party programme as "revisionist". Formed an extremist organisation in the CPI(M), the Marx-Engels Institute to wage inner-party ideological struggle. Actively supported the Naxalbari Peasant uprising of 1967 and was expelled from the CPI(M). Became a founder-member of the CPI(M-L) and elected to the party's Central Committee in 1970. Appointed Editor-in-Chief of *Deshabrati* and *Liberation,* the CPI(M-L) Bengali and English organs. Subsequently, developed ideological differences with Charu Mazumdar and was expelled from the party. Died of a heart attack in early 1971.

Santhal, Jangal

A tribal of the middle peasant origin in the Naxalbari area, Santhal is known as a professional tribal revolutionary leader. As a member of the Siliguri Local Committee of the CPI(M), Santhal had been active in the peasant front. Elected President of the Siliguri Subdivisional Kishan Sabha. Contested for a seat in the Assembly as a CPI candidate in 1962 and in 1967 as a CPI(M) candidate; was defeated on both the occasions. Acted as the "field-commander" of the Kisan Samiti's operations against landlords in the Naxalbari area in 1967. Elected a Central Committee member of the CPI(M-L) in 1970. Arrested in 1971.

Kanu Sanyal

Born in 1932 at Jalpaiguri, came in contact with Subhas Chandra Bose and learnt from him his early lessons in politics. Received early education at the Kurseong English School; joined the Jalpaiguri Ananda Chandra College at the Intermediate class, and became a very active leader of the BPSF, the students' wing of the CPI. Expelled from the college for organising a violent demonstration against Dr. B. C. Roy, the then Chief Minister of West Bengal, who was visiting the Jalpaiguri town. Joined the Darjeeling District Committee of the CPI and devoted himself as a full-time party worker among the Adivasis, poor peasants and agricultural labourers. Joined the CPI(M) in 1964 and became a close associate and right-hand man of Charu Mazumdar. Revolted against the CPI(M) leadership when the party became a partner at the UF Government in West Bengal and led the Naxalbari peasant uprising in the spring of 1967. Expelled from the party. Announced the formation of the CPI(M-L) at a May Day rally in Calcutta in 1969. Elected a Central Committee member of the party and held a position next to his mentor, Charu Mazumdar. A "Proclaimed Offender" with an award of Rs. 10,000 on his head, Sanyal was arrested at his Naxalbari hideout in early 1971. Now detained as an undertrial prisoner.

Sen, Asit

Born at Rangpur in East Bengal (now in Bangladesh) in the early 1920's; a Science graduate from Calcutta University. Was active in the BPSF, the student's wing of the CPI in the late 1930's; elected Secretary of the Local Committee of the CPI at Rangpur, his hometown. Joined the *Swadhinata Unit* of the party in 1950. Transferred to the Park Circus Local Committee and put in charge of the Education Branch of the Committee. Joined the CPI(M) after the split in 1964. Supported the Maoist faction in the CPI(M) after the Naxalbari Peasant uprising in 1967. Expelled from the party in late 1967. Presided over the May Day rally held in Calcutta in 1969 in which the formation of the Communist Party of India (Marxist-Leninist) was announced. Subsequently, developed ideological differences with Charu Mazumdar, resigned from the CPI(M-L) in early 1970 and formed a Maoist organisation, "The Preparatory Committee of the Revolutionary People's Struggle." Edited *Dakshin Desh* (Southern Country) and *Liberation War,* two Maoist journals.

Sen, Mary (née Tyler)

Born in London in 1943. Daughter of Earnest Tyler, a port Superintendent in North London. Became a School teacher in Willsden High School after graduating from King's College, London. Connected with the Marxist circles in London. Met Amalendu Sen, a committed Marxist from India during one of her trips to West Germany. Came to India in late 1969 by an overland route and because of her association with Amalendu Sen, joined the Naxalite movement, then at its height. They were married in April 1970. Arrested along with 51 others on May 28, 1970 from the dense forests of Jamshedpur, Bihar, immediately after their abortive attack on a nearby police post for seizing arms. Very recently the Government of India has withdrawn all cases against her and she has been sent back to United Kingdom. Speaks English, German, French, Italian, Spanish, Latin, Hindi and Bengali.

Singh, Satyanarain

Born in Bihar in 1923. Singh started his political career as a Congress volunteer; participated in the Quit India movement as a Congress Socialist whose idol was then Jayaprakash Narayan; became a Communist while working as an aircraftsman in the Royal Indian Air Force; arrested for refusing to salute the Union Jack on 15 August 1947 and released at the intervention of Mr. Jawaharlal Nehru; joined the CPI(M) in 1964 and became a member of the party's Bihar Secretariat, became a Maoist in

1967 after the Naxalbari peasant uprising Organiser of the Naxalite movement in Mushahari, Bihar, Singh had been one of the closest associates of Charu Mazumdar at the initial stages. He was elected Secretary of the Bihar Committee of the CPI(M-L) and a member of the party's Central Committee and politbureau. He staunchly defended Mazumdar's line when it came under attack from Nagi Reddi, Asit Sen and Parimal Dasgupta. In September 1970, he himself, however, questioned Mazumdar's line and in 1971 he along with several leaders of the CPI(M-L) Central Committee met in Bihar to review the party line. They rejected the political line laid down by Charu Mazumdar, and removed him from the party. Subsequently, Singh was elected General Secretary of the party. Declared an offender in 1970, Singh is now leading an underground life.

SELECT BIBLIOGRAPHY

The present author has relied heavily for information about the Communist movement in West Bengal on official party literature and the non-Communist publications as well. A few inner-party documents (meant for party members only) were made available to him and these have been sparingly used. Finally, the author worked for a few months in 1967 as a Lecturer in Political Science, University of North Bengal and collected first-hand information on the Naxalbari Peasant uprising of 1967. Chapter II of this book has been supplemented with this field work. The following catalogue of books, documents and articles includes, as far as practicable, all the important materials which have been cited in footnotes.

A. Primary Sources

I. *Restricted and Partly Published Documents of the Indian Communist Parties*

On *Telengana,* Information Document No. 7(2), 1950, Typescript.

Tactical Line, document prepared in Moscow in 1951 and circulated to the members of the Central Committee at the Third Congress of the Communist Party of India, Madurai, 1953.

Andhra Thesis, document placed by the Andhra Communist leaders before the Third Congress of the Communist Party of India, Madurai, 1953.

"On Certain Questions Before the International Communist Movement", Resolution of the Central Executive Committee of the CPI, 4-7 September, 1960 Typescript.

"Prithvirajer Dalil" (Prithviraja's Document), An inner-party document prepared by one Prithviraja (pseudonym) in Bengali in 1963. This document upheld the Maoist line as a strategy of the Indian revolution. Typescript.

"Chanakyae'r Dalil" (Chanakya's Document). An inner-party ideological document prepared by one Chanakya (pseudonym) in Bengali in 1963. This document challenged the ideological position of the CPI central leadership and took a completely pro-Chinese stand on the Sino-Soviet ideological dispute. Typescript.

"Bartaman Paristhiti o Partyr Karmaniti" (The Present Situation and Party's Policy). An inner-party document circulated by some un-identified CPI members in West Bengal in 1963. Typescript.

Tenali Convention of the CPI, a report prepared by Hare Krishna Singh Surjeet in 1964, Mimeographed.

Anonymous Letter to the Politbureau and Central Committee of the CPI(M), Mimeographed. This document was prepared by a section of extremists in the West Bengal State unit of the CPI(M) in 1966 challenging the party programme and the tactic of peaceful parliamentarism.

"Anashaner Darshan" (Philosophy of Hunger Strike). This document was prepared by the Marx-Engels Institute in Bengali in 1966. This Institute, originally set up by the CPI(M) West Bengal State Secretariat, was subsequently used by the Maoists in the Party to wage an inner-party ideological struggle.

"What Is the Meaning of The Spontaneous Revolutionary Outbursts in India ?" This document was prepared by the Maoist group in the Darjeeling District Committee of the CPI(M) in May 1965. Mimeographed.

Andhra Pradesh Revolutionary Communist Committee, *Immediate Programme,* 1966. Mimeographed.

——— *On Srikakulam Girijan Armed Struggle,* 1969. Mimeographed.

——— On *Armed Struggle in Andhra Pradesh,* July 1969. Mimeographed.

——— *Problems of People's War,* 1970. Mimeographed.

——— *Some Problems Concerning the Path of People's War in India,* 1970. Mimeographed.

Communist Party of India (Marxist-Leninist), *Constitution,* adopted at the Foundation Congress, May 1970. Typescript.

——— *Programme,* adopted at the Foundation Congress, May 1970. Typescript.

——— *Resolution on Party Organisation,* adopted at the Foundation Congress, May 1970, Typescript.

(These three documents were never published).

"Comrade Purnar Aviyoger Uttaré Comrade Charu Mazumdar" (Comrade Charu Mazumdar Refutes The Charges of Comrade Purna), inner-party ideological document circulated by the West Bengal State Committee of the CPI(M), 1970, 16 pp. Mimeographed.

"Pakistan O *Deshabrati-Liberation* Line Prasange Antarparty Dalil-2" (On The Question of Pakistan and The Deshabrati-Liberation Line), 1971, circulated by the West Bengal State Committee of the CPI(M-L). Mimeographed. 32 pp. This document contains charges and counter-charges of the Bengal-Bihar-Orissa Border Regional Committee and the *Deshabrati-Liberation* Editorial Boards on the liberation struggle in East Pakistan (now Bangla Desh).

"The Present Party Line and A Summary of Our Experience", A Self-Critical Report of the Bengal-Bihar-Orissa Border Regional Committee of the CPI(M-L), 1971. Mimeographed. This document is a critical review of the tactical mistakes committed by the Party in 1969-1970.

"Comrade Sourin Basu's Letter to Comrade Khokan", 1971, 32 pp. Mimeographed. This document analyses the tactical problems of the CPI(M-L) including the divergent views over the liberation struggle in Bangla Desh.

Naxalbarir Shiksha—Report of the West Bengal State Committee of the CPI(M-L), 1972.

II. *Published Documents and Policy Statements of the Indian Communist Parties and their leadership*

Political Resolution, adopted at the Third Party Congress of the CPI, Madurai, 1954.

"CPI Central Committee Resolution on the XX Congress of the CPSU", March 26-31, 1956.

Political Resolution, adopted at the Fourth Congress of the CPI, Palghat, April 1956.

Political Resolutions, adopted at the Fifth Congress of the CPI, Amritsar, May 1958.

Constitution of the CPI, adopted at the Extra-ordinary Party Congress of the CPI, Amritsar, April 1958.

"On India-China Relations", Resolution of the Central Executive Committee of the CPI, Calcutta, 25 December 1959.

"On India-China Border Dispute", Resolution of the National Council of the C.P.I., Hyderabad, 14-20 August 1962.

"Unite to Defend Our Mother Land against China's Open Aggression", Resolution of the National Council of the CPI, New Delhi, 31 October—2 November, 1962.

S. A. Dange, "Neither Revisionism nor Dogmatism is Our Guide", *New Age,* 21 April, 1963, CPI's reply to A Mirror for Revisionists. (*People's Daily,* 9 March, 1963; *Peking Review* 15 March, 1963).

"On Certain Ideological Questions Affecting the Unity of the International Communist Movement", Resolution of the National Council of the CPI, *New Age,* 28 June, 1963.

Deshraj Chadha, *Dange Unmarked—Repudiate Revisionists!* New Delhi, 1964. Preface by M. Basavapunniah, contains texts of "Dange Letters" and other documents related to the Dange letters Controversy.

"Draft Programme of the Communist Party of India", New Delhi, 1964. Rival draft circulated by the left group in the CPI before the formal split.

Deshraj Chadha, *A Contribution to Ideological Debate,* (P. Sundarayya and seven other members of the Central Executive Committee of the CPI), New Delhi, 1964.

——— *Programme of the Communist Party of India,* New Delhi, 1965. Adopted by the Communist Party of India (Marxist) at the foundation congress (Seventh Party Congress), Calcutta, October-November 1964.

E. M. S. Namboodripad, *Fight Against Revisionism,* Communist Party of India (Marxist), Trivandrum, 1965. Political Organisational Report Adopted by the Communist Party of India (Marxist) at its foundation congress, Calcutta, October-November 1964.

"New Situation and Party's Tasks", Communist Party of India (Marxist), Calcutta, 1967. Political Report adopted by the Central Committee in April 1967.

"Election Review and Party's Tasks", Communist Party of India (Marxist), Calcutta, 1967. Adopted by the Central Committee in April 1967.

"On Left Deviation", Communist Party of India (Marxist), Calcutta, 1967. Resolution of the Committee, Madurai, August 1967, and other information documents.

"Central Committee Draft for Ideological Discussion", Communist Party of India (Marxist), Calcutta, 1967. Adopted by the Central Committee at Madurai, August 1967.

"Our Tasks on Party Organisation", resolution adopted by the Central Committee of the Communist Party of India (Marxist), Calicut, October 28-November 2, 1967.

"Ideological Debate Summedup by the Politbureau", Communist Party of India (Marxist), Calcutta, 1968.

"Andhra Plenum Rejects the Neo-Revisionist Ideological Draft", Janasakthi Publications, Vijayawada, 1968.

"Resolutions of the Andhra Communist Committee Plenum at Palacole" (which rejected the Central Committee's Draft for ideological Discussion).

"Letter to Andhra Comrades", Communist Party of India (Marxist), Calcutta, 1968.

"Open Letter to Party Members" (Tarimela Nagi Reddy, Devulapath, Venkateswara Rao, Kolla Venkiah, and Chandra Pulla Reddy), 1968.

"Why the Ultra-'left' Deviation ?" Communist Party of India (Marxist), Calcutta, 1968. An Examination of the basic causes of the left-defections with special reference to Andhra Pradesh, adopted by the Central Committee in October 1968.

Political Organisational Report of the Central Committee to the Eighth Congress of the Communist Party (Marxist), Cochin, December 23-29, 1968.

"Declaration of the All-India Co-ordination Committee of Communist Revolutionaries". *Liberation,* June 1968.

"It is Time to Form a New Party", Resolution of the AICCCR, 8 February 1969, *Liberation,* March 1969.

"Resolution on Andhra State Committee" (by AICCCR), 7, February 1969, *Liberation,* March 1969.

"Political Resolution of the Communist Party of India (Marxist-Leninist)", *Liberation,* May 1969.

"Political Resolution," adopted by the Ninth Congress of the Communist Party of India (Marxist), Madurai, June 27-July 2, 1972.

Basavpunnaiah, M., "Letter To Nanda", *People's Democracy* January 30, 1966.

"Our Party's Stand on Naxalbari", *People's Democracy,* July 9, 1967.

"Rebels Come Out In Their True Colours", *People's Democracy,* July 16, 1967.

"Revisionist Approvers of Criminal Conspiracy", *People's Democracy,* July 23, 1967.

"Naxalism and Its Metamorphosis", *People's Democracy* December 6, 1970.

Konar, H. K., "Adventurists' Slogan of 'Armed Revolution' Here and Now", *People's Democracy,* March 31, 1968.

Mazumdar, Charu, "Time To Build Up A Revolutionary Party", *Liberation Miscellany,* No. 1, 1967.

——— "The Indian People's Democratic Revolution", *Liberation,* June 1968.

——— "One Year of Naxalbari", *Liberation,* June 1968.

——— "The United Front and the Revolutionary Party", *Liberation,* July 1968.

——— "Undertake the Work of Building a Revolutionary Party", *Liberation,* October, 1968.

—"To My Comrades", *Liberation,* October, 1968.

———"Develop Peasants' Class Struggle Through Class Analysis", *Liberation,* November, 1968.

——— "Boycott Elections—International Significance of the Slogan", *Liberation,* December, 1968.

———"To My Comrades Who Are Working in Villages", *Liberation,* March, 1969.

——— "To The Youth And The Students", *Liberation,* April, 1969.

——— "On Some Current Political And Organisational Problems", *Liberation,* July, 1969.

——— "Party's Call To The Youth and Students", *Liberation,* September, 1969.

——— "Fight Against The Concrete Manifestations of Revisionism", *Liberation,* September, 1969.

——— "Develop Revolutionary War To Eliminate War of Aggression Against China", *Liberation,* October, 1969.

——— "China's Chairman Is Our Chairman, China's Path is Our Path", *Liberation,* November 1969.

——— "Carry Forward The Peasant Struggle By Thoroughly Combating Revisionism, Struggle Against Revisionism, Develop The Mass Movement", *Liberation,* November 1969.

——— "Sum Up The Experience of Revolutionary Peasant Struggle", *Liberation,* December, 1969.

——— "The New Year Holds Promises of Still Bigger Victories", *Liberation,* January, 1970.

——— "Make The 1970's The Decade of Liberation", *Liberation,* February, 1970.

——— "A Few Words About Guerrilla Actions", *Liberation,* February, 1970.

——— "Party's Tasks Among Workers", *Liberation,* March, 1970.

——— "A Few Words To The Revolutionary Students and Youth", *Liberation,* March, 1970.

——— "The Peasant Revolutionary Struggle in Srikakulam is invincible", *Liberation,* March, 1970.

——— "Build Up People's Liberation Army And March Onward", *Liberation,* January-March, 1971.

——— "Seize The Rifles And Arm The Peasant Guerrilla Squads", *Liberation,* January-March, 1971.

——— "Red Salute To Comrades Behind Prison Bars", *Liberation,* January-March 1971.

——— "On The Questions Of Building People's Army And Base Area", *Liberation,* June, 1971—January, 1973.

——— "To The Comrades Of Birbhum", *Liberation,* July 1971-January, 1972.

Namboodiripad, E.M.S., "Mao's Struggle Against Dogmatism—Model for Indian Marxists" *New Age* (Monthly), November, 1957.

——— "Peasantry and Land Reform", *New Age* (Monthly), January, 1956.

——— "Agrarian Reforms : *A Study of the Congress and Communist Approaches,* The Communist Party of India, New Delhi, 1956.

— *Revisionism and Dogmatism in the Communist Party of India,* Communist Party of India, New Delhi, 1963.

——— *The Programme Explained,* Communist Party of India (Marxist) Calcutta, 1966.

Nishad (pseud.), "Soviet Social Imperialism's Stranglehold Over India", *Liberation,* February, 1969.

Observer, "To Win Victory in the Revolution We Must

Establish the Revolutionary Authority," *Liberation,* February 1970.

——— "Our Path : Guerrilla Warfare", *Liberation,* November, 1969.

Rao, C. Rajeswara, "Maoist Theories With Sugar Coating", *New Age,* October 29, 1967.

——— "CPM At Crossroads", *New Age,* October 22, 1967.

Ranadive, B.T. *On People's Democracy,* The Communist Party of India, Bombay, 1949.

——— "CPI(M) Follows Leninist Path", *People's Democracy,* July 16, 1967.

——— "Left Tactics Will Delink Party from Mass Struggle", *People's Democracy,* August 13, 1967.

——— "Left Opportunist Line Means Liquidation of Party As Central Organisation", *People's Democracy,* August 20, 1967.

——— "*The Two Programmes* : *Marxist and Revisionist,* Communist Party of India (Marxist), Calcutta, 1967.

Sanyal Kanu, "Report on the Peasant Movement in the Terai Region", *Liberation,* November, 1968.

Sen Asit, "The Indian Revolutionary Situation, Has it Matured?", *Liberation,* February, 1968.

Sen, Mohit, *The New Line and the Dogmatism,* Communist Party of India, New Delhi, 1964.

——— *Communism and the New Left,* Communist Party of India, New Delhi, 1969.

——— "Naxalbari and Revolution", *New* Age, July 1969.

——— "Naxalites—Crisis Within Crisis", *New Age,* Septembe 19, 1971.

——— and Pratap Mitra, *Communist Party and Naxalites,* Communist Party of India, New Delhi, 1971.

III *International Communist Publications*

Khrushchev, N. S., *Report of the Central Committee of the Communist Party of Soviet Union to the XX Party Congress,* February 14, 1956, Moscow, 1956.

"The Truth About How The Leaders of the CPSU have allied themselves with India against China" *People's Daily*, 2 November 1963, *Peking Review,* 8 November 1963.

Editorial Department of *People's Daily and Red Flag.* "The

Origin and Development of Differences Between the Leadership of the CPSU and Ourselves : Comments on the Open Letter of the Central Committee of the CPSU", *Peking Review,* September 13, 1963.

Lin Piao "Long Live the Victory of the People's War", *Peking Review,* September 3, 1965.

Observer, "What Shastri's Soviet Trip Reveals", *Peking Review,* June 4, 1965.

Shish Yen, "Non-Aligned India's Double Alignment", *Peking Review,* August 13, 1965.

"The Shift in US Global Strategy", *Peking Review,* February, 1966.

"India : Anti-Tyranny Struggle Rock Reactionary Rule", *Peking Review,* February 24, 1967.

"After the Indian Election, A Still More Reactionary Government", *Peking Review,* March 24, 1967.

Ting Chuan, "Food Crisis and Why", *Peking Review,* March 11, 1966.

"The Indian Food Crisis and Armed Revolution", *Peking Review,* September 22, 1967.

"Indian People Rise Up in Resistance", *Peking Review,* November 16, 1966.

"Student Movement in India", *Peking Review,* December 2, 1966.

Tung Ming, "The People's Revolutionary Struggles will Surely Triumph Over U.S. Imperialism's Counter-Revolutionary Strategy", *Peking Review,* September 9, 1966.

"Great New Era of World Revolution", *Peking Review,* January 13, 1967.

"Imperialist Camp Enters Gloomy New Year", *Peking Review,* January 20, 1967.

"Phrase-mongering Won't Help Empty Stomach", *Peking Review,* July 12, 1968.

"Revolution is the Only Way Out for Indian People", Hsinhua News Agency (3349), March 25, 1969.

"Experience Gained by Indian Peasants at the Price of Blood", *Peking Review,* September 22, 1967.

"Indian People Draw Lessons froom Telengana Uprising", Hsinhua News Agency (3479), August 4, 1967.

"The Darjeeling Peasant Armed Struggle", *People's Daily,* July 5, 1967.

"Spring Thunder Over India", *Peking Review,* July 14, 1967.

"India, Dozens of Naxalbaris", *Peking Review,* July 28, 1967.

"Let the Red Flag of Naxalbari Fly Still Higher", *Peking Review,* August 11, 1967.

"Historical Lessons of Telengana Uprising" *Peking Review,* August 11, 1967.

"Feudal System in Rural India Can Only Be Destroyed By Armed Agrarian Revolution", Hsinhua News Agency (3478), August 3, 1967.

"Mao Tse-tung's Thought Lights Up the Way to Victory for Indian Revolution", *Communist China Digest* (190), March 18, 1968.

"Let the Peasants' Revolutionary Storm in India Strike Harder", *Peking Review,* March 1, 1968.

"Historic Turning Point in the Indian Revolution", *Peking Review,* January 12, 1968.

"Indian Peasants Take 'Naxalbari Road' : Armed Seizure of Land in Bihar", *Peking Review,* February 16, 1968.

"Indian People Rise Up in Resistance", *Peking Review,* November 8, 1968.

"Revolutionary Struggle of the Indian People Grows in Depth", *Peking Review,* January 31, 1969.

"Revolutionary Armed Struggle of Indian Peasantry Surges Forward", Hsinhua News Agency (4248), September 24, 1969.

"Indian Peasant Armed Struggle Rages Like A Prairie Fire", *Peking Review,* September 19, 1969.

"Organising the Peasants, Building Up A People's Armed Force and Launching Armed Struggle for Complete Overthrow of Reactionary Rule", *Peking Review,* May 16, 1969.

"The Raging Flames of Srikakulam", Hsinhua News Agency (4283), October 29, 1969.

CPI(M-L) Leads Indian People Onward Along Victorious Path to Seizing Political Power By Armed Force", Hsinhua New Agency, March 28, 1970.

Indian Reactionaries Heading For Collapse At Quicker Tempo", *Peking Review,* February 27, 1970.

"Red Revolutionary Area in India Strikes Like a Beacon", *Peking Review,* reprinted in *Liberation,* February 1970.

B. Secondary Sources

I. *Books*

Brandt, C., Schwartz, B. and Fairbank, J. K., *A Documentary History of Chinese Communism,* Cambridge, Mass,, 1958.

Bandyopadhyaya, J., *Indian Nationalism Versus International Communism,* Calcutta, Firma K. L. Mukhopadhyaya, 1966.

——— *Mao Tse-tung and Gandhi,* Allied Publishers, Calcutta, 1973.

Broomfield, John H., *Elite Conflict in A Plural Society : Twentieth Century Bengal,* Berkeley, 1968.

Barnett, A. Doak, (Ed.), *Communist Strategies in Asia,* Praeger, New York, 1963.

The Bengal Chambers of Commerce, *West Bengal : An Analytical study.*

Bose, Sajal, *West Bengal : The Violent Years,* Prachi Publications, 1974.

Crankshaw, E., *The New Cold War : Moscow vs. Peking,* Penguin, Harmandsworth, 1963.

Ch'en Po-ta, *A Study of Land Rent in Pre-Liberation China,* Peking, Foreign Languages Press, 1958.

Cross, J. E., *Conflict in Shadows : The Nature and Politics of Guerrilla War,* Garden City. New York, 1963.

Debray, Regis, *Revolution in the Revolution?* Penguin Books, 1968.

Das Gupta, Biplab, *The Naxalite Movement,* Calcutta, Allied Publishers, 1974.

Fic, Victor, M., *Peaceful Transition to Communism in India,* Nachiketa Publication, Delhi 1963.

Franda, Marcus F., *Radical Politics in West Bengal,* M.I.T., 1971.

Floyed, David, *Mao Against Khruschev : A Short History of the Sino-Soviet Conflict,* New York, Preager, 1964.

Ghosh, Sankar, *West Bengal—The Disinherited State,* Orient Longmans, Calcutta, 1971.

——— *The Naxalite Movement,* Firma K. L. Mukhopadhyay, Calcutta, 1974.

Griffith, William E., *The Sino-Soviet Rift,* Allen and Unwin, London, 1963.

——— *Sino-Soviet Relations,* 1964-1965, Cambridge, M.I.T. Press.

Guevara, Che, *The Bolivian Diary,* National Book Agency, Calcutta, 1968.

——— *Guerrilla Warfare,* New Delhi, 1969.

Hudson, G., Lowenthal, and Mac Farquhar, R., *The Sino-Soviet Dispute,* Praeger, New York, 1961.

Irani, C. R., *Bengal : The Communist Challenge,* Bombay, 1968.

Johari, J. C., *Naxalite Politics in India,* Research, New Delhi, 1972.

Jerome, Ch'en, *Mao and the Chinese Revolution,* London, 1965.

Kan-Chih, Ho, *A History of the Modern Chinese Revolution,* Foreign Language Press, Peking, 1959.

Kabir, Humayun, *The Student Unrest : Causes and Cure,* Calcutta, Orient Book Company, 1953.

Kautsky, John, H., *Moscow and the Communist Party of India,* Wiley and M.I.T. New York and Cambridge, 1956.

Liddellhart, Captain, B. H., *Guerrilla Warfare by Mao Tse-tung and Che Guevara,* Cassell, London, 1963.

Lowenthal, R. (Ed.) *Issues in the Future of Asia : Communist and Non-Communist Alternatives,* Praeger, New York, 1969.

Labedz, Leopold (Ed.), *Revisionism : Essays on the History of Marxist Ideas,* Allen and Unwin, London, 1962.

Mao Tse-tung, *Selected Writings,* Compiled by Vichar Prakashan, Kanpur, 1969.

Charu Mazumdar, *Collected Writings,* Communist Party of India (Marxist-Leninist), Calcutta, 1973.

Overstreet, Gene, D. and Windmiller, M., *Communism in India,* California University, Berkeley and Los Angeles, 1959.

Ram, Mohan, *Indian Communism : Split Within A Split,* Vikas Publications, New Delhi, 1969.

——— *Maoism in India,* Vikas Publications, New Delhi, 1971.

Schwartz, B. I., *Chinese Communism and the Rise of Mao,* Cambridge, Mass, 1951.

Schram, Stuart, R., *Mao Tse-tung,* London, 1966.

——— *The Political Thought of Mao Tse-tung,* Praeger,

New York, 1963.—and Helene Carriere d'Encausse, *Marxism and Asia,* The Penguin Press, London, 1969.

Snow, Edgar, *Red Star Over China,* London, Victor Gollancz Ltd., 1968.

Scalpino, Robert A., (Ed.) *The Communist Revolution in Asia : Tactics, Goals and Achievements,* Prentice-Hall, New Jersey, 1969.

Selden, Mark, *The Yenan Way in Revolutionary China,* Cambridge Mass, 1971.

Sen, Asit, "Timing the Revolutionary Situation" in John Gerassi (Ed.) *Towards Revolution,* Vol. 1, Weidenfeld and Nicholson, London, 1971.

Sen, S. N., *The City of Calcutta : A Socio-economic Survey,* 1954-1958, Calcutta, Bookland, (P) Ltd., 1960.

Sengupta, Bhabani, *Communism in Indian Politics,* Columbia University Press, New York and London, 1972.

Soloman, Richard H. *Mao's Revolution and the Chinese Political Culture,* Berkeley, 1971.

Weiner, Myron, *Political Changes in South Asia,* Calcutta, Firma K. L. Mukhopadhyay, 1963.

Wilkes, John, *Communism in Asia,* Sydney, Angus and Robertson, 1967.

II. *Pamphlets and Articles*

Banerjee, Sumanta, "Naxalbari : Between Yesterday and Tomorrow", *Frontier,* May 17, 1967.

Bhargava, G. S., "The Spectre of Naxalbari", *China Report,* March-April, 1969.

Chakravarti. Satindranath, "A Party Is Born", *Now,* June 6, 1969 and June 13, 1969.

Dasgupta, Pannalal, "What Is the Naxalbari Path?", *Mainstream,* July 8, 1967.

Dutt, Gargi, "Peking, the Indian Communist Movement and International Communism", *Asian Survey,* October, 1971.

Frankel, F., "Agricultural Modernization and Social Change", *Mainstream,* December 13, 1969.

Franda, M., "India's Third Communist Party", *Asian Survey,* November, 1969.

Gelman, H., "The Indian CP between Moscow and Peking", *Problems of Communism,* May-June, 1963.

Ghosh, Sankar, "The Naxalite Struggle in West Bengal", *South Asian Review,* January 1971.

Naik, J. A. "The Communist Party of India and the Sino-Indian Conflict", *Eastern World,* March 1964.

Roy, A. K. : "Ideological Bases of the CPI(M-L)", *United Asia,* Jan-Feb. 1971. Vol. 23, No. 1; pp. 49-57.

Roy, A. K., "National and Communist Form At the Cross-Roads in Bangladesh", *United Asia,* May-June 1971.

Roy A. K., "India's Third Communist Party", *Institute of Defence Studies and Analyses Journal,* July-Sept. 1974.

Sangal, O. P. "Alphabet of Mao : AICCCR", *The Citizen and Weekend Review,* May 20, 1969.

Sen, N. C. : "Peking's Prescription for Indian Communists", *China Report,* Vol. 5, No. 2., March-April 1969. pp. 10-11.

Sengupta, Bhabani : "A Maoist Line for India", *China Quarterly,* January-March, 1968.

——— "Moscow, Peking and the Indian political Lee-lane after Nehru", *Orbis,* Summer, 1968.

——— "Indian Communism and the Peasantry", *Problems of Communism,* Jan-Feb. 1972.

——— "India's Rival Communist Models", *Problems of Communism,* Jan-Feb. 1973.

INDEX